BANDIT TERRITORIES

BANDIT TERRITORIES

BRITISH OUTLAW TRADITIONS

Edited by

Helen Phillips

UNIVERSITY OF WALES PRESS
CARDIFF
2008

© The Contributors, 2008

All rights reserved. No part of this book may be reproduced, stored in a retrieval system, or transmitted, in any form or by any means, electronic, mechanical, photocopying, recording or otherwise, without clearance from the University of Wales Press, 10 Columbus Walk, Brigantine Place, Cardiff, CF10 4UP.
www.uwp.co.uk

British Library Cataloguing-in-Publication Data
A catalogue record for this book is available from the British Library.

ISBN 978-0-7083-1985-7

The right of the Contributors to be identified as the authors of this work has been asserted by them in accordance with sections 77 and 78 of the Copyright, Designs and Patents Act 1988.

Typeset by Columns Design Ltd, Reading
Printed and bound in Great Britain by CPI Antony Rowe, Chippenham, Wilts

Contents

Acknowledgements	vii
Abbreviations	ix
Note on contributors	xi
Bandit Territories and Good Outlaws *Helen Phillips*	1
'Exempt me, Sire, for I am afeard of women': Gendering Robin Hood *Thomas Hahn and Stephen Knight*	24
Maid Marian in Twentieth-century Children's Books *David Blamires*	44
Welsh Bandits *Adrian Price*	58
Fouke Fitz Waryn III and King John: Good Outlaw and Bad King *Glyn Burgess*	73
Rabbie Hood: The Development of the English Outlaw Myth in Scotland *Stephen Knight*	99
Scott and the Outlaws *Helen Phillips*	119
Sketches by a Green Crayon: Washington Irving, Robin Hood and the Emerging American Frontier *Marcus A. J. Smith and †Julian N. Wasserman*	143
Robin Hood, King Arthur and Cold War Chivalry *Jeffrey Richards*	167

CONTENTS

'And for best supporting hero . . . Little John'
Laura Blunk — 196

'Begone, knave! Robbery is out of fashion hereabouts!' Robin Hood and the Comics Code
Allan W. Wright — 217

Robin Hood is Alive and Well in Cityton Prison
John Beynon — 233

Bibliography — 256

Index — 271

Acknowledgements

My greatest debt is to the contributors to this volume, for their expertise, their essays, their help and their patience. It is a great cause for sadness and regret that Julian Wasserman was not able to see the essay on Washington Irving in print before his death at a tragically early age. Deeply learned, Julian was also a proponent of the idea that academic studies should be fun. Like the hero of the *Gest of Robyn Hode*, Julian was brave, *curteys*, and 'dyde pore men moch god'. Thanks are also due to Sarah Lewis and Ennis Akpinar at the University of Wales Press, to the University of Wales Press's anonymous reader for helpful suggestions, and also to Jeff Wallace and Kathryn Sutherland for advice and encouragement.

Abbreviations

DT	R. B. Dobson and J. Taylor (eds), *Rymes of Robin Hood: An Introduction to the English Outlaw* (London: Heinemann, 1989)
Hahn	Thomas Hahn, *Robin Hood in Popular Culture: Violence, Transgression and Justice* (Cambridge: D. S. Brewer, 2000)
Hobsbawm	Eric Hobsbawm, *Bandits* (London: Weidenfeld & Nicolson, 1969)
Holt	J. C. Holt, *Robin Hood*, rev. ed. (London: Thames and Hudson, 1989)
Keen	Maurice Keen, *The Outlaws of Medieval England*, rev. ed. (London: Routledge and Kegan Paul, 1987)
Knight 1994	Stephen Knight, *Robin Hood: A Complete Study of the English Outlaw* (Oxford: Blackwell, 1994)
Knight 2003	Stephen Knight, *Robin Hood: A Mythic Biography* (Ithaca and London: Cornell University Press, 2003)
KO	Stephen Knight and Thomas H. Ohlgren (eds), *Robin Hood and Other Outlaw Tales*, TEAMS (Kalamazoo: Medieval Institute Publications, 1998)
MCS	*Medieval Cultural Studies: Essays in Honour of Stephen Knight*, ed. Ruth Evans, Helen Fulton, and David Matthews (Cardiff: University of Wales Press, 2006)

ABBREVIATIONS

RHMP   *Robin Hood: Medieval and Post-Medieval*, Helen Phillips (ed.) (Dublin: Four Courts Press, 2005)

Notes on contributors

John Beynon is Professor and Head of Communication, Cultural & Media Studies in the Cardiff School of Creative Industries, University of Glamorgan. His last book was *Masculinities and Culture* (2003). He is currently completing for publication the ethnographic study of 'prison masculinities' referred to in his chapter in this volume.

David Blamires retired in 2001 as Professor of German, Manchester University. His books include *David Jones: Artist and Writer* (2nd ed., 1978); *Herzog Ernst and the Otherworld Voyage* (1979); *Fortunatus in His Many English Guises* (1996); *The Book of the Perfect Life*, a translation with introduction of a late-medieval mystical treatise. He also produced the illustrated catalogue for an exhibition, 'Robin Hood: A Hero for All Times', John Rylands Library, 1998, and has written widely on children's literature, including the chapter on 'Children's Literature' in the *Oxford History of Literary Translation* IV (2006).

Laura Blunk is Associate Professor of History at Cuyahoga Community College, Ohio. Through more than thirty years of teaching history of civilization survey courses she has kept her classes fresh by integrating her love of popular culture into the course content. Her 'Red Robin: The Radical Politics of Richard Carpenter's "Robin of Sherwood" ' appears in *Robin Hood in Popular Culture*, ed. Thomas G. Hahn (2000). Outside of academia she is, along with Helen Avry, co-editor of the award-winning Robin of Sherwood fanzine *Albion*.

Glyn Burgess is Emeritus Professor of French and Honorary Research Fellow at the University of Liverpool. He has a particular interest in outlaw stories and is the author of *Two Medieval Outlaws: Eustace the Monk and Fouke Fitz Waryn* (1997). His other interests and publications include lexicology, the legend of St Brendan and twelfth-century French romance and short narrative. Recent books include (co-edited) *The Arthur of the French: The Arthurian Legend in Medieval French and Occitan Literature* (2006).

Stephen Knight is Distinguished Research Professor, English Literature, Cardiff University. His publications include books in the areas of political and cultural theory, Celtic and Arthurian Studies, Welsh writing in English, crime fiction, Chaucer and Robin Hood. His most recent book in the outlaw field is *Robin Hood: A Mythic Biography* (2003). He has just completed *Merlin: Knowledge and Power*, forthcoming.

Thomas Hahn is Professor of English at Rochester University, New York State. His research areas include cultural studies, theory and medieval literature. His publications include *Race and Ethnicity in the Middle Ages*; (ed.) *Robin Hood in Popular Culture: Violence, Transgression, and Justice*; *Reconceiving Chaucer: Literary Theory and Historical Interpretation*.

Helen Phillips is Professor of English, Cardiff University. Her publications are in the areas of medieval literature and Chaucer, Robin Hood and medievalism. She edited a collection of essays called *Robin Hood: Medieval and Post-Medieval* in 2005.

Adrian Price is Director of Teaching at the Cardiff and Vale of Glamorgan Centre for Welsh for Adults, at Cardiff University. His publications are in the areas of the Welsh language and second language learning, and they include *Welsh: The Essential Coursebook* (2007)&tab;

Jeffrey Richards is Professor of Cultural History at Lancaster University. His research areas include medieval history, the history of cinema, Victorian theatre, and national identity. His publications include *Popes and the Papacy in the Early Middle Ages*; *Swordsmen of the Silver Screen*; *Films and British National Identity*; *Imperialism and Music*; and *Sir Henry Irving: A Victorian Actor and his World*. He is also a well-known broadcaster, particularly on popular and cultural history.

Marcus A. J. Smith is Professor of English at Loyola University in New Orleans, Louisiana. He is currently working on a study of the Robin Hood legend in North America and in a

NOTE ON CONTRIBUTORS

global context. He has also written on Orwell, Walker Percy, Nathanael West and Thomas Pynchon. Additionally, he is a member of the Louisiana Bar and practices law in New Orleans.

The late **Julian N. Wasserman**, Professor of English at Loyola University, New Orleans, Louisiana, was an internationally known medievalist. With Marcus A. J. Smith he published 'In the Sheriff's Court: Robin Hood and American Jurisprudence, Or, Who is this Robin Hood and Why are the Lawyers Saying Nasty Things about Him?', in *Robin Hood in Popular Culture*, ed. Thomas Hahn (2000). He was also a major voice on the Pearl Poet and in Chaucerian scholarship.

Allen W. Wright is a Toronto journalist and media librarian. As a Robin Hood scholar and historian of comics, his contributions to these subjects include contributions to TV presentations about outlaws, conference presentations, participation in the preparation of the Robin Hood exhibition in 2001 at the University of Western Ontario, and the major Robin Hood website: http://www.boldoutlaw.com.

Bandit Territories and Good Outlaws

HELEN PHILLIPS

Bandits, outlaws and stories

The subject of this book is British bandits and outlaws: the changing reception and appropriation of bandit traditions in different centuries and for different ideologies and causes. Some of these traditions have travelled worldwide and, in the case of Robin Hood, received some of their most important representations in America. Most heroes of British outlaw tradition are historically documented men, including Fouke Fitz Waryn, Hereward the Wake, Dafydd ap Siencyn, Twm Siôn Cati, William Wallace and Rob Roy. The most famous, Robin Hood, was probably fictional, but the essays in this book are concerned with the cultural history, not just the historical phenomenon, of bandits and outlaws. These essays show how powerful the myth of the 'good outlaw' is: the stories told about bandits often depict as noble and sympathetic men individuals who in real life may well have been ruthless criminals, or they add glamour and playfulness to accounts of serious politicians fighting for kingship or national freedom. The good bandit is a figure which commands respect particularly in periods when authority is distrusted, but paradoxically it also evinces a strong belief in the ultimate triumph of justice, whether against mercenary clerics and unjust law-enforcers or against invading kings. This myth, with its potential for confronting assumptions about the control of social order and the use of power, often illuminates a range of other political issues: Glyn Burgess in this volume, discussing the narratives told of the twelfth-century Shropshire outlaw, Fouke Fitz Waryn, shows how contrasts between the good outlaw and the bad king, John, open up contemporary ideas about government.

The same kind of myth, of the thief and raider who, though outside the law, is justice-loving, generous, and kind to the poor, recurs in many eras and countries. Such a hero, and occasionally heroine, is also admired for audacious robbery, disguise, and trickery, especially against the powerful and privileged, triumphing over them as much with humiliation and ridicule as with force, and is often depicted as creating (whether materially, socially or – for the audience – imaginatively) an alternative realm and charisma to those of the orthodox powers. So pervasive is this cultural phenomenon, which Eric Hobsbawm famously called the myth of the 'social bandit', that, if we search for the roots of Britain's most celebrated bandit, Robin Hood, it seems likely that we may find his origins not in any specific historical medieval outlaw (though many researchers have searched through archives to find plausible candidates) but in other outlaw tales.[1] And the paradox at the myth's heart, the virtuous rogue, can be taken to an extreme, as Allan Wright's essay in this collection shows, when American comics in the post-war era were required to depict Robin Hood as a hero opposed to robbery and one who always respected the Church and even sheriffs. This diametrically contradicts the Robin Hood of the earliest extant ballads (*Robin Hood and the Monk*, *Robin Hood and the Potter*, *A Gest of Robyn Hode*, all dating from before 1501), where he robs the rich, without claiming to do this to help the poor, and where monks and abbots, or at least some worldly ones, are targets of his enmity and contempt, and Robin is said to have been murdered by an evil prioress. In the earliest extant play, from 1475, Robin kills the sheriff's officer (named as Sir Guy of Gisburne in a ballad version of the same episode) and the merry men violently rescue Robin from the sheriff's prison.[2] Yet such plays were put on by respectable medieval and Tudor parish leaders, to raise funds for the local church and good causes, and we know that the Norfolk landowners, the Pastons, had Robin Hood plays performed in the fifteenth century.[3]

Such heroes, good outlaws, have been popular with exponents of both radical and conservative ideologies (as is illustrated by the essay here on Walter Scott, a conservative writing about outlaws in a period when their traditions were often favourites with radicals). This alerts us to the legends' capacity for endless change and re-appropriation, adopted in seemingly contradictory fashion by diverse political camps, yet it also testifies to something at the core of the concept that remains a constant: one might call it the duality that unifies the tradition, the paradox of the good rogue. The paradox's power lies perhaps in the fact that it provides an attractive vehicle for the truth that issues of social good and bad, of law and resistance, are rarely clear-cut. The question to ask about any version of the outlaw myth is thus not only whether it is an adaptation for Left or Right but also how it treats the central paradox.

British outlaw tales may attribute the same motif to more than one hero. For example, an outlaw disguises himself as a potter in the fifteenth-century ballad *Robin Hood and the Potter*, the stories of the twelfth-century Norman outlaw, Eustace the Monk, and the Scottish national hero William Wallace (d.1305). Eustace's trick of eluding pursuers by reversing his horseshoes is also told of Fouke and the eleventh-century Fenland outlaw Hereward. In the past, outlaw tales were treated rather as a separate category by literary critics, often on the assumption, especially in the nineteenth century, that they belonged to 'folk' culture, together with other material that flourished especially in the ballad. Yet they share motifs with several medieval genres, including romances and beast fables. The outlaw tale is not a closed literary world: the courtly romance hero Tristan, for example spends time in the woods like an outlaw, and the escapades of the wily fox Renart, hero of the popular *Roman de Renart*, recall some outlaws' outwitting of their foes. Occasionally, outlaw traditions gain supernatural overtones. Thus Robin Hood and his men have been associated, particularly from the eighteenth century onwards, with prehistoric remains or large stones in certain landscapes, as if they were originally giants. In the nineteenth century such beliefs linked with a widespread scholarly tendency to believe that Robin Hood originated in ancient pagan beliefs, and was himself a wood spirit. Such hypotheses, like searches for a 'historical' Robin, may not feature very much currently in academic research into the outlaw but both questions continue to intrigue people, and they arouse lively debate in online discussions and television programmes, as well as engendering new books and theories. Interpreting the outlaw as ancient folklore or the survival of a god, sometimes a fertility god, has been particularly important in three periods, particularly, and in each case for historical reasons: the Elizabethan period, when protestants wanted to project a vision of English popular heritage without local – Catholic – saints' cults, so that Robin Hood, pucks, fairies and other folklore and customs appeared in both literature and antiquarians' writings; the nineteenth century, when comparative mythology, like comparative linguistics, was a major intellectual 'grand récit' for interpreting the ancient past; and the 1970s and 1980s, when 'New Age' ideals made 'Robin of Sherwood' into a cult phenomenon which still has many enthusiastic followers.[4]

Bandits and outlaws in history

Bandits, outlaws and political contenders who waged guerrilla warfare or took to the woods and wild places have been important forces in many eras of British history. These are distinct if overlapping categories of opponents of civil rule. The outlaw, as such, is a man deprived of his legal rights, by the king or, in reality, his courts, often for not appearing in court to answer a charge. Until the thirteenth century in England an outlaw could even be killed with impunity. After that, although an outlaw still suffered legal and financial deprivations, anyone who killed him was guilty of homicide.[5] Outlaw status sometimes lasted only a few months until the offender gained a pardon. Many outlaws were well-born and their opposition to the ruling power was political. Exciting narratives glorifying their stories are sometimes part of clear propaganda from their political camp. The narrative of Earl Godwin's conflict with King Edward the Confessor and his time as an outlaw and fugitive in Bruges (1050–2) manifestly falls into that class, being commissioned by his daughter, Queen Edith and written by her priest, to promote the views of the powerful Godwin clan.[6]

Bandits and highway robbers, whether technically outlawed or not, were an ever-present danger, lurking in woods and near roads to attack medieval travellers. A fourteenth-century English writer says '[o]ften in woods thieves are hidden . . . men passing by come and are despoiled and robbed and often slain', and records of the poet Chaucer record him being robbed more than once while travelling.[7] Highway robbers were often lowly men but among notorious gangs of this kind were the respectably born Folville brothers who waylaid travellers in the 1330s in Leicestershire.[8] The reign of terror and disorder engendered in localities by such gangs increased when national politics created conditions particularly conducive to their numbers and activities. Adrian Price observes that men returning from French wars and Lancastrian soldiers swelled the ranks of Welsh outlaw groups in the fifteenth century, though resistance to English rule meant that outlaws held a respected place generally in Wales. English baronial opposition to Henry III, led by Simon de Montfort, led to an increase in outlawry: among such gangs that of Adam de Gurdun operated in the Forest of Alton, where the London-Winchester road ran, and the perils of this favourite lair for medieval highwaymen entered popular imagination. *Piers Plowman* mentions it, as well as the Folvilles.[9] Langland uses the good outlaw myth in an apocalyptic vision, that when justice is finally, through Grace, restored to earth this will be like the Folvilles' 'law': restoring to men what has been wrongly taken. That a moralist like Langland uses such an image reveals not just popular romanticization of bandits but late medieval hopelessness about contemporary authorities' ability to dispense justice.[10] The fifteenth century, another period of aristocratic warfare, also sees an increase in local gangs, private armies, and outlaw disorder in England.

A third historically documented category of opposition to authority which often engenders romanticized outlaw-style narratives is that of nationalist guerrilla warfare against invaders, a tactic favoured by certain terrains: in medieval Wales, as Adrian Price's essay shows; in the Scottish highlands; and in the post-1066 English fenlands, the west midlands and Welsh marches.

It is illuminating to look at how bandit legends can emerge from historical outlawry and political disorder. William I's government was plagued in its first ten years by opposition both from figures like the outlawed landowner Hereward in the fens and other leaders of Anglo-Saxon resistance, such as Edric the Wild.[11] This Shropshire landowner and his allies, including two Welsh princes, sacked Hereford in 1067 in their campaign against William. He and other rebels appear to have taken to living in tents in the woods (hence 'Wild', paralleling his Latin and French labels, Edric 'Silvaticus' and 'Sauvage', meaning 'of the woods'). The fame of Hereward and Edric survived in popular legend, from a period when many others mounted campaigns against Norman power, because both became the subjects of oral and written accounts glorifying their deeds. Their real-life exploits acquired extra stories which can be paralleled elsewhere in folklore, romances and other outlaw legends, including supernatural adventures: Edric is said to have married a fairy and Hereward slew a giant and a half-human bear.[12] Similarly, the *Romance of Fouke Fitz Waryn* includes a story of this early-thirteenth-century opponent of King John rescuing a maiden from a dragon. The medieval Robin Hood differs from many medieval outlaw-heroes in being low-born and having wholly human adventures. Some outlaws, throughout the world, are believed to be not dead but able to return to help their country. In Britain this is claimed for Owain Glyndŵr and for Wild Edric, who rides with his horsemen to warn of war (last reported to have been seen locally before the Second World War).

The historical significance of bandit tales lies only partly in some heroes' historicity. While all bandit and outlaw traditions exhibit common elements of the pervasive 'social bandit' myth, their cultural significance includes the ways stories are used and re-used to serve political, ideological, and personal purposes, changing over time. For example, a Robin Hood play was performed in 1661 in Nottingham, expressly to persuade the citizens of the rightness of Charles II's Restoration, and in it the famous local outlaws debate contemporary political views.[13] Here long-established literary traditions and characterization are cleverly employed to serve contemporary politics. Little John voices Leveller-like arguments about the equality of men, contrasting with Robin's more headstrong, heroic attitudes – a dissenting voice, more sober, mature, even more principled than Robin's, which, as Laura Blunk's essay demonstrates, has frequently been one of John's roles throughout the legend's history. From the post-war twentieth-century period, Jeffrey Richards shows in his chapter on Hollywood how the evolving nature of the cold war left a clear ideological mark on films about Arthur and Robin Hood. We could also see the long first section of the silent film *Robin Hood*, 1922, starring Douglas Fairbanks, Sr., where Richard I and his knights go away to the Crusade on the continent, as paralleling the departure of American soldiers a few years before to fight in Europe in the First World War. Even Wild Edric's fairy bride may have been recounted, with other similar tales, by Walter Map in 1182, not as a mere fantasy latched onto a historical figure but as a compliment designed to interest Henry II, himself descended from the legendary fairy Melusine, ancestress of his dynasty.[14]

Hobsbawm's invaluable construction of a worldwide 'social bandit' can obscure the distinctive nature of outlaw figures, in a variety of periods and parts of Britain, as well as specific ways in which outlaw tales (and indeed, the academic study of outlaws) responds to sociopolitical situations. Though a common core of motifs reappears in the histories of these noble-rogue heroes, in some instances one can feel that little remains stable except a name and an outline of events. David Blamires's essay on Maid Marion shows this female outlaw getting remade almost every twenty years during the twentieth-century. She had also changed dramatically during the century leading to Ben Jonson's *Sad Shepherd* (*c*.1637): the sixteenth-century Marion often resembled a pantomime dame, a bawdy figure, performed by a man, dancing with a lewd Friar Tuck; Jonson's pastoral play creates in contrast a Marion who is a lively huntress of great beauty and charm. Anthony Munday's Earl of Huntington plays of the late 1590s had already turned Marion into Matilda, the noble and highly principled daughter of Lord Fitzwater. It is not clear how any of this relates, if at all, to earlier, medieval French, musical plays, in which 'Robin' and 'Marion' are a shepherd and shepherdess, though Stephen Knight argues for their influence on fifteenth-century English summer Robin Hood plays in his essay here on the Scottish Robin Hood. Such re-makings also occur with unequivocally documented outlaws. In Charles Kingsley's novel, *Hereward the Wake* (1877), which enjoyed great late Victorian popularity, Hereward, while retaining the courage and spirit of adventure of the medieval *Gesta Herewardi* (Deeds of Hereward), also becomes rather like a Victorian Anglican and the novel expresses a vision of England with aspirations that fit a nineteenth-century imperial ideal rather than the aims of the eleventh-century landowner attacking the Normans.[15]

Outlaw traditions need villains, and their heroes, whether upper or lower class, oppose either corrupt and harsh administration or a hated invader. Examples of the latter include Owain Glyndŵr fighting the English, 1400–15, and Robert Bruce and William Wallace resisting Edward I. The essays here show the power of the 'social bandit' myth in Welsh and Scottish responses to English imperialisms and in recent American global politics, in modern prisons and in young offenders' attitudes to their own opposition to authority. Allen Wright's exploration of the relationships between 1950s' American Robin Hood comics and their earlier counterparts in ballad and novel, shows how and why the comics' villains there became 'robber barons', rather than sheriffs, abbots, or kings. The national code regulating US comics forbade disrespect to legal authority or religious figures. If the system cannot be wrong, the outlaw-hero's enemies must become individualistic criminals – demonized by a subliminal link, through 'baron', to an unsavoury, pre-American, feudal bullying. In this world Robin Hood and his men cannot rob: they serve their true king, like undercover agents of justice and morality. In mid-twentieth-century films and comics it is common for any sheriff, royal figure or clergy who acts villainously to be designated as illegitimate or a pretender in his office, using it as a cover for evil. At the same time, as Wright shows, despite the distance this creates with earlier outlaw tales, the comics' wildly implausible narratives locate their new hero within detectably American virtues of democracy, freedom, respect for law, and frequently a distinct strand of zany fantasy. Besides its own bandit traditions, North America has its own Robin Hood history: Robin Hood ballads migrated with settlers and were printed in America, and the USA produced perhaps the finest children's version, by Howard Pyle (1883), besides great Robin Hood films.

Several essays here consider relationships between other outlaw traditions and that of Robin Hood. Stephen Knight's essay examines William Wallace alongside the Early Modern development of some distinctly Scottish versions of Robin Hood. In recent centuries Robin has become the English-speaking world's representative outlaw, through the influence and standardizing effects of printing, children's books and films, but perhaps also because his legend is not restricted by the existence of a documented historical figure or a single classic narrative, leaving the hero remarkably open to being appropriated for a variety of causes, places and eras.[16] Having not only, like many celebrated outlaw-leaders, a henchman, John, but also a company, Robin Hood gives writers opportunities for exploring alternative communal values and turning to the characters and adventures of other merry men. Laura Blunk comments that relationships are a more important theme in British Robin Hood films, whereas Hollywood often goes for individualistic adventures. Two of his band, Marion and the hitherto little researched John, are the subjects of essays here.

The most powerful nationalist outlaw tradition in British history is that of the Welsh bandits, and Adrian Price points to its unique features. Stephen Knight argues that the strongly national and political thrust of Scottish medieval outlaw narratives was, surprisingly, the cause of a sixteenth-century change in the Robin Hood tradition as a whole: a tradition which seems unpoliticized in its medieval form changes into the tales of a dispossessed, virtuous and patriotic earl, defending his rightful king, and versions of that hero appear from the end of the sixteenth-century in England. Knight also stresses the far-reaching importance of another Scottish intervention in the Robin Hood myth, that of Sir Walter Scott in the early nineteenth century. Helen Phillips examines the ambivalence with which Sir Walter Scott, as a lowlander and a Tory, treated the highland Scottish bandits, as well as – in one of his rare fictional forays into medieval Wales – the Welsh, whom Scott portrays, whether princes or bandits, as classic representatives of the noble savage. Marcus A. J. Smith and Julian Wasserman examine the complex ways in which Washington Irving, in the early nineteenth-century, both rejected and adopted the figure of the old English outlaw in his own redefining of the relationship of the New World and, particularly, the American West, to the Old Country. This is in the wake of American Independence and the nascent industrialization of England, compared with the American wilderness. Both Jeffrey Richards and Allen Wright trace the American political and social pressures that led, in films and comics, between the 1950s and 1970s, to the creation of outlaws who actually took over the role of the authorities and defended established government and law and order against antisocial elements, while the distinctive forms taken by the preferred categories of enemy in American comics and films of this period, 'robber barons' and a foreign 'evil empire' respectively, are figures with a wider significance in US political imagination, before and after.

Wasserman and Smith interpret Irving's complex use of outlaw myth as simultaneously his own engagement with the interest in such legends by intellectuals and writers of the early nineteenth century, and as a vehicle for a distinctive post-colonial mediation between the New World and the Old. The highly original images of outlawry and robbery in his oeuvre lead to Irving's striking claim that authorship itself and the world of scholarship are, through their intrinsic intertextuality, the actions of poachers. In his widening of the meaning of outlawry, poaching and purloining, especially as key symbols in his approaches to pre-industrial England and an American's reception of the Old Country, Irving seems to anticipate the ideas of Bourdieu and Deleuze on the nomadic mental acquisitions of the modern intellectual and the possibility of a deterritorialized position for the colonial observer.

Moral territory and authority – kings and outlaws

In fiction and popular tradition, bandit territory is often a moral territory, through its celebration of the rogue who paradoxically does good and dispenses truer justice than the ministers of official justice. The powerful attraction of this alternative moral territory for young male offenders is explored by John Beynon, who shows that holding to this 'mitigation strategy' prevents any advance by them into understanding their own effects on the real-life territory they inhabit, of their own lives and communities.

Kings and outlaws often enjoy symbiotic relationships in these traditions, an initially surprising point made by several authors. Glyn Burgess shows how the literary version of Fouke Fitz Waryn's outlawry, formulating the outlaw's exploits as a romance, depicts 'bad King John' and the 'good outlaw' in a contrastive relationship that makes the outlaw the embodiment of more of the ideal virtues of a good medieval king than the actual holder of the office. Walter Scott more than once creates outlaws and kings who change places with each other. And Jeffrey Richards examines the parallel and contrasting Hollywood treatment of a king and an outlaw, King Arthur and Robin Hood. Some tales adopt a motif found in some romances, where a king visits one of his subjects in disguise: in *A Gest of Robyn Hode* Robin entertains the king and fights with him, without recognizing him.

Outlaw legends often arise from literal struggles over territory. Most outlaw heroes are well born and the denouement may be of estates restored, as with Fouke Fitz Waryn or the fictional hero of the fourteenth-century poem *Gamelyn*, a young man who, after being robbed of his rights by a wicked brother, flees to the woods with a faithful steward and becomes king of the outlaws before finally winning back his land. Quite often too, and this can occur with outlaws of lowly origins, an erstwhile rebel ends up raised to royal service by an appreciative monarch. The heroes of the English ballad *Adam Bell, Clim of the Clough and William of Cloudesley* are yeomen. The tale appears to have been known at least by the fifteenth century and continued to be popular until the nineteenth. The trio of outlawed poachers are operating in Inglewood in Cumbria and their enemy is the Sheriff of Carlisle. Finally the king pardons them, impressed when William succeeds in the feat of shooting an apple on his son's head. The king makes William a rich man and his chief forest-ranger in the north and the queen makes William's wife her chief gentlewoman and governess to the royal nursery.

This picture of acclaim and rewards for outlaws by royalty is more than a happy ending. Such episodes validate the outlaws as ultimately respectful of true and just authority. This idea, that men prepared to break the law and attack law-enforcers, when these are corrupt administrative 'middle-management', can also be respectful towards higher forms of authority, is central to the image of the noble bandit: he is not usually a revolutionary against the system but typically depicted as antagonistic only to bad laws and bad administration of the law or usurpation of royal rule. In practice, historical outlaws, especially when these were powerful politicians or regional lords fighting to regain estates (like Fouke fighting King John or the eleventh-century Earl Godwin opposing Edward the Confessor), often ended up reconciled and pardoned, with lands and rights restored. Indeed, the apparent contrast, for modern readers, between the exiled outlaw and royal power actually hides a close connection in medieval law and administration between the strategies of outlawing and pardoning. Both royal measures are symptomatic of societies without adequate policing to control disorder and subversion. Mark Ormrod has shown that this pattern of late medieval outlaws readily reconciled to authority after a period in the wilderness, literally and legally, matches the fact that royal pardons were very often issued in the fourteenth and fifteenth centuries.[17]

Nationalist leaders and political contenders for government, not unexpectedly, rarely end in such an accommodation with the governing authority (though the Saxon Hereward apparently did). The poem *Wallace*, composed around 1474–9, attributed to a Scottish poet called Blind Hary, ends with Wallace, at his confession before execution, declaring that, far from repenting, if he had his will Robert Bruce, rightful king of Scotland, would control not only Scotland but England, and that he regrets not having killed more Englishmen in the fight for Scotland's rights.[18]

The form that the happy ending of an outlaw narrative takes varies. It tends in one way or another to remove the hero from his former life of crime and his exile from the social structure, and embody a strong sense of the bandit's essential devotion to virtue and ideals. This may take the form of endorsement by the monarch and reconciliation with authority; it may be a righting of wrongs, restored inheritance; or a restating of eternal opposition to an oppressed group's enemies. The last may speak specifically to the politics of a later age – those of a text's later author and readers. Thus, William Wallace's defiance of Edward I was celebrated by fifteenth-century Blind Hary, a century and a half later, to promote resistance to James III's pro-English policies, and it was recreated again in the film *Braveheart* (1995), which influentially coincided with the movement for Scottish devolution, leading to the referendum of 1997. Whereas Hereward was reinterpreted for the Victorian Empire by Kingsley as helping to mould the English into 'a great nation, and the parents of still greater nations in lands as yet unknown', in Geoffrey Trease's socialist *Bows Against the Barons* (1934), Robin Hood's followers vow to work towards Robin's dream of '[a]n England without masters'.[19]

When outlaws are credited with holiness, this may be used either to mitigate or underline their opposition to authority. *Wallace* compared its hero to martyred saints: all highly political – and, as it happens, English – national saints, Oswald, Edmund and Edward, all Anglo-Saxon kings killed fighting the Danish invaders, and St Thomas Becket, killed defending the Church's rights against Henry II. Recently there have been calls for Wallace's sanctification.[20] Hahn and Knight note Robin Hood's devotion to the Virgin Mary in the pre-Reformation ballads, although he readily attacks worldly churchmen. The ballads convey the same antagonism to worldly clerics, especially in religious orders, as appears in Chaucer's *Canterbury Tales*. Like the rebel's reverence for his true king, this attitude goes together with genuine piety. In *A Gest of Robyn Hode*, the hero wants to end his days quietly in the forest in religious devotion, building a shrine to St Mary Magdalene; the ideals behind this decision seem threefold: love of the simple forest life rather than the king's court, love for his men, and the desire to live penitently as his life approaches its close in this world.

In some post-medieval representations of outlaws the concluding motif of reconciliation and peace presided over by the king includes an ideal of new national or social unity. Scott's *Ivanhoe* (1819) combines the return of good King Richard with optimism that Norman and Saxon can live in harmony. Scott's Locksley is one of the best-behaved and most naturally order-loving outlaws known in legend. Yet all narratives in which the outlaw attacks corrupt officials or usurpers, while respecting a higher authority, present an essentially conservative pattern of hope in the ultimate triumph of good government, not a celebration of anarchy or revolution.

The counter-intuitive notion demonstrated by several of these essays, of close affinity between the king and the outlaw – the banished man – has become the subject of theoretical speculation in the writings of Giorgio Agamben. Drawing on Walter Benjamin's concept of the 'bare life', the *'blosse Leben'*, human biological existence reduced to essentials, introduced in Benjamin's discussion of tragedy, Agamben sees the power to banish men from their legal rights as the essential definition of sovereignty.[21] Agamben's banned and banished man is a figure who can be killed with impunity, though not a sacrifice. Some critics have considered in the light of this theory certain Shakespearean victims, heroes of medieval romance and some outlaw narratives.[22] As this collection of essays demonstrates, bandit legends may entertain the possibility of prince and outcast changing places, and of rapport between the noble rogue, the law-breaker, and his true lord, the king from whom genuine justice springs. As Ruth Evans has argued, Agamben's theory fits well the type of medieval narrative where a princely or aristocratic figure (Tristan and Sir Orfeo are examples) spends time in the wilderness for a period, mad and separated from human society.[23]

Yet Agamben's theory, that sovereign power is inherently linked with an absolute state of human abjection typified by the banished man who loses his rights, proves illuminating for late medieval British outlaw narratives also because of many respects in which it doesn't work with them. It reveals how distinct the patterns of these narratives are. English monarchs of the fourteenth and fifteenth centuries, the period when the Robin Hood plays and tales became popular, often lacked secure sovereignty in the sense in which continental theorists like Foucault or Agamben conceive it. The state of political disorder in fifteenth-century England in which real-life outlaws flourished was born from relatively weak royal government and power struggles between magnates and dynasties. Monarchy lacked central control over aristocrats who dominated factions and regions with private armies that included gangsters and outlaws. The law of outlawry had already changed: an outlaw might no longer be killed with impunity and was not in a state of absolute helplessness in relationship to the king's law. And, although the life of robbers and political outcasts may often have been bleak, in late medieval fiction the outlaw's territory is a fantasy of luxury rather than Lear-like nakedness: it is not the opposite of aristocratic life but (notably in *A Gest of Robyn Hode*) more like an alternative court, a sylvan land of Cockaigne, where guests and captives may be feasted royally and loaded with expensive horses, goods, and clothes, when they leave the lordly king of the outlaws.[24] It seems clear that 'greenwood', like 'merry men', acquired a glamorized image and a specific association with outlaw tales as early as the early thirteenth century.[25] Several Early Modern visions of the outlaw merge it with the similarly romanticized vision of the pastoral, as in Shakespeare's *As You Like It* and Ben Jonson's *The Sad Shepherd*.[26] Like virtually all features of the myth of the noble bandit, this image of the banished man in the wilds as enjoying a life of delight and luxury – at times as a quasi-lord with his court – is richly paradoxical, particularly when, as with the *Gest*, the outlaw leader is a yeoman and no exiled aristocrat. While Agamben and Hobsbawm focus on the features that unite versions of the outlaw, across centuries and cultures, the essays collected here, like the history of British bandits and outlaws in general, also show how very specific to period, place and ideology their narratives are.

Kings have enjoyed appropriating the imagery of romantically wild and courageous outlaw life. Henry VIII and his courtiers dressed up as Robin and the merry men to amuse Katherine of Aragon and her ladies one May morning (1510). In 1515 Henry and Katherine enjoyed a *fête champêtre* at Shooter's Hill near Greenwich, being met by two hundred men dressed as outlaws and enjoying a breakfast of venison. Outlaw pageants have a long history as princely entertainments. Royal appropriation of the imagery of subversiveness, apart from the opportunities for fun (and fun can have political capital), has symbolic potential for dramatizing menace and displaying royal control over disorderly subjects. When the defeated French King Jean II was being escorted towards

London in 1357, as a hostage after the battle of Poitiers, the English arranged for his cavalcade to be met by five hundred green-clad men disguised as merry outlaws with bows and swords, which the royal captive was informed was an English tradition – men enjoying life in the woods and issuing forth in the fashion that they had accosted the cavalcade. This holds barbed political symbolism: the royal victim-spectator is met by play-bandits and play-huntsmen; and after an English victory, due in part to long-bow success, is faced with a sylvan reminder of English archery prowess. The chronicler does not mention Robin Hood's name in association with this pageant, though it occurred at Whitsuntide, the time for parish Robin Hood plays.[27] One reason for Robin Hood's long domination over later British culture, compared with the many other medieval British outlaws, must be his appearance from at least the fifteenth century onwards, if not (as is likely) one to two centuries earlier, in plays and pageants. These Whitsuntide festivities were often called the 'May games'. Stephen Knight shows how much these were, in sixteenth-century Scotland particularly, expensive urban celebrations, organized by the town council and chief citizens, not merely 'folk' or peasant entertainments.

Political outlaws

There is scholarly debate about whether outlaw traditions embody conservative or radical ideals. This arose in the historical journal *Past and Present* in the 1950s. Starting from R. H. Hilton's suggestion that Robin Hood ballads reflected the 1381 Rising, the debate embraced contending views about the legend's origins and its sociopolitical import. Where Hilton and others proposed affinity with peasants' aspirations, J. C. Holt suggested the earliest audiences may have been pre-1381 and gentry households.[28] Outlaw stories do sometimes exhibit opposition to hierarchy: in *Robin Hood and the Monk* a striking thread of ideas runs through the portrayal of the outlaw group about leadership and deference, embodied in Little John's opposition to Robin's attempt to impose himself as master in a conventional sense. The outlaw band also has the potential to become a microcosm for exploration of alternative social orders and ideals, as several novelists have shown, whether the ideals are, for example, socialist, like Henry Gilbert's *Robin Hood and the Men of the Greenwood*, 1912, or feminist: see David Blamires's discussion. *Robin Hood and the Monk* is a ballad where Little John is the real hero, and Laura Blunk traces the tradition's use through ensuing centuries of John and Robin as a source of opposing views, where occasionally, as in the film *Robin and Marion* (1976), John proves the wiser. In *Wallace* the hero is reprimanded after his spying adventure, disguised as a potter, by his fellow-commander of the Scottish army, Sir John the Graham, that such escapades ill befit a chieftain: Wallace replies that to free Scotland it will be necessary for himself and even men of high rank to do dangerous deeds and even sometimes break accustomed rules. In Wales, English imperialism ensured that bandit activity and guerrilla warfare were often conducted by respected leaders, commanding widespread public support: Adrian Price records that the followers of Owain Glyndŵr are triumphantly celebrated in poetry, as 'Birds of Crime' and chivalric knights of the forest.

Bandits, sex, and relationships

Blamires shows how children's authors used Maid Marion to raise feminist challenges to conventions in two very different ways. In some books and films Marion is a tomboy, equal or (in Robyn MacKinley's *The Outlaws of Sherwood Forest*, 1988) superior to men in masculine skills like archery. In Gayle Feyrer's *The Thief's Mistress* (1996) Marion becomes on occasion a brutal killer. In Theresa Tomlinson's *The Forest-Wife* the social criteria are altered, not the degree of female participation in a masculine society. Marion is a healer and Robin proves in need of her skills. Such remakings of the female outlaw myth propose not acceptance of women in a man's world but a re-thinking of that world's values. An active and courageous Marion appears as early as the seventeenth-century ballad *Robin Hood and Maid Marion* and in Peacock's *Maid Marian* (1822) and Tennyson's play *The Foresters* (1891). Yet the essentially masculine values and dreams of the greenwood myth, such as toughness and escape from social ties and home, create problems for writing about Maid Marion. Novels, where relationships must be developed over time, have always found it hard to decide what Robin and Marion's relationship is: are they married, sexually attached or platonic?

The duo of Robin and John has been at the tradition's heart since its earliest appearance. Laura Blunk explores this history, revealing the extent to which changes in the rank of John have equalled the changes in Robin (ranging from yeoman or even serf to earl), and how shifting images of masculinity affect this figure in film. In several Victorian novels and some late twentieth-century British TV versions, John and other merry men have been devoted married men. In *Prince of Thieves* (1991) the hero's relationship to a male companion, more powerful than that with Marian, is with the black Muslim, Azeem: a development that parallels the appearance in Hollywood buddy movies of black–white comrades (from *The Heat of the Night* to *Lethal Weapon*).

Knight and Hahn explore the territorial and cross-territorial subject of gender definition and encounters or negotiations between masculine and feminine spheres. From its earliest medieval origins, the Robin Hood tradition has been a source of masculine motifs and wish-fulfilment. It involves plots of action and conflict, a landscape for individual activity and control, the charm of the sort of adventures Hahn and Knight call 'phallic narcissism', as well as the myth of the little man defying authority, and the myth of freedom from the responsibilities of home and workplace. Its emotional bonds are homosocial and sometimes, Hahn and Knight show, homoerotic. The myth has been used by several gay writers. The presence of Maid Marian in later versions of the legend means that the hero operates emotionally in two distinct territories, bonding with men and with the opposite sex. At times, as with the great American children's author, Howard Pyle, the result is a hymn to the joys and values of masculine bonding, with Robin's final return to the forest as a return to, above all, his male friends.[29] The bachelor brigand of early Robin Hood ballads and some later versions differs from many British outlaws, including

Hereward and William Wallace, who have romantic entanglements and wives, and Fouke Fitz Waryn, whose loyal wife gives birth while accompanying him in the forest, or the Inglewood outlaws, who owe their escape from the sheriff's clutches to a resourceful outlaw's wife.

Outlaw traditions have been used also as fantasy territories: Robin Hood is a favourite for 'fanzines' and 'slash' fiction, where fans invent and publish on the web their own stories about existing characters, often with sexual encounters between characters, and frequently queering the heterosexual relationships of the established versions. Shenagh Pugh has argued powerfully for these as a new democratization and de-commercialization of the production of fiction. The catalyst for such personal fictional bandit spin-offs is usually the TV series 'Robin of Sherwood', with its strong ecological and pagan themes.[30] Graeme Morton has discussed the socio-economic contexts and the commercial potential of what he calls 'Wallace.com', the fan spin-offs and commercial promotions associated with *Braveheart*, in terms both of globalization of cultures and specific economic opportunities for Scotland, with the film creating 'a niche market for Scottish culture'.[31] The processes by which history becomes myth, particularly the myths that compose narratives of national identity, are evident in the histories of outlaw traditions in Britain. Since Robert Burns composed the song in 1787, Scots have often taken 'Scots wha hae wi' Wallace bled' as a national anthem – while its words, about 'oppression's woes and pains' and 'tyrants' and 'liberty', suggest Burns was thinking as much about contemporary political radicals as Scotland's early fourteenth-century battles against Edward I. Robin Hood has recently been nominated one of the 'icons of England', together with cricket and red 'Routemaster' buses (the website declares him a 'champion of the poor' and a figure 'derived from ancient legendary figures who represented the spirit of spring-time rebirth', a belief that goes back mostly to the 1980s TV series *Robin of Sherwood*, and also 'a Celtic warlord': all three claims representing relatively modern additions to older concepts of Robin Hood and the last probably confusing him with King Arthur).[32]

Places and territories

British bandits are often local heroes and, on occasion, national heroes. The territory, in a literal sense, where such a hero operated becomes a revered – or contested – place. Today, Yorkshire and Nottinghamshire contend over ownership of Robin Hood, and both Yorkshire and Sherwood locations are named in the earliest ballads. Newspaper articles and claims to have discovered the 'real' Robin Hood continue to show this, only fairly, friendly rivalry. A formulaic statement, 'Robin Hood in . . . stood' seems to have been widely used from the fifteenth century on (whether it originated in the plays or ballads or in some other context remains mysterious), but it is recorded with three alternative locations named: 'Sherwood', 'Barnsdale' (Yorkshire), and the neutral 'greenwood'. Yet Robin Hood plays were performed in many parts of England and Scotland in the late medieval and Early Modern periods: it looks as if, early on, he was neither a regional hero nor even an exclusively English one. As Adrian Price shows, the historical Shropshire landowner, Fouke Fitz Waryn, became in Welsh folklore Fouke Morgannwg, 'Fouke of Glamorgan'. In Early Modern Scotland riders dressed as Robin Hood and Little John replaced two earlier leaders of civic pageants: the Abbot of Unreason and Monk of Misrule (these might themselves be relabelled as Abbot and Prior of Bonacord, less subversively). Possibly an originally English outlaw tradition has moved north, though Knight also discusses the possibility that Robin Hood originated in Scotland.

Material memorials may follow literature: tourism is not just a modern phenomenon. Sometimes these then engender further legends and alleged associations. Visitors in the thirteenth-century were being shown 'Hereward's Castle', a wooden house in the fens, and Robin Hood's alleged grave at Kirklees had to be railed, in the eighteenth-century, because enthusiasts were chipping bits off it.[33] 'Little John's Grave' in Hathersage churchyard, Derbyshire, prompts the question of whether it was named after the ballads or whether Little John's size in the ballads derives from the existence of this long grave. Perhaps the tale of Robin shooting an arrow to mark his grave at Kirklees was introduced to explain the half mile or so separating the alleged grave of the hero from Kirklees Priory: is this the legend following upon the geography, or did the grave's location, oddly amidst woods, follow from the tale of his murder at Kirklees, found already in *Gest*? The present gravestone dates from the late eighteenth century and there is no sign of a grave under it.

The title, *Bandit Territories*, reflects the fact that most of the essays are concerned with crossing between territories – lowland/highland; gay/straight; male/female; Scotland/England; Wales/England; king/rebel – as well as the fact that bandit literature generally claims that the outlaw inhabits his own territory in the sense both of lurking in the forest, mountain or cave, and also as representative of a higher justice than the current holders of power, be those imperialist invaders or corrupt authorities.

A statement by the Scottish historian Andrew of Wyntoun (*c.*1420), discussed by Knight, touches many of the issues associated with the figure of the bandit. Wyntoun says Robin Hood and John operated in Inglewood, a comment possibly mirroring the ubiquity of their traditions in Britain before printing fixed them down to Sherwood or Barnsdale, or perhaps reflecting the fluidity with which outlaw stories interact – for it was famously Clim of the Clough and his comrades, rather than Robin, who operated in Inglewood. Wyntoun then says Robin and John were highwaymen, 'Waithmen', and 'commendit guid', praised highly.[34] Is this apparent oxymoron the attitude towards English troublemakers of a partisan Scot, delighting in any disruption in adjacent English territory, or does it encapsulate the paradox always at the heart of the bandit myth – that of the robber who is admired?

NOTES

[1] Hobsbawm, passim.
[2] Texts in KO, pp. 169–83, 269–80.
[3] KO, pp. 269–80 (includes text), esp. pp. 269–70. Thomas Ohlgren explores the relationship of the Pastons to late medieval Robin Hood texts in his *Robin Hood: The Earliest Poems, 1465–1560* (Newark: University of Delaware Press, 2007).

4   An important anthropological-folkloric study is Joseph F. Nagy, 'The Paradoxes of Robin Hood', *Folklore* 91 (1980), 198–210.
5   Keen, pp. 9–10.
6   'The Outlawry of Earl Godwin from the *Vita Ædwardi Regis*', Timothy S. Jones (trans.), in *Medieval Outlaws: Ten Tales in Modern English*, Thomas H. Ohlgren (ed.) (Stroud: Sutton, 1998), pp. 1–11.
7   John Trevisa, *On the Properties of Things: John Trevisa's Translations on Bartholomaeus Anglicus 'De proprietatibus rerum'*, M. C. Seymour (ed.) (Oxford: Clarendon Press, 1975), p. 124 a/b; Derek Pearsall, *The Life of Geoffrey Chaucer: A Critical Biography* (Oxford: Blackwell, 1992), p. 213.
8   Keen, pp. 197–201.
9   William Langland, *Piers the Plowman, The A, B, C, and Z Versions*, A. V. C. Schmidt (ed.), 2 vols (London: Longman, 1995), vol. 1, pp. 564–5, B 14:301, C 16:137.
10 Ibid., pp. 704–5, B 19:247, C 21:247.
11 See on Hereward, and other medieval outlaws, Ohlgren, *Medieval Outlaws*, esp. pp. 12–60; on Edric, Susan Reynolds, 'Edric Silvaticus and the English Resistance', *Bulletin of the Institute of Historical Research* 54, no. 129 (1981), pp. 102–5.
12 Walter Map, *De nugis curialium, Courtiers' Trifles*, M. R. James, rev. C. N. L. Brooke and R. A. B. Mynors (eds), Oxford Medieval Texts (Oxford: Clarendon Press, 1983), pp. 154–9; *Gesta Herewardi*, Michael Swanton (trans.), in KO, pp. 633–67; Reynolds, 'Edric', pp. 104–5.
13 Knight 1994, pp. 143–8; text in KO, pp. 441–51.
14 Jennifer Westwood, *Albion: A Guide to Legendary Britain* (London: Granada, 1985), pp. 300–4.
15 Victor Head, *Hereward* (Stroud: Sutton, 1995), pp. 123–37.
16 See Bennett A. Brockman, 'Robin Hood and the Invention of Children's Literature', *Children's Literature* 10 (1982), 1–17.
17 W. M. Ormrod, 'Robin Hood and Public Record: The Authority of Writing in the Medieval Outlaw Tradition', in *MCS*, pp. 57–74.
18 *Hary's Wallace*, Matthew P. McDiarmid (ed.), Scottish Text Society, 2 vols (Edinburgh: Edinburgh University Press, 1968, 1969), vol. 2, p. 120, ll. 1373–90.
19 Charles Kingsley, *Hereward the Wake, The Last of the English* (London: P. R. Gawthorn, 1949), p. 362; Geoffrey Trease, *Bows Against the Barons*, rev. edn (London: Hodder and Stoughton, 1966), p. 152.
20 *Hary's Wallace*, p. 118, ll. 1307–8. See Graeme Morton, *William Wallace, Man and Myth* (Stroud: Sutton, 2001), pp. 59–61, 139–52.
21 Giorgio Agamben, *Homo Sacer: Sovereign Power and Bare Life*, Daniel Heller-Roazen (trans.) (Stanford: Stanford University Press, 1998); see also Walter Benjamin, 'Ursprung des deutschen Trauerspiels', *Gesammelte Schriften*, Rolf Tiedemann (ed.), 4 vols (Frankfurt-am-Main: Suhrkamp, 1980), vol. 1, pp. 203–409, esp. pp. 245–55.
22 Paul Strohm, 'York's Paper Crown: "Bare Life" and Shakespeare's First

23 Tragedy', *Journal of Medieval and Early Modern Studies* 36:1 (2006), pp. 75–103; Ruth Evans, 'Sir Orfeo and the Bare Life', in *MCS*, pp. 198–212.
23 Evans, '*Sir Orfeo*', esp. pp. 200–6.
24 On the alternative ideals of community in such narratives, see Douglas Gray, 'Everybody's Robin Hood', and Derek Pearsall, 'Little John and *Robin Hood and the Monk*', in *RHMP*, pp. 21–41 and 42–50 (esp. 29–30 and 48–9).
25 See my '"Merry", "Merry Men" and "Greenwood": A History of Some Meanings', in Joshua Calhoun and Lois Potter (eds), *Images of Robin Hood* (Newark: University of Delaware Press, 2008).
26 Richard Wilson, '"Like the Old Robin Hood": *As You Like It* and the Enclosure Riots', *Shakespeare Quarterly*, 43 (1992), 1–19; Stephen Knight, '"Meere English Flocks": Ben Jonson's *The Sad Shepherd* and the Robin Hood Tradition', in *RHMP*, pp. 129–44
27 *Anonimalle Chronicle 1333–1380*, V. Galbraith (ed.), (Manchester and New York: Manchester University Press, 1927), p. 41.
28 See Thomas Hahn's analysis, relating this to the birth of cultural studies, 'Robin Hood and the Birth of Cultural Studies', *MCS*, pp. 39–54.
29 *The Merry Adventures of Robin Hood of Great Renown in Nottinghamshire* (New York: Scribner, 1883).
30 Sheenagh Pugh, *Democratic Fictions* (Bridgend: Seren, 2006); Henry Jenkins, *Textual Poachers* (New York and London: Routledge, 1992), 168, 239, 252, 282.
31 Morton, *William Wallace*, 139–52.
32 *www.icons.org.uk/theicons*.
33 On questions and mysteries raised by the grave see David Hepworth, 'A Grave Tale', in *RHMP*, pp. 91–112.
34 KO, p. 24.

'Exempt me, Sire, for I am afeard of women': Gendering Robin Hood

THOMAS HAHN AND STEPHEN KNIGHT[1]

Robin Hood and women

Riding hard the horse between his thighs, speeding target-splitting arrows from his bow, surrounded by tall sprouting trees, Robin Hood would seem to represent hetero-masculinity in its archetypal form. But is that all?

The tights that reveal the manly legs were in fact first worn by nineteenth-century actresses in pantomime and musical, using the role of principal boy to reveal their own alluring thighs. Robin's green-tighted display might, perhaps, be acceptable as male narcissism, if a little disconcerting in its origins; but more discomposing to the notion of an all-male outlaw is the all-male relationship he has with his rival for Marian: as Eve Kosofsky Sedgwick has shown in *Between Men*,[2] the interaction of such male rivals is freighted, even fraught, with same-sex emotion. At the end of the 1938 *Adventures of Robin Hood*, the sword-fight between Robin and Guy comes to a complex climax as, with swords locked together, the two men are face to face, panting, excited, close enough to kiss.

Another twentieth-century work overtly indicates that Robin's sexuality is not exclusively heterosexual male. The title of this essay quotes a caption from the landmark Douglas Fairbanks film of 1922. The Earl of Huntingdon, the future Robin Hood, has just won the tournament that opened the movie, and King Richard – played by a robustly patriarchal Wallace Beery – instructs him to receive the victor's chaplet from the fair Maid Marian, who stands upon a dais across a clearing. The woman-fearing caption flashes on the screen

'EXEMPT ME, SIRE, FOR I AM AFEARD OF WOMEN'

after Huntingdon, having turned his curious and then anxious gaze upon Marian, speaks with the king in earnest distress. The king finds his knight's apprehensions hilariously funny, and pushes him off to take his prize. After the Earl has awkwardly accepted his reward, he lurches backwards down the steps of the dais with an acrobatic quasi-ineptitude reminiscent of Chaplin. Back in the clearing, a mob of young women – encouraged by the king, and dressed more like flappers than medieval ladies – descend upon the Earl, and throw him into a full-blown panic. The Earl, still clothed in knightly attire, pushes through the women, dives into the river, and swims underwater to escape their clutches; when he finally surfaces on the other bank, near a maid-servant washing clothes, the next caption reads: 'Another Woman!'.

The scene dramatizes the Earl's masculine prowess and his sexual naivety, and even suggests some link between these features of his heroism: tournaments are not won by woman-lovers. As far as the Earl is concerned, his relationship with his Sire and his usefulness to the king as a loyal knight do not entail any connection with women; Huntingdon's boyish charm and the ethos of homosocial competition make the exclusion of women seem appropriate, even natural. That evening in the castle – the last night before the departure on the Great Crusade – King Richard attempts to give the Earl some explicit tutelage on the central importance of heterosexuality to mature masculine gender identity. As the camera pans the great hall of the castle, men and women pair off to say their last goodbyes, wandering off to talk and embrace by themselves. When the king looks for Huntingdon, however, he espies him with a bunch of his comrades, literally rolling on the floor, clutching each other in a series of wrestling holds. The king speaks with him, gesturing towards the heterosexuality so vividly illustrated in the surrounding couples, but Huntingdon takes little notice. In fact, he becomes engaged with heterosexuality only negatively, when Prince John – who himself shows no direct interest in women, and who is clearly coded as homosexual – attempts to procure Marian not for himself, but for his traitorous fellow conspirator, the dastardly Guy of Gisborne, the very man Huntingdon had defeated in the tournament. The Earl follows John upstairs to one of the private parts of the castle and intervenes when he lays hands on Marian. When Huntingdon draws his sword the cowardly John exits. This is followed by several minutes running time of intense and spectacular gazing at Marian by the hero; this scene clearly does what the king failed to do, that is activate the power of heterosexuality and assimilate the Earl to it. Following all these wordless stares, the caption declares: 'I never knew a woman could be this way!' The boisterous hero is conquered, and so has become a real man.

Marian is the link that holds the two halves of this disjoint film together: she calls the Earl back from the crusade to help their troubled country, and it is after her supposed death that he becomes Robin Hood, elusive rebel against the usurper Prince John. In making a woman the linchpin of the narrative, and in making romance an indispensable component of the adventure plot, Fairbanks's *Robin Hood* established the model for every succeeding version of the hero produced in Hollywood (including those starring Flynn, Costner, Bergin, and, in part parodically, Elwes). Before the Fairbanks film, the heterosexual romance had formed part of the Robin Hood tradition as it developed in the nineteenth century, in lengthy novels like Pierce Egan's *Robin Hood and Little John* (1840), and very influentially in theatrical treatments. There existed by 1822, a new romantic Robin Hood tradition started with Thomas Love Peacock's *Maid Marian* and widely popularized from the same year throughout the century in J. R. Planché's *Maid Marian, or The Huntress of Arlingford*.[3] There were many pantomimes and musicals developing this overtly heteronormative theme, the most prestigious being Tennyson's *The Foresters*, successfully produced in America in 1892 with music by Sir Arthur Sullivan. But film was most influenced by Reginald de Koven's musical *Maid Marian*, first performed in 1890: this was the premier vehicle for the story in the early twentieth century, and MGM planned to film it, with Jeanette McDonald and Nelson Eddy, in 1935.[4] In all these versions Marian plays a significant, though rarely an active role, but she is on stage at crucial moments, as a desired object, captive and finally legitimate heterosexual partner.

Marian's recurrent role in film is generically inspired. The origin of her presence in the tradition seems involved with dramatic production, for in the first Robin Hood play in the professional theatre – Anthony Munday's *The Downfall of Robert, Earle of Huntington* (1598–9) – she plays a part and she consistently appears throughout eighteenth-century ballad operas, nineteenth-century stage productions, ranging from Tennyson's gravity, through Planché's light opera, to the many farcical entertainments and pantomimes in which Victorians celebrated the outlaw tradition. There were practical reasons for her presence: once the tradition became musical, well-established by the eighteenth century in the ballad operas, then female voices were essential for variety, and parts had to be found for them; further, the need to attract and hold the attention of a female paying audience had a good deal to do with it. In terms of ideology, her early role may relate to class rather than gender: it is noticeable that she only appears in texts, whether play or novel, where Robin is gentrified – she is originally a lady rather than a woman, and the only broadside ballad where she appears, and fights Robin vigorously in male incognito is also the only one where he is identified as the Earl of Huntingdon, 'Robin Hood and Maid Marian'.

The absence of the early Marian and the contrary force of the theatrical tradition were both factors in the development of the screenplay for the Warner's film of 1938: in an early memo, Rowland Leigh (the first of the writers for the movie) said:

> I would strenuously put forward the suggestion in this case either that Maid Marian be omitted completely, in that she is a later . . . addition to the story of Robin Hood, or that she be brought in as little as possible, because women had no place in the scheme of life of Robin Hood and his band of merry men.[5]

Leigh's scholarship is accurate (though there is more to be said on gender in the early texts, as will be explored below), but the tradition of nineteenth-century theatre and the Fairbanks film dominated. In the Warner's version and in later films, the relationship with Marian becomes the touchstone of Robin's masculinity, marking the hero's move from the naive phallic narcissism of the Greenwood – a potentially endless cycle of competitive adventures, blithely insensible to the teleologies of history and story – to his identification with the Law of the

Father, a political and social awareness symbolized by generational distinctions, the giving and taking of women in marriage, and the possession and inheritance of property. Rather than reflecting the authenticity of the scheme of life of Robin Hood and his band of merry men together in the forest – itself a fantasy with little historical underpinning – the centrality of romance in these screenplays reproduces the historical pressures exerted by a dominant heteronormativity within Western popular and mass culture. The heterophobia induced by the female riot in the Fairbanks film sets the stage for the advance to mature masculinity and 'proper' gender identification: loyalty to the Sire requires more than phallic performativity and bumptious homoeroticism; as Huntingdon's return to England against the king's explicit command makes clear, the Law of the Father seals patriarchal claims to land, law, offspring, titles and social status through active engagement with the normative force of heterosexuality.

Hollywood cinema, which has brought Robin Hood stories to a far broader and more diverse audience than any previous medium, has insisted upon heteronormativity as the foundation of the hero's identity and of the narrative's meaning; each of the five best-known films ends as a romance, with a marriage scene presided over by that symbolic sire, the king. In the Fairbanks and Flynn pictures, the hero's manliness is set off by the illegitimate semi-masculinity of the two Prince Johns (played by Sam Jaffe and Claude Rains), who are characterized as self-absorbed yet ineffectual, wrongfully coveting political power, without overt heterosexual interests of their own, and committed to holding the attachment of male subordinates like Guy. In their effete personal demeanour, habitual nervousness, and distaste for action, the characters represent a homophobic inverse of true masculinity. More recent films have offered subtler versions of normative male identities: in *Prince of Thieves*, for example, when Robin and Azeem are about to be launched over the castle wall by the trebuchet, the Moor asks 'Is she worth it, Christian?', repeating Robin's query to Azeem from earlier in the film. The scene allusively reproduces the memorable leap made by Butch Cassidy and Sundance in the 1969 film, but without its rich ambiguity; as a decisive heterosexual disclaimer made from a position of racial difference,

Azeem's rhetorical question renders the bond between man and man innocent, and the union of man and woman universal. A shot in *Robin Hood* with Patrick Bergin and Uma Thurman, made in the same year as *Prince of Thieves*, comes much closer to open homosexual panic: Thurman, unconvincingly cross-dressed as the boy Martin, has enabled Robin's close escape from an ambush by the authorities; when Martin celebrates their freedom by kissing Robin *right on the lips*, the camera offers a close-up of Bergin's face, conveying a sequence of expressions from dismay and confusion at this aggressive and preposterous overture to a dawning and ambiguous interest or pleasure. The succeeding episode dissolves any uncertainty that may have surrounded the sexual encounter, however, for Martin/Marian and Robin are shown as a couple, attentive both to the injustices in the countryside and to their own heterosexual desires. The Law of the Father challenges other possible gender relations.

Robin Hood and men

The interdependent homosocial and homophobic elements that underpin cinematic versions of the Robin Hood story receive fullest acknowledgement in the latest Hollywood production, Mel Brooks's *Robin Hood: Men in Tights*, where they are perhaps the central target of the allusive satire. In a scene that Brooks reruns as his signature in the credits, Rabbi Tuchmann casts a suspicious eye over the band of merry men – whom Robin has introduced – and, shaking his hand dubiously, intones, 'Fagelles?', the Yiddish for homosexuals. Robin, responding to this 'natural' misperception of an exclusively male group dressed in revealing clothing, says: 'No, we're straight; merry, but straight'. Throughout, the film plays with the contradictions embedded in this fantasy of merry masculinity, which ranges from a symbolization of the Law of the Father – a medallion containing the key to Marian's genitals and land – through homosocial phallic narcissism in various scenes of competition and bonding, to heterosexual triumphalism, in the male audience's raucous response to the shadow-projection of Robin's self-erecting sword as he sings romantically (and also parodically) to Marian. The presence of homophobia as an uneasy partner to legitimate masculinity – whether narcissistic or heterosexual – emerges most forcefully in the decidedly camp production of the title song, whose refrain is: 'We're men, we're men in tights . . . If you get us wrong, we'll put out your lights'. This self-parodic spectacle presents a chorus line of singing and dancing men celebrating their 'right' masculinity; their instinctual conviction that they are 'real men' takes the form of spontaneous aggression against any imputation of non-straight identity. Their dissonant performance enacts a version of homophobic panic, disclosing the insecurity and mobility of masculine gender identity; its lack of fixity to exclusively heterosexual desire. In the same way, it is notable by the end that in fact none of the merry men are gay: Little John, though frightened and indeed flattened by Marian's massive Germanic maid, has in fact accepted her as partner. The film raises the possibility of gay outlaws – like black sheriffs in *Blazing Saddles* – only to provide assurance that they are only a joke.

Such an overt awareness of and anxiety about sexuality, of whatever kind, is a long distance from the earliest representations of Robin Hood. The early ballads, popular narratives that detail the potentially endless cycles of traditional masculine adventures, have had a less tense relationship with a representation of male-male feeling. Yet plainly by the sixteenth and seventeenth centuries, in its close attachment to masculinity and the unstructured world of the forest, 'merry' already occupied a peculiar cultural register, and the actions of the 'merry men' constructed a specific meaning, a characteristic, though obviously idealized, milieu of normative homosociality. For a man to be merry is to act outside the constraints of ordinary class structures and social identities, to move in an unalienated world of spontaneous potency; here, without any external coercion or incentive beyond the pleasure in performance and achievement, a man really *can* do what a 'man's gotta do'. And, as the proliferating *mano-a-mano* struggles in the early ballads make clear, what a man's got to do is to find mates, make matches and enter bonds with other men. Same-sex competition and violence lead to deep attachments in the merry Greenwood, for this natural, unsocialized locale defines an ideal space where a man can know a man for what he is and does, rather than for his socially enjoined identity. In this space, physical encounters produce no destructive rivalries, for merry men seek no deferred object through their competition; without the exchange of women or the possibility of inherited social position and property, seeking and meeting one's match produces masculine amity and egalitarian union. In a world where the Law of the Father ostensibly does not obtain, there is no future, and no need for exclusive triumph.

Yet if the space of the outlaw is defined by the opposing frontiers of authority, then the law – especially the law of that symbolic father, the king – always lurks as a structural feature of this identity. Moreover, in all Robin Hood stories, at some point the hero becomes the king's man; in the early narratives, notably in *A Gest of Robyn Hode* (*c*.1500), this is a temporary condition which the hero escapes by reverting to the merry Greenwood, whereas in the Hollywood films Robin's acceptance of the Father's Law is the premise of his heroism. The texture of the merry world produced in the early ballads, and the contradictions inherent in the unconstrained life of the Greenwood, are illustrated in a memorable episode in *A Gest of Robyn Hode*, in which King Edward enters the forest disguised in 'monkes wede': after Robin has distributed twenty pounds to his 'mery men' and 'bad them mery to be', the seeming monk announces:

> Well the greteth Edward our kynge
> And sent to the his seal. (1534–5)[6]

He draws out from under his cloak an image of the monarch. Robin, who 'coud his courteysy . . . set hym on his kne', and declares:

> I love no man in all the worlde
> So well as I do my kynge;
> Welcome is my lordes seale. (1542–4)

Michael Clanchy has characterized the capacity of medieval kings to reproduce themselves in authorized effigies as a Weberian bureaucratization of charisma, and it is this aura, rather than the masculine person of the king, that Robin venerates.[7] The ballad's image of the king holding an image of the king and proving the loyalty of even his outlaw subjects emblematizes how the Law of the Father in a non-sexualized form runs through the forest, licensing the Greenwood as merry space not simply for the band, but for interpellated readers and listeners as well. Moving deeper into the Greenwood, the king discovers that natural relations among men result in an order that exceeds the regime imposed by custom, law, or fear: when Robin's men kneel before him without prompting, the king remarks:

> Here is a wonder semely syght:
> Me thynketh, by Goddes pyne,
> His men are more at his byddynge
> Then my men be at myn. (1562–5)

The Law of the Father, though it takes the king as its symbolic source and guarantor, retains its potency beyond any particular intervention by the person of the king or statute.

The king, however, remains a man among merry men in an untroubled homosocial world, as the remainder of the episode makes clear. After a great feast, Robin arranges an archery contest so that the 'monk' may report back to the king 'what lyfe we lede' (1578) together in the forest. The game, pluck-buffet, demands that anyone who misses his mark receives a blow from his competitor. When Robin is outdone by Gilbert of the White Hand, he asks the disguised king to administer the 'buffet on his hede' (1598); at first the king demurs, but, catching the spirit of the event, he gives Robin a stroke that nearly knocks him to the ground. Robin responds immediately to his opponent's manliness:

> Thou arte a stalworthe frere . . .
> There is pith in thyn arme . . .
> Thus our kynge and Robyn Hode
> Togeder gan they mete. (1633–7)

The physical exchange spurs Robin to look the king 'wystly in the face', and at this moment he recognizes the royal countenance, and again kneels. Robin agrees to attend the king, and as they proceed back to court through the Greenwood, the king throws off his monk's disguise and dresses himself and his entire retinue in 'Lyncolne grene . . . Outlawes as they were'

'EXEMPT ME, SIRE, FOR I AM AFEARD OF WOMEN'

(1686, 1693). Recognition of authority does not disrupt the homosocial games. 'Our kynge and Robyn rode togyder', and Robin engages Edward in another game of pluck-buffet:

And many a buffet our kynge wan
Of Robyn Hode that day,
And nothynge spared good Robyn
Our kynge in his pay. (1698–1701)

The two behave towards each other as equals, matching shot for shot, and trading blow for blow within the framework of manly competition. The merry Greenwood – the world of phallic masculinity – sanctions what would be unthinkable in the real social or political sphere. The Law of the Father underwrites the merriness of a universalized phallic narcissism, so that direct assaults on the king's person – treasonous acts once back in court – reflect a total equality between men.

The gentrified tradition, especially on the stage, brought this all-male story into the awareness of gender, with some occasionally odd results – in the 1730 *Robin Hood: An Opera* Will Stutely and other outlaws plan to rape Marian and her friend Marina, till Robin smoothes things over; the opposite of such heterosexual aggression appears in Pierce Egan's long novel *Robin Hood and Little John* (1840), where Robin and Will Scarlet deliberately share kissing sessions with, between them, as it were, Maude, Will's fiancée.

Apart from these exotic instances of gender raising its ambiguous head in the tradition, a major transmitter of the early ballads indicates both its relation to and nervousness about the deep homosociality of the early ballad tradition. Howard Pyle's *Merry Adventures of Robin Hood* (1883), directly addressed to the boy culture of the later nineteenth century, reproduces the plots and details of many of the early ballads in what is perhaps the most compendious and influential collection of the modem era. Women make up no part of this idyll: Robin thinks of Marian once, Allan a Dale marries his love (the notable heterosexual disclaimer in the book), but, beyond the treacherous Prioress of Kirklees who plays out the stereotypical misogynist ending, women have no substantive roles whatsoever. The bonds between the merry men are strong and intimate: when Little John has rescued Will Stutely, the latter turned and

> looked him in the face till the tears ran down from his eyes and he wept aloud, and kissing his friend's cheeks, 'O Little John!' quoth he, 'mine own true friend, and he that I love better than man or woman in all the world beside . . .'. And Little John could make no answer, but wept also.[8]

Like the proliferating episodes of the early modern ballads and prose lives, Pyle's *Merry Adventures* provides not a 'history' of Robin Hood that progresses towards 'maturity' as a teleological narrative, but a series of adventures that celebrate the energy and prowess of narcissistic, phallic masculinity, deemed appropriate for pre-adolescent boys. The reiterated type-scenes, usually designated 'Robin Hood meets his match', function not only as contests, but as same-sex matches, in both senses, providing structures for males to come to know one another physically, and to bond with one another psychically.

But nevertheless, like the films of the next century, this homosocial world guards itself against accusation of homosexuality through a clear representation of homophobic attitudes. The dangerous potential for excess in such relationships surfaces in the initial encounter with Will Scarlet, who stands in the key relationship of mother's brother's son with Robin (what old English called a sister-son). Little John, Arthur a Bland, and Robin are lolling in 'sunny silence' when a 'fine figure' of a man appears in the road:

> with doublet of scarlet silk and his stockings also . . . his cap was of scarlet velvet, and a broad feather hung down behind and back of one ear. His hair was long and yellow, and curled upon his shoulders, and in his hand he bore an early rose, which he smelt at daintily now and then.
>
> 'By my life!' quoth Robin Hood laughing, 'saw ye e'er such a pretty mincing fellow?' (p. 89)

Though Arthur defends the stranger's masculinity, observing that 'his shoulders are broad and his loins are narrow', Robin is put off:

> Pah! . . . the sight of such a fellow doth put a nasty taste into my mouth! Look how he doth hold that fair flower betwixt his thumb

and finger, as he would say, 'Good rose, I like thee not so ill but I can bear thy odor for a little while' . . . What a pity that such men as he, that have no thought but to go abroad in gay clothes, should have good fellows, whose shoes they are not fit to tie, dancing at their bidding . . . it doth make me mad to see such gay lordlings from over the sea go stepping on the necks of good Saxons. (pp. 89–90)

Little John expresses in good manly, and yeomanly, terms his sense that Robin's disgust seems at once unmotivated and overdetermined:

'Why, how now, master', quoth Little John, 'what heat is this? Thou dost set thy pot a-boiling, and mayhap no bacon to cook? . . . He may be a good man and true for aught thou knowest.'

'Nay,' said Robin, 'my head against a leaden farthing, *he is what I say*. Whenever saw ye Saxon mince along like that . . . I will pluck him as close as ever a goose was plucked . . . Thou sayst he is a sturdy fellow . . . watch till I show thee how woodland life toughens a man . . . till I show thee how I drub this fellow.'(p. 90, emphasis added)

Robin's rage and the ensuing violence are incited – to the surprise even of the characters in the story – solely by the appearance of this stranger, by his somehow appearing not a proper man. Will's ostensible deviance from the normative masculinity of the Greenwood – hard, ready for action, clubbable – prompts homophobic panic in Robin's desire to 'drub', to bash this soft, elegant, remote figure. Only when Will's identity has been established – through his manly thrashing of Robin, and his genealogical connection – is Robin calmed; within the confines of a secure masculinity, he can even tease his kinsman that 'I should have known thee by that pretty maiden air of thine – that dainty, finicking manner of gait' (p. 95). Homophobia here transmutes itself from the source of panicked violence into the ritualized aggression of masculine insult, a further contestive structure that cements male cohesion.

The match with Will Scarlet sets in motion the linked sadistic and masochistic features of masculine phallic narcissism; Robin Hood, the text makes clear, takes active pleasure in having Will beat the stuffing out of him, and this – even more than the family connection – becomes the basis of their shared relationship in the Greenwood. The features of Will's appearance that provoke the conflict – he is a 'gaily-feathered bird', a 'gay lordling' wearing 'gay clothes' – form a notable part of the medievalesque, archaizing idiom that Pyle invented to enhance and distance the Middle Ages for his readers, but at the same time have an uncanny ring for late twentieth-century audiences. Pyle produced his book, with its nervous recognition of male-male feeling, precisely at the moment when historians have identified the emergence of distinctive forms of gay culture, yet there can be no question of connecting Pyle's use of 'gay' with the adjective that has come into use in the last decades. Nonetheless, Pyle's use of this term – and its ubiquitous counterpart, 'merry' – to define masculinity in its most distinctive, its broadest, and even its deviant forms and activities invites analysis, both in terms of the semantic histories that attracted Pyle's attention and in terms of their characteristic role in narratives of Robin Hood.

In the early ballads, which Pyle diligently used as his sources, *gay* occurs infrequently, and Pyle seems to have multiplied its use as an equivalent to *merry,* which is a frequent and significant adjective in a wide range of poems. The band of outlaws appear as 'merry men' or a 'mery meyney' in at least nine of the early ballads, and six of these poems fix the masculine pasimes of the band in the 'Merry Greenwood'. In 'Robin Hood and the Potter' the leader assures his men amidst the forest: 'Here het ys merey to be.' For modern writers, from Pyle to Brooks, 'merry' (taken straight or satirically) invokes the archaic and nostalgic world of 'Merrie England'.

In both Pyle's *Merry Adventures* and the *Gest,* Robin Hood's boyish homosociality – his indifference to a legitimated masculinity, assimilated to society and history – prevents his remaining within the King's Law – the law of the Sire. He is driven back to the Greenwood as the merry space of phallic, narcissistic masculinity; here he can indulge the immediately gratified, object-less desires of an 'innocent' masculinity of a kind that continues to have popular appeal for adults in martial arts films and for children in classic boys' fiction and the endless cycles of phallic narcissism played out in arcade games. These stand in contrast to the reconciliations and marriages that in the Hollywood films produce a smooth transition from the Greenwood to the enacted Law of the Father. But this transition creates strain, and requires the delineation of simple homosociality as possibly being an unacceptable heterosexuality. Robin's postulation, in *Men in Tights,* of a masculinity that is 'straight; merry, but straight' defines the double-bind – the imperative for intense homosocial relations, and the strict homosexual taboo – that incites the homophobic panic. This may seem to be a modern anxiety imported into the tradition in the nineteenth century, but recent work in Renaissance studies suggests an expanding interest in that period in multiple, deviant and so worrisome patterns of masculine identity – not to mention Chaucer's Pardoner. Those elements of masculine gender anxiety do not seem to be integral to the early outlaw ballads – though the disagreement between Robin and John in 'Robin Hood and the Monk' could be read as a lover's tiff, and Robin's apparently special relationship with the sheriff's wife in 'Robin Hood and the Potter' is as unconvincing as the assertion of Robin's masculinity in *Men in Tights.*

Nevertheless, it seems broadly true that the early ballads represent an unselfconscious and so unanxious representation of a homosocial world of male-male activity and feeling, where the nineteenth and twentieth centuries increasingly feel there may be some reprehensible elements of homosexuality in that structure. More was to come.

Gay Robin Hood

If Howard Pyle withdrew officially from homosociality into homophobia and the early ballads show no negative awareness of the implications of their gender relations, the twentieth century did occasionally show the tradition moving closer to recognizing an overt and even tolerated element of homosexuality in the tradition. In Alfred Noyes's highly nostalgic early twentieth-century poem 'Sherwood', the charms of masculinity seem relished from not only a female viewpoint:

> Merry, merry England is waking as of old,
> With eyes of blither hazel and hair of brighter gold.[9]

There seems to be a male head on the pillow in this forest bedroom scene. Noyes's companion in Georgian poetry, J. C. Squire, goes closer still to an overtly camp note in the *dramatis personae* to his play *Robin Hood* with descriptions like: 'Alanadale (Very elegant, all, unperturbed, precise, high voice, foppishly dressed at first appearance)' and the knight's squire ('Bright, manly, luxuriant hair)', not to mention 'Marian de Burgh (Rosalindish, vivacious, but more daring and pert)'.[10] At this time E. M. Forster used the greenwood legend to create an arena where men can love each other without social disruption,[11] and there seems to have been throughout the century a recurrent possibility that the greenwood myth of merry men could be appropriated to a homosexual viewpoint, whether seriously as with Forster or in low-camp playfulness descending through pantomime, as was evident in both the title and a good deal of the innuendo of Lionel Bart's musical *Twang!*, which – perhaps partly for this reason – failed disastrously in London in 1965.

At the *fin de siècle* such sub-surface possibilities came into the open. In the summer of 1999 there was a brief but moderately intense media flurry about the possibility of Robin Hood being gay. It was late July and August, when the senior editors are on holiday and the media mice come out to play, but the range and intensity of the reaction, worldwide, suggested that this was something more than a silly season story. It started with the title of a paper to be delivered by Stephen Knight to the second international Robin Hood conference at Nottingham. The paper was called 'The Forest Queen', and it gave an account of a novel published in 1849 by Joachim Stocqueler. The novel's full title is *Maid Marian: The Forest Queen*, and in one paragraph Knight was to suggest that, since Marian plays a very minor part in the story and since Stocqueler was a well-known wit and theatrical personality, it might be conceivable that the sub-title was a waggish reference to a possible aura of homosexuality hovering about the hero. This possibility was acutely detected, from the mere title of the paper, read in a Nottingham University publicity release, by a journalist from the London *Sunday Times*, Jonathan Leake: he deserves identification for his initiating part in this imbroglio. Having familiarized himself with the outlaw tradition, he held a lengthy telephone discussion with Knight (who still feels there was some ominous significance in the fact that he spoke to Leake while overlooking the ruins of King John's hunting lodge in Sherwood Forest). Leake's interest was in controversy, the law of the newspaper proprietor, not the Law of the Father, and scholarly though the discussion was, it kept returning to the possibility of the gay Robin Hood, and that weekend's *Sunday Times* carried the story on page three, usually reserved for damaging political news. Led by a large photograph of Errol Flynn at his most thigh-revealingly winsome, the story outed the outlaw as having had lots of fun in the forest with men. Leake dwelled on the late arrival of Marian in the tradition, and quoted the distinguished historian and Robin Hood scholar Barrie Dobson as saying that homosexuality was certainly known in the Middle Ages. It also had Peter Tatchell, a leading British gay rights campaigner, expressing his enthusiasm for the idea of a gay Robin Hood; the fiction of balance was respected with a quote from the present Earl of Huntingdon, who sounded thoroughly dismayed.

This story was boiled down by Reuters and went round the world, from the grubby street-level London tabloids to the *South China News* and, in at least a paragraph, most points in between. There was lively radio interest, notably from regional stations in cities near to, and rival to, Nottingham, but also from New Zealand, Australia, South Africa, Sweden, Norway, Canada and America, where people had grown up on stories of the blade-straight outlaw hero.

Most of the interviews followed the same pattern – a sensationalist introduction, then a request for Knight to defend this outrageous idea. He always took the same line, now somewhat developed: the proposal was not, as the English press preferred, that Robin Hood was capering about the medieval forest in pink tights, but rather that just as he stood for resistance to authority in political and even nationalist terms, so the tradition could be read as also embodying some elements of resistance to heteronormative gender relations. None of the broadcasters seemed outraged, and indeed most seemed interested in, even pleased by, the idea in its rational form. A few stations were more thoroughgoing: the Chicago Lesbi-Gay line conducted a lengthy and distinctly scholarly interview, though also in cheerful mode; and on the British Forces Network two serious-sounding men held an in-depth discussion about gay warriors through history. In the broader context of the popular modes in which the Robin Hood tradition has always been communicated, it is striking that the oral media were the most interested in the story – there were two requests for television interviews, but Knight demurred as they came from the lower depths of British provision – the adolescent-oriented and structure-free *Big Breakfast* and *The Graham Norton Show*, a late night compote of heavy innuendo compered by a witty gay Irishman. None of the Anglophone newspapers or magazines expressed any interest, but (probably indicating more the all-round intellectual interest of Germany and France rather than a gay focus) the weeklies *Der Spiegel* and *L'Evènement* conducted lengthy telephone interviews and ran full-page pieces in a mode basically interpretative rather than investigative – though the French woman journalist was the only person to ask Knight if he was himself gay.

Almost all of these interviews were inherently serious – though there was one fairly hysterical one with a Sydney commercial station, but that was counterpoised by a very long and thoughtful, even earnest, interview with the ABC, a government-run national network, in Melbourne. Most of the journalists could not see anything particularly outrageous about suggesting that one of the possibilities of the outlaw tradition was a sexual politics that privileges male-male desire of various kinds. There was a semi-negative London tabloid response that ran a short account, without of course reference to Leake or the *Sunday Times*, and merely meant to support a joke headline: 'Robin Not the Marian Kind' and 'How Big was Little John?' were typical.

If the general media response was curiosity and calm interest, there was nevertheless opposition to be found. The Nottingham newspapers carried a good deal of spluttering from outraged councillors and *soi-disant* experts. The local tourist office was particularly put out, and was involved in some radio interviews – frequent suggestions by interviewees that they should follow up the story and seek the pink pound did not in any way calm their discomposure. That response was familiar enough: Nottingham is always upset by any other claims on Robin Hood, whether topographic from York or interpretative from anyone outside the sheriff's domain. Much more interesting and revealing were the hostile letters that Knight received, including a few poison emails. The letters tended to be written, as if by some form of collective compulsion, on poor paper in small hands, mostly fully literate. The remarkable thing was that very few were anti-gay. This view was just visible: one correspondent to the *Nottingham Evening Post* asked: 'What's next? Saying Robin Hood was gay is like saying Santa Claus is a pederast.' Apart from the conflation of homosexuality and pederasty, this correspondent's concern with children was in tune with most of the hostile letters. A recurrent, clearly obsessional, theme was the idea that the argument had affronted childhood. It was an obscure affront, without specifics or imagined results, but it filled the space of outrage left by the complete lack of any defenders of a heterosexual regular-guy Robin Hood. The issue was between a benign Robin Hood who typified innocence and an offensive Robin Hood who was sexualized, no matter what form his sexuality took. These responses made it clear that the thrust of the news story was not in fact that Robin Hood was gay, but that Robin Hood actually had sexuality. To deal in terms of gender had engendered a different Robin Hood, one who was to some deeply disturbing and to others rather enticing and convincing, no matter what their own sexual preference. It was not the return but the turn of the repressed.

These letter-writers had their own tradition. The concept of a desexualized innocence of Robin Hood was a major force in the most extraordinary boom in the long career of the outlaw tradition. Under the combined developmental forces of mass literacy, primary and secondary education in English literature and the rural ideal in Anglophone society, Robin Hood publishing for children multiplied enormously around the beginning of the twentieth century. Plays for teenagers, story-readers, poetry anthologies, rechauffées of the ballads in prose, these all poured off presses in England and America between 1900 and about 1930. In the search for material simple enough and decent enough to help the young to learn language, literature, good citizenship and appropriate ideals, Robin

Hood must have seemed in overt terms far more acceptable than Malory's Round Table adulteries or classical myths of bestiality and family violence.

But as the letter-writers indicated, there is a shocking flipside to this image of innocence, a reverse that can seem perverse. As a glance at the films and a scan of the texts will show, the Robin Hood myth is in fact steeped in gender in its symbolized, and therefore all the more potent, form, and the intensity of that innate (if also inchoate) gendering is all the more widely appealing for its non-specific character. While there is heterosexual musing and romancing, of a mild kind, between Robin and Marian, and often between other outlaws and appropriate maidens, and while arrows, trees, horses, nooses, escapes, dungeons, shackles, tortures all express subliminally the *sturm und drang* of sexuality, the gendering need not be heteronormative. Whatever Stocqueler might or might not have meant by his subtitle, Pierce Egan created in the Robin-Maude-Will triangle a classic of the woman as mediator of physical contact between men, and this sense of pervasive male-male feeling tradition goes right through to Will a Gamwell, Robin's friend in the 1938 film, whom Little John, wielding a bigger staff than both, addresses as 'pretty fellow'.

What early ballads saw as normative, what Pyle and the films both celebrate and constrain, the contemporary world can to a large degree contemplate as difference, something interesting, diverting, even exciting, but recognized as simply existent. But that public response to the gay Robin Hood debate seems ahead of the creators in the tradition: the spoiled innocence party were clearly in the minority among the audience, but in terms of production – or of those who control production – they still prove dominant.

Robin Hood: Men in Tights plays with gender as both urgently heterosexual – the chastity belt running gag – and possibly homosexual – the butch men in tights. But finally, in a moment that curiously re-adopts the position of the outraged letter-writers, it denies both: none of the outlaws is in fact gay, and in the last moment of the film we hear that the key does not fit the chastity belt. The last irony is to ironically proclaim the undergendered character that has been for so long, and for such importance, the official position of the outlaw tradition,

'EXEMPT ME, SIRE, FOR I AM AFEARD OF WOMEN'

whether the hero eventually marries or not. The film epitomizes the ambiguous gender position of Robin Hood, hero of a pattern of stories that overtly appeal to those who are, like Fairbanks's Robin, 'afeard' of gender, yet are also fascinated by narratives that are unconsciously, insistently and multiply gendered all the time.

NOTES

1. The authors would like to thank William Spurlin for his help with this paper.
2. Eve Kosofsky Sedgwick, *Between Men: English Literature and Male Homosocial Desire* (New York: Columbia University Press, 1985).
3. For a discussion of the popular tradition in the nineteenth century see Stephen Knight in Chapter 5 of this volume, parts 3 and 4, and Stephanie L. Barczewski, *Myth and National Identity in Nineteenth-Century Britain: The Legends of King Arthur and Robin* Hood (Oxford: Oxford University Press, 2000), pp. 191–200.
4. See Rudy Behlmer, '"Welcome to Sherwood!" The Adventures of Robin Hood' (1938), in his *Behind the Scenes* (Hollywood: French, 1990), p. 62.
5. Ibid., p. 64.
6. 'A Gest of Robyn Hode', in Stephen Knight and Thomas H. Ohlgren (eds), *Robin Hood and Other Outlaw Tales*, TEAMS Middle English Texts Series (Kalamazoo: Medieval Institute Publications, 1997), pp. 80–168.
7. Michael T. Clanchy, *From Memory to Written Record: England, 1066–1307*, 2nd edn (London: Oxford University Press, 1993), *passim*.
8. Howard Pyle, *The Merry Adventures of Robin Hood of Great Renown in Nottinghamshire* (New York: Scribners, 1883), p. 43.
9. Alfred Noyes, 'Sherwood' in *Sherwood* (New York: Frederick A. Stokes, 1911), p. 83.
10. John Collings Squire, *Robin Hood: A Farcical Romantic Pastoral* (London: Heinemann, 1928), p. 1.
11. Knight 1994, pp. 216–17.

Maid Marian in Twentieth-century Children's Books

DAVID BLAMIRES

Maid Marian is a late arrival in the development of the Robin Hood stories. She is not found in the early ballads, but seems to have joined Robin through the May games and is first mentioned in conjunction with Robin Hood by Alexander Barclay, soon after 1500.[1] The 'Marian' of the Whitsun May games seems to have been a comic figure and partnered by the Friar. The ballad 'Robin Hood and Maid Marian' is of the seventeenth century and portrays Marian disguised as a page going in search of Robin, her lover, in the greenwood, where the two only discover their identities after fighting and wounding each other.[2] This encounter figures in many later accounts of Robin's adventures.

More important for the future tradition, however, is the equation of Marian with Matilda, daughter of Lord Fitzwater and the object of Prince John's amorous attentions, that was first made by Michael Drayton in his historical poem 'Matilda, the Faire and Chaste Daughter of Lord R. Fitzwater' (1594) and taken up by Anthony Munday in his two plays *The Downfall of Robert, Earl of Huntington* and *The Death of Robert, Earl of Huntington* (printed 1601).[3] Marian in these literary treatments of the late sixteenth and seventeenth centuries has become not only a beautiful young noblewoman and the beloved of Robin, rather than the comic dancing-partner of the Friar, but also a fine archer and huntress:

> [Robin's] Mistris deare, his loved Marian
> Was ever constant knowne, which whersoere shee came,
> Was soveraigne of the Woods, chiefe Lady of the Game:
> Her Clothes tuck'd to the knee, and daintie braided haire,
> With Bow and Quiver arm'd, shee wandred here and there,

> Amongst the forests wild; Diana never knew
> Such pleasures, nor such harts as Mariana slew.

This description comes from Drayton's 'Poly-Olbion' (1622).[4] Another element in the development of Maid Marian came with Ben Jonson's *The Sad Shepherd* (printed 1641), which introduces Maudlin, the witch of Papplewick, who causes trouble through disguising herself as Marian.[5] Knight suggests that Jonson constructs the witch to represent a negative image of the female in the play to counter the relatively explicit depiction of sexual desire and happiness between Robin and the true Marian.[6] Nearly two centuries later Thomas Love Peacock, in his *Maid Marian* (1822), was the first to make Marian the central figure of a romantic novel, using the ballads printed by Ritson (1795) as a basis but giving them a satirical and political twist.[7] All these disparate sources provided material for retellings by twentieth-century children's writers.

The problem with Maid Marian is that she does not belong in the core stories of Robin Hood, which are fundamentally about tests of strength and cunning between men, in which social equals and those down on their luck are enlisted on Robin's side and the wicked and powerful are defeated. There is place for betrayal (and a woman betrays Robin in the *Gest*) but none for romance. The 'merry men' are a homosocial company. When Marian is introduced into the stories, her presence raises the question: how do men relate to women? The ballad episode in which she is disguised as a page suggests that she may be treated as an honorary male and acquire the skills and capacities of a man, in which case the sexual question is largely side-stepped. On the other hand, where the heterosexual issue is paramount, she may become the essentially passive focus of a contest between Robin and another would-be husband, the latter always identified as a villain. In either case Marian is a member of the aristocracy in her appearances in the literary tradition from the late sixteenth century on, so Robin too has to become a nobleman rather than remain the 'gode yeman' of the *Gest*. The matter of Marian's social class is profoundly important for authors and readers up to the end of the nineteenth century, but it can be seen to diminish in the twentieth as the social position of women changes. Marian becomes a figure who can have power in a man's world without the status added by high birth. In the course of the twentieth century Marian underwent profound transformations. In looking at how Marian was portrayed in a range of twentieth-century children's books, we can see how the traditions have been adapted to reflect changing patterns in society and, in particular, concerns about the role of women; Marian is an outline figure that each writer fills in differently. The only thing that all agree on is that she and Robin are devoted to each other. There is no consensus about her parentage, her physical appearance, the disagreeable suitor that she escapes from to be with Robin, the manner of her death and whether she died before Robin or after. By the end of the twentieth century even the traditional episodes in which she figures had undergone a radical change.

Let us look first at descriptions of Marian's appearance. At the beginning of the century H. E. Marshall (1905) idealizes her before her marriage to Robin. She looks 'like a fairy princess. She wore an underdress of glittering white, and over it a robe of lovely satin, green and shimmering like beech leaves in early spring. Her dark hair was caught up in a net of pearls, and a soft white veil fell about her face' (78).[8] At the end of the century Monica Furlong (1994) also gives her dark curly hair, but says because it was short her head 'looked like that of a boy' (24), and later at the shooting contest she was 'slim and graceful in her boy's outfit' (112).[9] Furlong's Marian is the complete antithesis of Marshall's. When Dummy, the dumb boy who is the novel's central character, arrives in the greenwood, he is surprised to find her wearing 'leather leggings, and a leather tunic like a man's' (25). Marian, whom Robin calls 'the best archer among us' (60), teaches Dummy to shoot and is cold and severe to begin with because she thinks he may be a spy. This is a cool, rational Marian, referred to as 'the Woman of the greenwood' (76), but in every way equal to the men.

E. Charles Vivian (1927) declares in old-fashioned words, 'She was slim and fair, the chroniclers tell, with great blue eyes and hair of gold, a right fair maid' (136), while Roger Lancelyn Green (1956) depicts her at the age of twenty-five as 'tall and beautiful, but strong and fearless also, a very fitting wife for such a man [as Robin]' (26).[10] Rosemary Sutcliff (1950) provides no separate description, but mentions her '[l]ong golden-brown hair' (86) when Robin pulls off her hood after their fight.[11] Robert Leeson (1994) refers to her as a 'fair-haired girl' (48), but Michael Morpurgo (1996) shatters the traditional image totally by making Marian an albino.[12] She has 'a willowy figure', and '[h]er hair was white, not silver like an old person's, not fair as [Robin's] mother's had been, but white, pure white. Her eyes seemed to glow red in the early morning sun' (23). She does not like Robin staring at her. She is one of the company of Outcasts, which includes hunchbacks, cripples and lepers as well as albinos, 'creatures of the forest, creatures of the dark'. Conventional ideals of physical beauty are subverted here. What matters is self-worth, actions matching words, sticking to principles. It is not surprising that at the end of Morpurgo's story, when King Richard wants to keep Robin at court as a knight, Marian refuses to stay, stating roundly: 'I have stayed too long in this place. It is too comfortable, and full of sycophants and title-seekers. There is corruption in the very air we breathe' (111). Marian is made of stronger stuff than Robin.

The episode, first appearing in the ballad 'Robin and Marian', in which Marian goes looking for Robin in disguise, crops up in several, but not all the twentieth-century children's books. Marshall, Tilney (1913), and Oman (1939) all have her as a knight in armour, but showing her as a young woman and stressing her noble background.[13] Sutcliff, Hayes (1989), Leeson, and Williams (1995) all portray her as looking like a boy.[14]

Oman's 1930s Marian is 18-years-old and looking for 'the only man in this world in whom I can put trust' (177). She has been trying to get Robin to marry her for three years. She can do embroidery, but not darn stockings. She has never seen an egg boiled or a hen plucked and expects banquets to descend any time as from heaven. She spends time fencing, drawing the long bow, playing single-staff, rides cross-saddle and knows everything about horses, hawks and hounds. With her bold self-confidence and witty remarks she seems just the sort of character that Noel Coward or P. G. Wodehouse would have adored.

In almost every book Marian has to escape the unwelcome attentions of an older powerful nobleman. She is the personification of virginity threatened by a forced marriage, from which only Robin can save her. Her father, Lord Fitzwalter, or her guardian is powerless to protect her. Vivian curiously makes Marian the daughter of Sir Richard at Lea, though this is not revealed till very late on in the book. She is the ward of Abbot Hugo de Rainault, and the would-be husband is Isambart of Belame with his dread castle known as Evil Hold. The virginity theme is emphasized through the fact that Marian is at first under shelter at the nunnery of Kirklees, and Robin and his men fight Guy of Gisborne to prevent him taking Marian from there to Evil Hold. She prefers to stay with Robin rather than return to Kirklees. She first has Will Scarlett's wife for company, but is soon married to Robin by Friar Tuck and becomes 'Queen of Sherwood' (138). Vivian's Marian is essentially passive. When Robin goes to attack Evil Hold, she says, 'I could do naught but sit and pray for you' (204). She is abducted by Isambart in Robin's absence at Ravenscar, but is of course rescued. Many years later Abbot Hugo conspires with Robin's enemy, Roger the Cruel, who, disguised as a pedlar, stabs and kills Marian. Before she dies Marian thanks Robin for 'all the happy years' (328) that they have been together. When Robin himself dies in the traditional way at Kirklees, his last words are 'Marian, my Marian'. Marian's role in Vivian's tale harks back to Victorian (and indeed much earlier) preoccupations with the idea of the sexually attractive woman as a victim and, more importantly, as a pawn in the power struggles of men. In expanding Marian's role from that found in the ballads and transmitted by Marshall and Tilney, Vivian has altered the balance of Robin's adventures. Traditionally they were concerned with economic injustice and the misuse of political power, but Vivian puts greater emphasis on the weakness of the female sex and women's need for male protection.

Vivian is perhaps the clearest exponent of the theme of the weak and defenceless Marian. Other writers make use of the unwanted suitor motif, but do not depict Marian in quite the same way. Sutcliff names the suitor as Sir Roger of Doncaster, picking up the name from the *Gest*.[15] With Green the opponent is Prince John. Hayes and Williams name Sir Guy of Gisborne, while Mitchell (1998), following his model in Peacock's *Maid Marian*, has Sir Ralph Montfalcon. This plethora of names demonstrates the fact that the identity of the opponent is of less consequence than his role as villain. Equally, Marian simply has a role to fulfil in relation to this opponent. Marian's flight from a suitor who is not Robin fits both the tomboy role found in some stories and the romantic role. The traditional stories are told from Robin's angle. Like the princess who marries the hero at the end of the traditional fairy tale, Marian has no independent, rounded existence of her own in the early twentieth-century children's books, but is merely the focal point of another of Robin's adventures.

By the mid-twentieth century, however, attempts are made at making Marian a more active character. We have noted this already with Oman in 1939. Sutcliff too pursues this strategy, but expresses it in terms of Marian's suppression of supposedly feminine traits. After three months in the greenwood, during which the outlaws overcome their shyness of her, Marian becomes:

> a worthy comrade. When Roger Lightfoot had cut his hand half off she had neither shrieked nor swooned, but held the edges of the gash together while Robin stitched it. She had not been afraid when there was an alarm of an attack, but had calmly strung her bow and taken her place beside Robin. She had not complained when the nights were cold. She took her turn at cooking and cleaning, and her place among the younger outlaws at the daily target-practice (89–90).

She is also mentioned frequently in the accounts of Robin's later adventures, though not as a particularly significant participant.

Roger Lancelyn Green utilizes virtually all the traditional Marian themes, combining traditional feminine qualities with masculine capacities. When her marriage to Robin is broken off by Sir Guy of Gisborne's proclamation from Prince John, Brother Michael (i.e. Friar Tuck) says of her: 'Has she not beauty, grace, wit, good sense and high valour? Can she not fence with the sword, ply the quarter-staff and shoot with the long bow all but as well as – as Robin Hood himself? Truly a worthy mate for a worthy man' (35). Green unusually and adroitly manages to include the Clorinda episode from the ballad 'Robin Hood's Birth, Breeding, Valour, and Marriage' (c.1662), which he interprets as a May Day dance at Gamwell that Marian joins disguised as a peasant girl.[16] In the altercation with Sir Guy afterwards, Clorinda shows her mettle by shooting an arrow that transfixes his hand.

The nature of Robin and Marian's relationship proves a challenging problem for many writers. Anthony Munday and Thomas Love Peacock had both begun a plot with the wedding of Robin and Marian, interrupted by the forces of an unjust authority. Several authors have Robin and Marian wed as soon as she arrives in the greenwood, but Green postpones the marriage till near the end of his story and has the bride given away by King Richard Coeur de Lion. The unspoken assumption is that Robin and Marian lived a celibate life in the greenwood before this wedding.

While Green's book weaves together many strands of tradition about Marian, Antonia Pakenham (1955; Antonia Fraser 1971) invents a great deal, beginning by associating Marian with Whitby.[17] The man who wants to marry her is called Oswald Montdragon, and he forces Marian into leading Robin into an ambush, ostensibly in return for saving Marian's mother's life. It turns out afterwards that she is already known to be dead. Pakenham also invents a treacherous companion for Marian, Barbara Nevill, known as Black Barbara, who is infatuated with Robin herself and through various kinds of trickery betrays Marian to Montdragon.[18] Both Marian and Robin fall into Montdragon's clutches, but with the help of Much, the miller's son, Marian rescues Robin from hanging and the two return to the greenwood. After the return of King Richard, Marian goes disguised as a boy to a tournament at Nottingham, but is recognized and taken hostage by Montdragon. Robin gains help from a stranger who turns out to be the King, he is made Earl of Locksley, and requests Marian as his wife. When Robin later dies at an unnamed convent, the nun who bleeds him to death reveals herself as Black Barbara: treacherous to both Marian and Robin. There is no doubt that Pakenham has created a much fuller role here for Marian through the sub-plot with the wicked, scheming Black Barbara, and Robin and Marian act as a pair in many adventures, but she remains very much the noble lady subjected to inhuman pressures from her would-be husband.

With Bernard Miles (1979) we have a very different Marian.[19] She is the daughter of a farmer on the North York Moors with a twin brother aged fourteen, and Robin has been adopted by the farmer after his father's death in raids by the Scots. After being caught poaching Robin is forced to run away. We are told Marian 'was a real tomboy, tall and strong, yet quick as lightning, especially with her sword. Indeed, she would often challenge Robin himself and he would find it quite difficult to hold her off. Some brothers would have been jealous of such a sister, but Mark was proud of her' (25). When Marian is seventeen, she pretends to agree to Sir Guy of Gisburn's desire to marry her, but takes flight southward to Sherwood. Here Miles has a neat variation on the traditional encounter of Robin and Marian as strangers: Marian defeats Robin in combat, forces him to take her to his outlaw band and says she has come to marry their leader. Only then does she reveal her identity. The two are married a few days later at Edwinstowe by Friar Tuck. In this version Marian dies accidentally as a result of a bough of an oak tree falling on her. Miles's Marian is robust and down-to-earth and knows her own mind. She is not merely Robin's equal in male pursuits; she is his superior. The romanticism that colours most twentieth-century adaptations of the traditional tales is largely absent. This is a Marian who in great measure exemplifies the advent of women's liberation. Germaine Greer's *The Female Eunuch*, for example, was first published in 1970. Yet Miles's Marian, perhaps understandably as imagined by a man, is still just a character operating in a male-dominated world.

Robin McKinley's *The Outlaws of Sherwood* (1988) indicates with its very title a different approach from that of earlier authors.[20] Not only is Robin's name not mentioned, but he is also not the most brilliant archer of the company. In the climactic contest for the golden arrow it is actually Marian in male garb, and widely thought to be Robin Hood, who shoots and wins it. Robin has a reputation for making excellent arrows, but Marian is the most accurate shot. Physically the two are very alike, and this is particularly emphasized on one occasion:

> Robin looked at her where she stood, lithe and slender, wearing one of the dark-green woolen tunics that nearly all his forest folk now wore; probably one originally cut for him, for they were nearly of a size. Her hair was tied back, and her boots and breeches tied too as the outlaws did, she might have been a young man (71).

Though Marian acts the part of the young noblewoman at her father's house, she displays remarkable independence in her actions and is both brave and intellectually adroit. It is she who outmanoeuvres Blaise de Beautement when he attempts to take advantage of Sir Richard of the Lea's financial troubles.

Marian is present in McKinley's narrative from the start, together with Robin and Much the miller's son, and she is a stronger character than Robin in many ways. She is at first a visitor to his camp after he is forced to hide in Sherwood following his accidental killing of a friend of the Chief Forester. She is, in outlaw skills and initiative, Robin's superior. While still living at her father's house, she brings them information about the sheriff and what people think about the outlaws as well as practical things like leather, twine, salt and cooking pots. 'It was a dangerous task she had set herself', we are told (38). Danger is no deterrent to Marian or the other women who join the outlaws. McKinley's multiplication of the number of resourceful women marks a feminist advance: previously, where Marian was brave, clever at strategy, or skilled at archery or other masculine skills, these presented her as exceptional among women. McKinley represents women in general as capable of these qualities. Will Scarlet's young sister Cecily disguises herself as a boy to escape being married to an unwanted suitor, and she survives as Cecil for quite a considerable time before her gender is discovered. Gradually mutual love grows between her and Little John, comrades in arms and hardships. The theme of young women escaping from an unwanted marriage partner is strongly articulated by McKinley. She does not avoid the idea of romantic love, but, in a novel concerned with adventure and the struggle for justice and mercy, it is very much played down. At the end of the book King Richard the Lionheart makes Robin the heir of Sir Richard and suggests before they depart on the crusade: 'The heir of a lord like Sir Richard might consider himself a suitor for the hand of lady Marian. I believe there should be time to celebrate such a marriage before we set sail' (274). He also suggests Marian would make the best Sheriff of Nottingham. The marriage of Robin and Marian is based on a mutual acceptance of their weaknesses and strengths, a knowledge gained through struggle and hardship. That the book ends with a marriage and the outlaws' submission to King Richard is a gesture towards the romance genre, perhaps inevitable when Robin has been moved from the centre. The story does not continue to Robin's fateful death at the hands of the prioress. That would be to introduce a female character completely out of keeping with McKinley's ideals, which are to portray a Marian who is able to make decisions for herself and act independently.

The 1990s provide more books that put Marian in the foreground, and to a greater degree even than *The Outlaws of Sherwood*. Theresa Tomlinson's *The Forestwife* (1993) and *Child of the May* (1998) are thoroughly re-imagined narratives, in which Robin and his men inhabit the periphery rather than the centre of the action.[21] Both books focus on women and women's values, the importance that women have in sustaining communities both materially and spiritually and in healing and discouraging violent conflict. From her double incarnation as Matilda/Marian, her evil double in the form of Maudlin the witch, and the story of her disguise as a man, Marian has always switched from one identity to another, and these dual identities have always reflected writers' attempts to perceive a place for the female within the essentially homosocial focus of the tales. This, in contrast, is a tale of a young woman developing a new role and skills. This is Marian's own tale; Robin enters into it as Marian once entered the Robin-centred narratives. *The Forestwife* is a story about three generations of women. The motif of flight from an unwelcome husband has the potential to present a heroine not just moving to a better man, but moving beyond the static role of romantic heroine, entering a new world. Here, at the beginning, Mary (later identified as Marian) runs away from home to escape marriage to an elderly nobleman. Together with her nurse, Agnes, she finds her way to the Forestwife's solitary house only to find that she has just died. The Forestwife symbolizes the power of nature and healing, and Agnes now takes her place.

Mary becomes known, in her new life, as Marian, 'the beautiful green lady of the woods', and the together the two women provide help and support for the poor, the wounded and oppressed, developing the theme, from the *Gest* on, of Robin Hood as a communal benefactor to the oppressed. A small community of nuns is helped to escape from exploitation by lay brothers, and an anchoress, known as the Seeress, turns out to be Marian's own mother, doing penance for having given birth to her as a child fathered by a minstrel. Unlike earlier books, Tomlinson's takes on the complexities of sexual relationships and childbirth. A girl that Mary meets when she is first escaping gives birth to a stillborn child. Much later she has a child by Little John. Marian first comes across Robert (i.e. Robin) lying wounded in the undergrowth, and learns later that he is actually Agnes's son whom she left with her brother at the age of two so that she could earn her living as Mary's wet-nurse. Agnes tells Robert and Marian: 'You two are the ones that I love best in the world. T'would be a blessing on me, if you could manage to agree' (67). Much later, after Robert has been wounded by Guy of Gisburn, whom he manages to kill, Marian looks after him at Baytown and sleeps with him (literally) to keep him warm. Agnes is later drowned by the tyrant William of Langden, leaving Marian to become the Forestwife in her place. In this capacity she is not permitted to marry, so Robert announces he will be 'the Knight of the Forestwife, devoted to the Sisters of the Magdalen' (166), as the community of nuns is known.[22]

The Forestwife is a striking achievement, using some traditional material that had developed in the history of Maid Marian, but with a radically refocused vision. Its emphasis on Marian as a healer – a role she continues in *Child of the May* – is shared by Morpurgo, who says about the albino Marion (spelt here with an 'o'): 'Among the Outcasts, it was only she who had the healing powers, so she took Robin's father aside and bathed his eyes and dressed them' (38). Robin feels he can only be himself with Marion, another indication that her emotional power transcends his success in adventures. Robin and Marion marry and have a child, wondering before its birth whether it will have white or black hair and whether it will be a boy or a girl. The child has white hair (like Marion), but is a boy (like Robin) and is baptized Martin after his grandfather. Marion is for life. She persuades Robin to have mercy on the sheriff and not kill him, but she is prepared to risk her own life in order to rescue her abducted son from the sheriff. It is entirely appropriate in this story for Marion to survive Robin. When all his adventures are over, she is still there.

Monica Furlong's Marian is another strong figure, tougher and psychologically more complex than most earlier portrayals of Robin's eventual spouse. She also belongs to the liberated band. So too does Marcia Williams's cartoon Marian, who 'proved herself to be a skilled fighter, joined the merry outlaws and shared all their adventures'.[23] But Williams has a light, humorous touch when she has Robin saying, 'We'll have to call ourselves a band of merry persons now', while one man sitting by a tree glumly declares, '"Merry men" had such a fine ring to it', and two others say, 'The more women, the merrier persons we'll be, I reckon!'. Perhaps Williams is a post-feminist, but in any case she displays an attitude towards the traditional tales that is shared by Adrian Mitchell: both treat the stories as material for comedy. This is an aspect that goes back as far as the ballads and folk plays and is apparent in Mitchell's chief source, Peacock's *Maid Marian*, but when Robin Hood is told as a boys' adventure story or as high drama à la Munday, Tennyson, or Noyes, the tales are taken seriously. Williams and, much more so, Mitchell poke fun at them. Mitchell turns the stories into pantomime entertainment, with extraneous characters such as the two black children called the Hoghigs and jokes round every corner.[24] His Marian is the romantic Lady Matilda Fitzwater. We are back to the beginnings of the Maid Marian stories, but the mood is that of late twentieth-century irony and burlesque where content is utterly subordinate to style. The books that I have looked at are a fair cross-section of children's versions of the Robin Hood stories, and they display a vast range of attitudes towards Maid Marian. Over the twentieth century everything seems possible, but the treatment of Marian reveals itself as a very telling index of the changes in social views about women. Because Marian's role in the ballads is tangential or absent, modern authors have felt at liberty to modify it or add to it extensively. With her, invention becomes more important than tradition.

NOTES

1. Stephen Knight, *Robin Hood: A Complete History of the English Outlaw* (Oxford: Blackwell, 1994), pp. 102–5; Adam de la Halle wrote *Robin et Marion*, a *pastourelle*, in 1280; the name 'Marion' may have influenced, or become conflated with, the 'Marian' of the Early Modern May games. See Malcolm A. Nelson, *The Robin Hood Tradition in the English Renaissance*, Elizabethan and Renaissance Studies, James Hogg (ed.), Salzburg Studies in English Literature (Salzburg: Institut für Anglistik und Amerikanistik, 1973), pp. 57–67. See also Stephen Knight's proposal that the French *pastourelle* perhaps entered English summer celebrations, in the late Middle Ages, in his essay in this volume on 'Rabbie Hood', and his 'Robin Hood: The Earliest Contexts', in Calhoun and Potter, *Images of Robin Hood*.
2. Text in KO, pp. 493–8.
3. KO, pp. 296–440.
4. Michael Drayton, 'Poly-Olbion', in *Works*, J. W. Hebel (ed.), 4 vols (Oxford: Clarendon Press 1961), vol. 4, ll. 350–8.
5. *The Sad Shepherd*, C. H. Herford and F. and E. Simpson (eds) in *The Works of Ben Jonson*, vol 7 (Oxford: Clarendon Press, 1941).
6. Knight 1994, pp. 140–2.
7. Thomas Love Peacock, *Maid Marian*, George Saintsbury (ed.) (London: Macmillan, 1895).
8. H. E. Marshall, *Stories of Robin Hood*, with pictures by A. S. Forrest (London, New York: Dutton, 1905).
9. Monica Furlong, *Robin's Country* (London: Hamish Hamilton, 1994).
10. Evelyn Charles H. Vivian, *Robin Hood* (London: Ward, Lock, 1927); Roger Lancelyn Green, *The Adventures of Robin Hood*, illustrated by Arthur Hall (Harmondsworth: Penguin, 1956).
11. Rosemary Sutcliffe, *The Chronicles of Robin Hood*, illustrated by C. Walter Hodges (London: Oxford University Press, 1950).
12. Robert Leeson, *The Story of Robin Hood*, illustrated by Barbara Lofthouse (Boston and London: Kingfisher, 1994); Michael Morpurgo, *Robin of Sherwood*, illustrated by Michael Foreman (London: Hodder, 1996).
13. F. C. Tilney, *Robin Hood and his Merry Outlaws* (London and New York: Dent, 1913).
14. Sarah Hayes, *Robin Hood*, illustrated by Patrick Benson (London: Walker Books, 1989).
15. Lines 1806–20. Roger of Donkesly, paramour of the Prioress of Kirklees, is involved in Robin's murder.
16. Text in KO, pp. 527–40.
17. Antonia Pakenham, *Robin Hood*, illustrated by Geoffrey Whittam (London: Heirloom, 1955); Antonia Fraser, *Robin Hood*, illustrated by Rebecca Fraser (London: Orion, 1971).
18. This motif of a malign and treacherous female, the counter to Marian's fidelity and virtue, and her rival for Robin, goes back to Jonson's

invention of Maudlin, the Witch of Papplewick, who disguises herself with magic as Marian, deceiving Robin and creating trouble between the true lovers.

[19] Bernard Miles, *Robin Hood: His Life and Legend*, illustrated by Victor G. Ambrus (London: Hamlyn, 1979).
[20] Robin McKinley, *The Outlaws of Sherwood* (New York: Greenwillow, 1988).
[21] Theresa Tomlinson, *The Forestwife* (London: Corgi, 1993).
[22] Tomlinson here adapts to a feminist theme the motif of Robin building a chapel to Mary Magdalene, found in the *Gest*.
[23] Marcia Williams, *The Adventures of Robin Hood* (London: Walker Books, 1995).
[24] Adrian Mitchell, *The Adventures of Robin Hood and Marian*, illustrated by Emma Chichester Clark (London: Orchard 1998).

Welsh Bandits

ADRIAN PRICE

The terrain of Wales in the medieval and Early Modern periods was ideally suited to the needs of the outlaw. The land was mountainous and densely forested, communications were poor and until 1536 the country was fragmented into a mosaic of independent native principalities and Marcher lordships. In medieval Wales, three legal systems coexisted. The native Welsh adhered to the Laws of Howell the Good. In royal lordships the Englishries were governed according to English Law and in the March, the Law of the March prevailed which varied from lordship to lordship. As stated in the Statute of Westminster (1275): 'In the Marches of Wales . . . the King's writ does not run.'[1] The legal situation in Wales was of advantage to the outlaw. For instance, an outlaw who committed a crime in Glamorgan could escape arrest by fleeing northwards over the Brecon Beacons into the Lordship of Brecon. He could also flee westwards across the River Tawe into the Gower or eastwards across the River Rhymney into Newport. The modern analogy would be the United States where criminals can escape arrest by fleeing across the state line.

If we add to this picture of administrative complexity a further element, that of long-term social disruption, one can easily see how Wales became a breeding ground for outlawry. The Welsh Wars of Independence lasted intermittently from 1067 to 1282, when Wales was finally conquered by Edward I. This 215-year piecemeal war of attrition inevitably took its toll on Welsh society. Then there was the additional disruption of the Black Death of 1348–9, which killed one-third of the Welsh population and destabilized the economy. Finally, in the fifteenth century there was the Rebellion of Owain Glyndŵr and the Wars of the Roses, which resulted in what could be described as the golden age of the Welsh outlaw.

There is a final ingredient which led to the rise of the Welsh outlaw: that of nationalism. There was no nationalist element to the medieval Robin Hood tradition, though in later tradition he was visualized as a member of a conquered and oppressed people, the Saxons, but many of the fifteenth-century Welsh outlaws had formerly been soldiers in Glyndŵr's rebel army. They refused to submit to or recognize English Law.

Therefore, when one considers all these elements, the terrain, the legal situation, the deprivation, and the nationalism, it is hardly surprising that Wales produced numerous outlaws. A number of them survive today in the popular consciousness in Wales as does Robin Hood in England.

Fouke Fitz Waryn

The first outlaw who merits attention is the Norman Lord of Whittington, Shropshire, Fouke Fitz Waryn. Although not strictly speaking a Welsh outlaw, he was a Welsh Marcher lord who became an outlaw and whose exploits, in fiction at least, have similarities to other outlaw tales, including tales of Robin Hood. Fouke III was a historical character who regained possession of the family estate, Whittington, Shropshire, in 1204 after a period spent as an outlaw between 1200 and 1203. He allied himself with Llywelyn the Great against the English in 1217 but they were enemies by 1223 when Llywelyn captured Whittington. Fouke died *c.*1256. The basis of Fouke's fame as an outlaw derives from the romance of *Fouke Fitz Waryn*, an Anglo-Norman prose 'history' of *c.*1320, a prose rendering of a lost thirteenth-century verse romance.[2] It recounts many of Fouke's adventures in Europe and North Africa. However, what is most interesting from the perspective of this paper are his exploits as the leader of a band of outlaws and the numerous references to Wales. The text begins with a narrative describing the establishment, after the Norman Conquest, of Norman lords in the Welsh Marches. This is historically garbled, combining events of the eleventh century with those of the twelfth, but it tells of family territorial acquisitions, feuds and alliances, involving Norman and Welsh landowners, and thus explains the background to the young Fouke's own career as depicted in the romance, which is devoted to attempts to take vengeance on his family's enemies, especially King John, and recover the Fitz Waryn's Whittington estate. King John outlawed Fouke. Fouke, with a company of outlaws who included his brothers and cousins, hid in forests and other strongholds. The romance says that he only did harm or robberies that would injure the King: John functions in this romance as the Sheriff of Nottingham does in the Robin Hood tales, as an authority against whom illegality is justified. The narrative of Fouke's life is remarkable for its many references to Welsh princes: Owain Gwynedd, Iorwerth Goch, Iorwerth Drwyndwn, Llywelyn the Great, Owain Cyfeiliog, and Gwenwynwyn of Powys. At one point, having slain Morys Fitz Roger, Fouke seeks refuge with Prince Llywelyn and their friendship endures, despite the fact that Morys was Llywelyn's cousin. Llywelyn's wife, King John's sister Joan, is presented as reconciling the two men.[3] Fouke's good agency persuades Llywelyn to make peace with Gwenwynwyn of Powys. Kelly points to this as one of many ways in which the romance presents Fouke as a good outlaw.[4] Similarly, it presents John's gift of Fouke's estate to Morys, which provoked Fouke's vengeance, as an act of unjust use of authority.[5] The romance is a family romance, written to glorify the Fitz Waryn family; it records marriages, births, and the gain or loss of estates. Nothing of this kind is present in the medieval Robin Hood tradition. Prophecies embedded in the romance, one of them by Merlin, help to promote the idea of Fouke, the 'Wolf' (a wolf's head, an outlaw), as a divinely ordained revenger against the 'Leopard', King John, and the 'Boar', Morys.[6] Fouke's adventures include battles against fabulous enemies, including a dragon, flying serpents and a giant: again, things unknown in the Robin Hood tradition. The romance, however, does include elements, however, found in other outlaw tales, including those of Eustace the Monk and Robin Hood, such as tricks involving disguise, and in one story Fouke robs merchants and measures the stolen cloth and rich furs against his lance before generously distributing it and giving the merchants a forest feast. Similarly, in the *Gest of Robyn Hode*, Little John measures cloth against his bow and is particularly generous with it. Good outlaws, as presented in tales like this, are men of magnificent generosity, like greenwood princes, and they are not motivated solely by a desire for sordid gain. Both as outlaw and as lord of his estates, Fouke is presented as munificent and hospitable. There was a Middle English romance, now lost, about Fouke.[7] English and Anglo-Norman tales of Fouke perhaps formed part of the background for the Robin Hood stories.[8]

Particularly intriguing is the romance's statement that Prince John, Fouke and Llewellyn ap Iorwerth in boyhood were raised together in the court of Henry II of England: the author attributes to a boyhood quarrel over chess the lifelong malevolence from Prince John towards Fouke.[9] The romance depicts the friendship between Fouke and Llywelyn ap Iorwerth as also going back to this shared upbringing. Later, however, John prevails on Llywelyn to plot to try to capture Fouke, though Fouke escapes. At the end of the romance Llywelyn marries Fouke's daughter as his second wife. The era the romance depicts, that of the Norman acquisition of estates along the Welsh borders, is not one of simple national conflict between Welsh and Norman but of shifting alliances, both political and marital between princes and lords from both nations. Another historical outlaw, about whom there appears to have developed a literary tradition, is Sir John Giffard of Brimpsfield, who operated in the 1260s during De Montfort's rebellion with a band of followers in the Forest of Dean, and he also made alliances with Welsh princes and extended his robberies to the Welsh border.[10]

Though there is no extant Welsh version of the romance of Fouke, it would appear that the Welsh were familiar with the tradition.[11] This is attested by the fairly frequent references to *Syr Ffwg* and *Ffwg ap Gwarin* by the 'Poets of the Gentry', including Iolo Goch (*fl.* 1320–98) and Tudur Aled (*fl.* 1480–1526). However, these poets do not refer to the content of the romance or to Fouke's fame as an outlaw. *Syr Ffwg* for them is merely a symbol of knightly prowess and gracious hospitality: his name is invoked, like Guy of Warwick's, as a compliment in praise poems.[12] However, Fouke reappears in a moral parable printed by the aptly named Isaac Foulkes in his collection of folklore, *Cymru Fu* (1862–4), as both Ffowc Ffitswarren and Ffowc o Forgannwg (Fouke of Glamorgan).[13] The hero of this tale is sheriff of Cardiff and lives in Cardiff Castle but is clearly the same as the hero of the romance because we are told of his combats with Saracens. This association with Glamorgan is further corroborated by a reference to Fouke as a generous lord, under the title *Ffwg Morgannwg*, in an *englyn* to Ifor Hael, his patron, a landowner in south-east Wales, by the fourteenth-century poet, Dafydd ap Gwilym.[14]

Owain's Children

The Glyndŵr rebellion, between 1400 and 1412, involved guerilla raids, with Owain Glyndŵr using woods and mountains as secure bases for attacks. After the defeat of the last national rebellion in Wales and the disappearance of Owain Glyndŵr, many of the rebel soldiers became outlaws. They were referred to as *gwerin Owain* (Owain's children or folk). Indeed, it became very difficult for the Welsh to live within the law after the Penal Code had been passed during the Revolt by Parliament against the Welsh:

> It is ordained ... that no Englishman shall be convicted by any Welshman ... within the land of Wales.
>
> It is ordained ... that from henceforth no Welshman shall be armed nor bear defensible armour.[15]

One of the first such outlaws that we come across is Gruffudd ap Dafydd ap Gruffudd, a Welsh bandit and former rebel. He wrote several letters from his hideout in Dyffryn Clwyd to Lord Reginald Grey (1411). In the letters he states that he is willing to submit in return for seemingly outrageous demands: a royal charter of pardon, an important local office, and military service overseas.

Robin Hood was celebrated in drama, ballad and legend.[16] Owain's Children became celebrated in poetry and song. Welsh outlaw tradition includes poetry composed by the outlaws themselves. The poet, Llewellyn ap Moel y Pantri (d.1440) of Llanwddyn, Powys, was a Glyndŵr rebel turned outlaw and he wrote several poems about his band, the outlaws of Coed-y-Graig. The most notable is 'The Battle of Waun Gaseg' which is a frivolous and self-mocking account of his band's ignominious flight from more than a hundred horsemen:

> happy band on the hill slope
> Were we that day, in high hope,
> All at stretch and in good heart,
> Resolute to play our part,
> With doughty deeds in winning fame,
> In men's mouth's for Owain's name.[17]

There survives a verse of folk song about one of these outlaws, entitled *Marwnad yr Hedydd* (*The Elegy of the Lark*):

> *Mi a glywais fod yr hedydd*
> *Wedi marw ar y mynydd,*
> *Pe gwyddwn i mai gwir y geirie*
> *Awn â gyrr o wŷr ac arfe,*
> *I gyrchu corff yr hedydd adre.*[18]

> I have heard that the lark
> Has died on the mountain,
> If I knew that the words were true
> I would take an armed band of men,
> To bring the lark's body home.

The hedydd would appear to be the alias of an outlaw leader and it is possible that it could be either Owain Glyndŵr (the place of whose death is unknown) or the famous outlaw, Dafydd ap Siancyn (*fl.* mid-fifteenth century).[19]

As the fifteenth century wore on, the number of outlaws in Wales was increased by soldiers returning from the Hundred Years War (1337–1453) in France, well-versed in pillage and robbery. The Wars of the Roses (1455–85) greatly added to the numbers of outlaws because the armies brought desolation and, when defeated, would take to the woods. One of their number was the most celebrated outlaw of this period, Dafydd ap Siancyn (Siencyn) ap Dafydd ap y Crach of the Vale of Conwy. He was a captain on the Lancastrian side and a poet, who became an outlaw for a period during the reign of Edward IV. He was also the grandson of Rhys Gethin, one of Owain Glyndŵr's captains and was related to the Tudors. He and his followers were clad in green (perhaps a connection with the

Lincoln Green of Robin Hood?). On seeing these individuals at night dressed in green the local people, according to Sir John Wynn (*c*.1580), would take them for fairies and run away.[20] Tudur Penllyn (*c*.1420–85) wrote a *cywydd* in praise of Dafydd ap Siancyn, describing his eyrie at Carreg-y-gwalch, Llanrwst:

> *Cai Hir y coed ir a'r dail . . .*
> *Dy gastell ydyw'r gelli,*
> *Derw dôl yw dy dyrau di.*[21]

> The tall Sir Kay of the lush trees and the leaves . . .
> Your castle is the depth of the forest,
> Your towers, the oaks of the vale.

The hero's woodland hideout is the equivalent of an Arthurian court and fortress. Ieuan ap Gruffudd Leiaf, says his the outlaws' court, roofed with green foliage is like the glass house of Merlin; he is a golden warrior-knight of Rhos, his men are raid-loving 'adar o greim ar dir Grwst', birds of crime on the land of St Grwst.[22] Llywelyn ab y Moel described his own outlaw hideout in romance terms: a castle with turrets and tapestries of leaves.[23] The outlaw seems to have been assimilable to romantic and courtly associations in Welsh poetry to a degree that does not happen in the extant English tradition.

Another Lancastrian soldier and poet turned outlaw was Lewys Glyn Cothi or Llywelyn y Glyn (*c*.1420–89). After taking part in the Lancastrian defeat at Mortimer's Cross (1461), he fled and became an outlaw on the eastern slopes of Pumlumon, Cardiganshire. In one *cywydd*, he mentions that he had been an outlaw before with Owain ap Gruffudd ap Nicolas in Gwynedd, possibly as early as 1442:

> *A mi'n nhiredd Gwynedd gynt*
> *Yn herwa, yno hirhynt,*
> *Owain i gadw fy einioes*
> *Ei aur a'i win im a roes.*[24]

> When in the lands of Gwynedd of yore
> I was an outlaw, there a long time,
> Owain to save my life
> Gave me his gold and wine.

We have seen that some outlaws hid out in the forests and mountains but others used castles abandoned after damage during the Wars of the Roses. For instance, brigands used Castell Carreg Cennen in Carmarthenshire as their hideout until some 500 men were set to work with crowbars to demolish the castle in 1462.[25] Finally, there was a notorious outlaw near Mold in Flintshire named Rheinallt ap Gruffudd ap Bleddyn (c.1438–65/6) and described by the poet Howell Cilan as *braw'r Mars* (the terror of the Marches); according to tradition, he captured the mayor of Chester in 1464 and hanged him from a pillar in his house, y Tŵr.[26]

It is without doubt that these outlaws appealed to a number of poets. The poetry composed in praise of outlaws can be seen as a kind of condemnation of the settled lifestyle of court and city. The bandits were also outside English law, and this gained the sympathy of the bards who on the whole were Anglophobic.[27] The figure of the outlaw in relation to society and culture was inevitably more complex in Wales than in England. We have seen that, in the early thirteenth century, Fouke Fitz Waryn was at one time an outlaw, at others a legitimate Marcher lord, and he shifted between Welsh and English political and military alliances. Despite the misery caused by lawlessness, many late medieval Welsh gentry had themselves some experience of banditry.[28] However, late medieval outlaws kept the country in constant chaos, and the people became accustomed to violence through them. Blood feuds were fomented and according to Sir John Wynn:

> so bloody and ireful were quarrels in those days, and the revenge of the sword at such liberty as almost nothing was punished by law whatsoever happened.[29]

It is hardly surprising that Sir John claims that no one 'went abroad but in sort [in a posse] and so armed as if he went to the field to encounter with his enemies'.[30] It is further believed that this period of banditry and lawlessness gave rise to the English rhyme 'Taffy was a Welshman, Taffy was a thief'.[31] It is also possible that the verb *to welsh* or *to welch*, meaning to abscond without paying, entered the English language at this time: it may have been based upon a Welsh reputation for lawlessness in the fifteenth and sixteenth century.[32] Nevertheless, one should be wary of the accounts of this period written by Tudor commentators such as Sir John Wynn. They may well have deliberately painted the picture blacker than it was in order to magnify the supposed Tudor achievement of bringing law and order to Wales. That there were numerous outlaws in fifteenth-century Wales is beyond doubt, but it is unlikely that they were as prevalent as was formerly claimed.

The man credited with the restoration of law and order in Wales is Rowland Lee, Bishop of Lichfield and Coventry. He was appointed by Thomas Cromwell as President of the Council of Wales and the Marches in 1534 and given the task of pacifying the country in readiness for the Acts of Union 1536–43. He went about his job with great enthusiasm. He was suspicious of every Welshman: as a certain William Gerard informs us, he was 'not affable to any of the Walshrie, an extreme ponisher of offenders'.[33] He was disgusted at the Act of Union of 1536, which allowed Welshmen for the first time to become Justices of the Peace. His comment was: 'If one thief shall try another, all we have here begun is foredone.'[34] The contemporary claim that he hanged 5,000 Welsh felons is exaggerated but it is indicative of the fear he inspired. An example of this is the occasion when he caused the dead body of an outlaw to be 'brought in a sack trussed upon a horse' to a market town and hanged on the gallows before a crowd of 300; he gleefully wrote to Cromwell: 'The manner thereof had not been seen heretofore.'[35]

However, at least one band of outlaws escaped Rowland Lee's reign of terror: the celebrated Red Bandits of Mawddwy. They were reputed to be descended from Owain Glyndŵr's rebels and they terrorized the area around the mountainous and inaccessible commote of Mawddwy, now in Gwynedd. Until the nineteenth century there were houses in the area with scythe blades lodged in the chimneys, said to have been placed there centuries before as protection against the bandits. They gained their epithet from their red hair and the red-haired denizens of the area today are reputed to be their descendants. The commote had traditionally formed part of Powys. However, in 1536, instead of forming part of the newly created shire of Montgomery, it was added to the well-established shire of Merioneth which had been set up in 1284. This, it seems, was done because of the disorder caused by the Red Bandits and it was felt that the settled administration of

Merionethshire would be better able to suppress the bandits. According to Thomas Pennant in his *Tours of Wales* (1778), little time was lost in subduing them. Baron Lewis Owen (High Sheriff of Merioneth, 1554–5) hanged over eighty of them on Christmas Eve, 1554. According to tradition, the mother of two outlaws who were hanged, cursed Baron Owen, saying: 'These breasts have nurtured other sons who will wash their hands in your heart's blood.'[36] Less than a year later (11 October 1555) her surviving sons murdered Baron Owen at Dugoed Mawddwy. However, this did not save the clan of brigands, as it is believed that all the males were executed following this murder.[37]

Twm Siôn Cati

Finally, we turn to the outlaw often described as the Welsh Robin Hood: Twm Siôn Cati (*c*.1530–1609). His official names were Thomas Jones or Johns or Tomas Siôn Dafydd Madoc and he was an antiquarian and heraldic bard. There is no historical record of his ever being an outlaw apart from the fact that he received a pardon under the Great Seal in the first year of Elizabeth I's reign (1559). We are not, however, told what the nature of his crime was. However, this pardon, coupled with his confusion with others of the same name who were robbers and highwaymen in the Tregaron area of Cardiganshire, gave rise to a number of tales. In some of the stories, Twm is portrayed as a man to be feared, hence, this well-known rhyme:

> Mae llefain mawr a gweiddi
> Yn Ystrad-ffin eleni,
> A'r cerrig nadd yn toddi'n blwm
> Gan ofon Twm Siôn Cati.[38]

> There is great weeping and shouting
> In Ystrad-ffin this year;
> And the hewn stones melt into lead
> In fear of Twm Siôn Cati.

The majority of tales and anecdotes, however, portray him positively, as a Welsh Robin Hood: the people's champion who stole from the rich and gave to the poor. He is reputed to have had two hideouts, both caves, one near Ystrad-ffin, Tregaron and another at Rhandir-mwyn, near Llandovery, Carmarthenshire. He may have been an inspiration for Henry Fielding's *The History of Tom Jones, A Foundling* (1749), with its honourable-rogue hero: 'Tom Jones' is an anglicized form of his name. Nevertheless, the earliest printed account of Twm Siôn Cati's adventures appeared in a pamphlet entitled 'Tomshone Catty's Tricks', printed by John Ross, Carmarthen, in 1763. A number of tales about Twm Siôn Cati were included by Samuel Rush Meyrick in his *History of the County of Cardigan* (1808). They were expanded by William Frederick Deacon in his books, *Twm John Catty, the Welsh Robin Hood* (1822) and *The Welsh Rob Roy* (1823). The main reason for his fame is T. J. Llywelyn Prichard's novel, *The Adventures and Vagaries of Twm Shon Catti* (1828), which is based on traditional material. A Welsh-language version was published later and a much more extensive English-language version was published in 1839, followed by a third edition in 1873.[39] Many other books recounting the adventures of Twm Siôn Cati, mainly for children, have followed, including Lynn Hughes's *Hawkmoor* in 1977. This was made into a television series where he is portrayed as a hero defending the Welsh from the injustices of English rule. The novel was republished in 1983 under the title *Twm Sion Catti's Men*.

In conclusion, we can now see that the heyday of the Welsh outlaw was the fifteenth and sixteenth centuries; more specifically, the period extended from the end of the Owain Glyndŵr's Rebellion to Elizabeth I's accession. The outlaws were, in the main, Glyndŵr's rebels who refused to submit to English law. They chose to live outside it or were forced to do so by the extreme Penal Code introduced against the Welsh during the Glyndŵr revolt. Because of their nationalism they were praised by the bards and a number were poets themselves. Whereas the medieval Robin Hood is a yeoman, most of the medieval Welsh outlaws of literary tradition were of gentle birth. With the Act of Union and the introduction of a uniform administrative and legal system to Wales, the outlaws, perhaps the last vestigial survival of Welsh independence, were suppressed. However, the fame of one did survive to posterity, Twm Siôn Cati: the Welsh Robin Hood.

NOTES

1. Ivor Bowen, *The Statutes of Wales* (London, 1908), p. 2.
2. *Fouke Le Fitz Waryn*, E. J. Hathaway, P. T. Ricketts, C. A. Robson, A. D. Wilshere (eds), Anglo-Norman Text Society (Oxford, 1975). For translations see Glyn Burgess, *Two Medieval Outlaws: Eustace the Monk and Fouke Fitz Waryn* (Cambridge, 1997), *Fouke Fitz Waryn*, Thomas E. Kelly (trans.), in Thomas H. Ohlgren (ed.), *Medieval Outlaws: Ten Tales in Modern English* (Stroud, 1998), pp. 106–67.
3. Historically, Joan was John's daughter not sister.
4. Kelly, *Fouke Fitz Waryn*, pp. 108–9.
5. Ibid. See Burgess, *Two Medieval Outlaws*, pp. 91–131.
6. The use of the prophecies with animals' names for people is probably drawn from Geoffrey of Monmouth, though the genre is common in Welsh poetry. See R. Wallis Evans, 'Prophetic Poetry', in A. O. H. Jarman and Gwilym Rees Hughes (eds), revised by Dafydd Johnston, *A Guide to Welsh Literature 1282–c.1550*, (Cardiff, 1997), pp. 256–74.
7. A summary is preserved in John Leland's *Collectanea*: see *Fouke le Fitz Waryn*, ed. Hathaway, pp. xxi–xxvi, and *Fouke Fitz Warin*, ed. Louis Brandin, Les classiques français du moyen âge (Paris, 1930), pp. v–vi. Langland's *Piers Plowman*, B 396, refers to 'rymes of Robyn Hode and Ranulf erl of Chestre', as if these are very popular; the reference to poems about Randolph has never been satisfactorily explained but Randolph appears in the romance of Fouke, perhaps further evidence that narratives of, or connected with, the Fouke saga were known in fourteenth-century England, possibly influencing the *Gest*.
8. The reference to Lady Matilda de Caus (Mahaud in the text, a Norman name equivalent also to modern Maud) could perhaps, through knowledge of Leland's summary of the English romance, have encouraged sixteenth-century writers to call Maid Marian 'Matilda' and make her father a Norman lord, see *Fouke le Fitz Waryn*, ed. Hathaway, p. xxxiii.
9. The use of this motif, found in some other romances, including *Les Quatre Fils Aymon*, helps justify Fouke's lawlessness against John: as in the Robin Hood tradition, the hero fights unjust authority. The fact that *Fouke* sets Fouke's adventures in this period may have influenced the move towards setting Robin Hood in that era.
10. Keen, pp. 194–5; Keen compares Gifford, as a 'baronial rebel', to Fouke.
11. They could have known the tradition from Anglo-Norman or Middle English texts, though he may also have appeared in now lost Welsh narratives.
12. The romance Fouke, a knight, fights on horseback, mounts some

large-scale military assaults and wins a tournament in disguise against French King's knights: for comparisons and contrast with Robin Hood narratives see Keen, pp. 45–51. Tudur Aled refers frequently to Syr Ffwg as a standard for complimentary comparison with other lords: *Gwaith Tudur Aled*, ed. T. Gwynn Jones, 2 vols (Cardiff, 1926), I, pp. 38, 41, 133, 171; II. pp. 403. Iolo Goch presents his hospitality as legendary: a complimentary poem to Ieuan ab Einion of Chwilog says that besides Ieuan's princely munificence 'there was less expenditure in the castles/Fulk's court by the side of the road', referring to the story that Fouke diverted a main road to brings travellers to be entertained at his house; he also compares a ship riding a wild sea to 'a cold serpent like Sir Fulk's horse': 'I Ieuan ab Einion o Chwilog' and 'Cywydd y Llong', in *Iolo Goch: Poems*, trans. and ed. Dafydd Johnston (Llandysul, Dyfed, 1993), pp. 10–11, 134–5. A powerful strand in the tradition, and the language, of Welsh outlaw poetry sees outlaws as gracious and courtly. Ieuan Tew ai Cant praised two Welsh outlaws for their graciousness, both in robbing the rich to help the poor and in their generosity to the poet: 'Kind Robin Hood was a magician, an outlaw who scattered money; if you bribe, bring me wine, bribe as Robin used to bribe! To avoid discourtesy is to make life in the world longer', T. Gwynn Jones, 'Cultural Bases: A Study of the Tudor Period in Wales', *Y Cymmrodor*, 31 (1921), 161–92, text pp. 181–3.

13   Isaac Foulkes, *Cymru Fu: yn Cynnwys Hanesion, Traddodiadau yn nghyda Chwedlau a Dammegion Cymreig* (Wrexham, 1862), p. 84.

14   'Englynion I Ifor Hael', *Gwaith Dafydd ap Gwilym*, ed. Thomas Parry (Cardiff, 1952), pp. 16–17.

15   See E. A. Rees, *Welsh Outlaws and Bandits: Political Rebellion and Lawlessness in Wales, 1400–1603* (King's Norton, 2001), pp. 17–18, on English punitive legislative measures to curb Welsh rebellion and lawlessness, which provoked further Welsh resentment and popular support for Glyndŵr.

16   The Robin Hood tradition seems to have been current in late medieval and early modern Wales: there is a song, 'Robin Hwd ai Kant', in a manuscript from *c*.1500, and evidence of Robin Hood plays, especially in towns in the Marches area: see Knight 1994, 262–88 and note 41, on the assumption of a play at Brecknock.

17   *The Oxford Book of Welsh Verse in English*, ed. Gwyn Jones (ed.) (Oxford, 1977), 59. J. E. Caerwyn Williams comments 'no one but a man confident of his reputation for bravery would deliberately set out to make himself a laughing-stock for running away', 'Guto'r Glyn', in A. O. H. Jarman and Gwilym Rees Hughes (eds), revised by Dafydd Johnston, *A Guide to Welsh Literature 1282–c.1550* (Cardiff: University of Wales Press, 1997), pp. 197–221, p. 200.

18   *Lleisiau'r Werin* (Arfon, 1980), p. 36.

19   E. A. Rees, *Welsh Outlaws and Bandits: Political Rebellion and Lawlessness in Wales, 1400–1603* (King's Norton: Caterwen, 2001) 17–18, discusses the development of a legend that Glyndŵr had not died and would return to help his country, as well as the ascription of

magical powers to Owain, ideas which Hobsbawm, pp. 56–62, finds in the 'noble outlaw' mythology attached to other outlaw-heroes.

20 Sir John Wynn, *The History of the Gwydir Family and Memoirs*, ed. J. Gwynfor Jones (Llandysul, 1990), pp. 29, 33, 41, 41, 50–1, 127–9; story about green-clad outlaws, p. 51. Dafydd ap Siencyn, poet and outlaw, was kin to the powerful Hywel ap Rhys, often helping him in quarrels with Sir John's ancestor, John ap Maredudd. Gwynfor Jones observes: 'In times of political and economic stress [outlaws] were regarded often as popular leaders of discontent and local unrest', while 'In the political climate described by Sir John Wynn renegades could easily become the tools of others in their efforts to seize the main chance in the acquisition of land or to pay back old scores' (p. 129). Fifteenth-century England and Wales both saw gentry maintaining private armies, often using gangs and outlaws in pursuit of their aims, but the phenomenon had more complex and nationalist dimensions in Wales.

21 *Gwaith Tudur Penllyn*, ed. Thomas Roberts (Cardiff, 1958), no. I, p. 1. The poet describes Dafydd as a man of gentle family, who became an outlaw and suffered deprivations under an unjust English law; Thomas Parry, *Hanes Llenyddiaeth Gymraeg Hyd 1900* (Cardiff, 1979), p. 122.

22 *The Dictionary of Welsh Biography Down to 1940* (Cardiff, 1959). The phrase proudly adopts to garrison men's slang for outlaws.

23 *Cywyddau Iolo Goch ac Eraill*, ed. H. Lewis, T. Roberts and I. Williams (Cardiff, 1925), pp. 198–9. Rees, *Welsh Outlaws*, p. 82, points out that the outlaw is sometimes a metaphor for the courtly lover, unrequited in love, by several poets, including Dafydd ap Gwilym and Tudur Aled.

24 Gwynfor Evans, *Aros Mae* (Swansea, Cardiff, 1971), p. 199. The poet describes Dafydd as a man of gentle ancestry who became an outlaw and suffered deprivations under an unjust English law.

25 Linsday Evans, *The Castles of Wales: A Guide* (London, 1998), p. 75.

26 'Cywydd to Rheinallt ap Gruffudd', by Gutun Owain, *Ouevre poétiques de Gutun Owains*, 2 vols, ed. E. Bachellery (Paris, 1950–1), no. 16.

27 Llewellyn ap y Moel praised outlaws for undermining English law and encouraging opposition in the border regions, Lewis, *Cywyddau Iolo Goch*, lxiii, pp. 191–2. Rees, *Welsh Outlaws*, pp. 128–9, observes that Henry Tudor was praised as 'Harri Herwr', Harry the Outlaw, when opposing the Yorkists: he is *herwr* (both 'outlaw' and 'challenger'), while Richard III's followers are, more pejoratively, *gwylliaid* ('bandits'). Gwynn Jones, 'Cultural Bases', pp. 163–5, points to bards' praise of outlaws in contrast to the despised 'garrison men'.

28 The nation's leaders, Glyndŵr, Jasper Tudor and Henry Tudor, all at times operated like guerilla leaders. Knight (1994), pp. 116–18, on the performance of a Robin Hood play-within-a-play, in George Peele's *The Famous Chronicle of Edward I* (by 1593), comments that the subject is chosen by Lluellen and his followers, and is a parallel to their

actual role as Welsh nationalist guerilla-fighters in the rest of the drama. Peele has Lluellen say: 'Weele get the next daie from Breacknock the booke of Robin Hood . . . ile be maister of misrule, ile be *Robin Hood*, that once', p. 117.

29 David Williams, *A History of Modern Wales* (London, 1977), p. 17.
30 Ibid.
31 *A Most Peculiar People: Quotations about Wales and the Welsh*, compiled by Meic Stephens (Cardiff, 1992), p. 30. There are many variants.
32 Clearly an oral tradition, OED finds it first recorded in writing in the context of racing slang, in the mid-nineteenth century.
33 'Rowland Lee', in Meic Stephens (ed.), *Cydymaith i Lenyddiaeth Cymru/Companion to the Literature of Wales*, rev. edn (Cardiff, 1997), pp. 430–1.
34 Ibid.
35 Williams, *History*, p. 31.
36 Robin Gwyndaf, *Welsh Folk Tales* (Cardiff, 1995), p. 57.
37 L. Dwnn, *Heraldic Visitations of Wales and Part of the Marches* (Cardiff, 1848). J. Y. W. Lloyd, *The History of the Princes, the Lords Marcher, and the Ancient Nobility of Powys Fadog, and the Ancient Lords of Arwystli, Cedewen, and Meirionydd* (Cardiff, 1882), p. 236.
38 Gwyndaf, *Folk Tales*, p. 67.
39 The early nineteenth century was a period both of the scholarly investigation and publication of folklore and also of radicalism and revolt. Publications in both areas sometimes had common ideals; see Lois Potter, 'Sherwood Forest and the Byronic Robin Hood', in *Robin Hood in Popular Culture*, ed. Thomas Hahn (Cambridge, 2000), pp. 215–24, on Robin Hood imagery in radical writings in Nottinghamshire and London literary circles at this time, and John Beynon on Robin Hood references in the Rebecca Riots in west Wales of 1839 and 1842: p. 237, in this volume.

Fouke Fitz Waryn III and King John: Good Outlaw and Bad King

GLYN BURGESS

A medieval king had a number of duties. He was expected to preserve peace and stability, to maintain good laws and customs and to administer justice to all men equitably.[1] He was also expected to live his life according to Christian principles, which included attendance at church and the protection of the Church and the clergy.[2] To be successful, a king needed to be strong and decisive; in war he had to show himself to be both a brave warrior and an effective leader. In addition, it was important that the king should be able to deal appropriately with his barons, in whom much of the wealth of the kingdom resided; a difficult task as the barons were immensely powerful. The barons expected to enjoy a good deal of personal freedom and individual authority, but they respected a king who acted firmly, provided he did so with justice. Indeed, in order to achieve peace and harmony it was wise for a king to instil into his subjects as a whole a certain degree of fear, even at the risk of being called a tyrant (*'fortes reges tyranni vocabantur'*, 'strong kings were commonly called tyrants', Isidore of Seville, *Etymologiae*, IX, III, 18–20). For it was better to be regarded as a tyrant than as a weak and incompetent king who failed to control power or who used it foolishly; such a king was called useless, a *rex inutilis*.[3]

Literary works from the medieval period contain an array of kings, some good, some bad, some strong, some weak. Epic poems often include real kings, such as Charlemagne, without their portraits having much basis in reality; romance kings, headed by King Arthur, are largely fictional.[4] The present article will focus on the presentation of kingship in a text in which eight real kings and several fictional kings are depicted:

the ancestral romance, *Fouke le Fitz Waryn*.[5] The original version of this text, composed in verse around 1260, is now lost, but a prose version, written in the 1320s and 1330s, has been preserved.[6] Of the various kings, it is John who merits particular attention, as his hostility towards Fouke Fitz Waryn III creates the core of the action. This point was not neglected by the romance's modern editors, who comment on the 'bitterly satirical and disdainful' portrayal of King John (p. xxix). My intention here is to expand on this observation and to explore the way in which the author, writing some forty-five years after John's death in October 1216, transformed a real king into an effective literary figure.[7] Fouke became an outlaw but the issues were land-holding and justice, and the romance shows King John to be the source of social disruption and not the upholder of peace, order and justice.

The first king to be mentioned in the text is King Harold, about whom we are told summarily that he was killed by William the Bastard, Duke of Normandy, who conquered the entire land of England by force and had himself crowned in London (p. 3, ll. 9–12). The narrative then concentrates on William's activities as king. He is presented as doing exactly what a king should do, making proper use of force in order to establish peace and law according to his will (*'estably pees e leys a sa volenté'*, p. 3, ll. 8–9); his success enables him to bestow lands on his supporters (*'donna terres a diverse gentz qe ou ly vyndrent'*, p. 3, ll. 13–14). William is clearly aware of his responsibilities and kingship in his hands is seen as a force for good. Thus the text opens with a very positive vision of Norman kingship.

The author then concentrates on a particular area of Britain, the Welsh March, beginning with the county of Shrewsbury, which, we are told, is claimed by the Prince of Wales, the most feared of all the king's opponents. But such is the strength of William's army that the prince abandons the territory, thus allowing William to distribute the lands as he wishes. The author is evidently impressed by a king who has the military might to frighten off an opponent and to put his plans into effect without any need for fighting. William is therefore a man to be admired, an effective ruler, one who sets the standard by which later kings can be judged. William gives the county of

Shrewsbury to Roger de Bellême, but when Roger's heirs later prove hostile to the crown by building adulterine castles it becomes the turn of William's son, Henry I, to act firmly and swiftly. Henry banishes the Bellême family and gives the land to his own knights. The Norman kings are thus presented as strong, energetic and just; they are very sensitive to the issues of land and the need to reward those knights who have given good service.[8]

There is no mention of Henry I's successor, King Stephen, but as he prepares us for the outlawry of Fouke III the author comments favourably on the actions of Henry II, and even more favourably on those of his son Richard. When Walter de Lacy has captured Joce de Dynan and seized the lands belonging to Fouke le Brun, the latter, grievously wounded, seeks help from Henry who declares his intention to avenge himself on the criminals (*malfesours*) responsible. On learning who Fouke is, he states that he will help him because he is of his blood. He has Fouke's wounds tended to and sends for his mother and wife; he has the latter reside in the queen's chamber until she gives birth to the child who will become the principal character in the romance. Henry sends Walter a letter threatening him with dire consequences and duly secures the release of Joce and his men; he receives them in Gloucester with joy, promising Joce the support of law and reason ('*ley e resoun*'). He later makes Fouke le Brun constable of the entire army (pp. 20, 30–8; 31, ll. 30–8).

Henry is presented as a king who does what is right and knows how to reward excellence and make proper use of the law. On his death, his son Richard continues where his father left off. Richard cherishes Fouke le Brun because of his loyalty (p. 23, ll. 6–7) and it is Richard himself who dubs the young Fouke '*molt richement*' (p. 23, ll. 8–11). When Fouke Le Brun dies, the young Fouke is abroad seeking '*pris e los*' (p. 23, l. 12) and again it is Richard himself who writes to him, telling him to return home and receive his inheritance. On his return Fouke is duly welcomed by Richard and put in possession of all his father's lands (p. 23, ll. 21–3). Moreover, when Richard is making preparations to travel to the Holy Land, he is said to place the entire March under Fouke's protection (p. 23, ll. 17–25). The author is clearly keen to stress the very positive relationship between Richard and Fouke and he gives reasons for it: '*Le roy l'ama mout e chery pur sa lealté e pur la grant renomee qu'il aveit*' ('The king loved him dearly and cherished him for his loyalty and great renown') (p. 23, ll. 25–6). Fouke was thus on excellent terms with Richard ('*molt bien de le roy*') during the whole of his reign. Richard maintained his father's high standards as king.

This situation provides the background for a dramatic change in the fortunes of the Fitz Waryn family. The author is at pains to make clear that Fouke III, an ideal knight in the making, has great potential as a supporter of the monarch, something which heightens the feeling of loss to the community when King John comes to the throne and fails to build on the harmonious relationship between the Fitz Waryns and his predecessors.[9] Thus far, the Norman kings have been the very models of kingship, displaying a caring attitude towards their supporters and doing their best to create a just society. At this point it is appropriate to recall the Prologue, in which the author states that his aim is to recall the adventures and brave deeds of those who strove to act with honour and loyalty (p. 3, ll. 6–7), and also the comment that William the Bastard, who was '*mout sages*', gave lands in the March to his most valiant knights so that they could defend them '*a lur profit e al honur lur seignour le roy*' (p. 3, ll. 22–6). Society is presented as being dependent for its proper functioning on the balance between royal wisdom and chivalric honour and loyalty. Loyal service, properly rewarded, was to the advantage of both knights and king. The issue of the justice of the king's distribution of lands will be the key to Fouke's rebellion and outlawry.

The transition from Richard to John is succinctly handled, with no mention of the uncertainty concerning the succession: '*Aprés cui mort, Johan, le frere le roy Richart, fust coronee roy d'Engletere*' ('After Richard's death, John, King Richard's brother, was crowned King of England') (p. 23, ll. 28–9).[10] From this point onwards the relationship between Fouke III and King John dominates the text. The first specific reference to John had appeared a little earlier when the author created a link between the five sons of Fouke le Brun and the four sons of Henry II (p. 22, ll. 23–6). The impression given is that these nine boys were all fine specimens with the exception of John, about whom it is said: '*Tote sa vie fust maveys e contrarious e envyous*' (pp. 22, ll. 29–30): thus from the start we are informed of John's negative characteristics: 'wicked, quarrelsome and envious'.[11] We are consequently prepared for the conflict between John and Fouke III, so it comes as no surprise when John turns out to be a stumbling block to Fouke's ambition to regain possession of Whittington. But when the author recounts the story of a game of chess played by Fouke and John as youngsters, it becomes even clearer that there is trouble ahead:

> It happened that John and Fouke were sitting all alone in a chamber playing chess when John took the chessboard and struck Fouke a mighty blow with it. Realising he was injured, Fouke raised his foot and kicked John in the chest so hard that his head went crashing against the wall, with the result that he became giddy and fainted. Fouke was dismayed, but glad that there was no one in the room apart from the two of them. He rubbed John's ears and he regained consciousness. He went to his father, the king, and complained bitterly. 'Hold your tongue, wretch', said the king, 'you are always trying to pick a quarrel. If Fouke did anything to you which was harmful, it was just what you deserved'. He summoned John's master and had him well and truly beaten because he had complained. John was very angry with Fouke, so that afterwards he could never feel any true love towards him (pp. 22, ll. 32–9 – 32, ll. 1–5).

This crucial episode reveals a number of aspects of John's character, and it certainly depicts a youth whose personality and behaviour do not augur well for the future. We are not told specifically why John reacts as he does during the game. It is tempting to assume that he is losing, or that he is in some way frustrated by the progress of the game, but the author may simply have wished to convey the notion that John was unpredictable and likely to pick a quarrel at any time for no particular reason (he had earlier been described as *contrarious* 'quarrelsome, perverse', pp. 22, l. 29). Whatever the reason, John behaves here with unexpected anger and an inappropriate level of aggression. The impression conveyed is that he is already a dangerous individual, one who can be a threat to the welfare of others, even when they have done no wrong. It is the future king who has a disruptive personality, not the future outlaw. The conclusion of the episode shows John as a bad loser and as someone who harbours grudges. On the other hand, the episode also allows us to see that, even as a youth, Fouke is not a person to be trifled with; he demonstrates that if wronged, even by the king's son, he is capable of swift revenge. He also shows himself to be capable of reacting sensibly and honourably in a crisis; when he sees that John has lost consciousness, he does his best to help him, while at the same time remaining mindful of the possible consequences of what he has done. The episode also confirms Henry's sense of justice and thereby continues to show him in a good light, both as father and as king. From Henry's reaction it would appear that John had been guilty of unruly behaviour in the past (*"maveys"*, *fet le roy, "touz jours estes contreckaunt"'* ('"Wretch", said the king, "you are always trying to pick a quarrel"'), pp. 22, l. 39 – 23, l. 1[12]), so Henry was not willing to take John's side merely because he was his son and therefore to inflict unjust punishment on Fouke. In this episode John acquires the image of a cry-baby,[13] of someone whose actions backfire on him and of a man who deserves what is coming to him ('*ce fust par vostre desert demeyne*' ('it was just what you deserved'), p. 23, l. 2).[14]

The chessboard incident has the distinction of being the only anecdote which has come down to us concerning the real King John's childhood. W. L. Warren states that the story is 'probably apocryphal', but he does quote it in full, presumably to suggest that it provides an early indication of John's personality.[15] Janet Meisel comments that she is unable to dismiss the story entirely: 'The very absurdity of this story helps to make it convincing'.[16] Richard Eales cites Meisel's comment, but he prefers to see the quarrel over the chess game here as a literary *topos*.[17] If Fouke were John's cousin, as is stated in the text, this could explain his presence at court as a playmate for John, but there is no evidence that the two were related. If the quarrel did take place in the way described, it would presumably have happened in the mid to late 1170s. We can note that the anecdote requires Fouke, John and Henry to have been at court at the same time (the location of the court is not specified and Henry was constantly on the move). The episode is chronologically plausible; John, born in 1167, saw little of his parents in the first years of his life, but after the elder sons' rebellion (1173–4), he did remain with his father.[18]

The consequences of the chessboard incident are revealed very soon, in the pivotal scene of the narrative. Fouke has learned that John, now king, has made Morys de Powys, the occupant of Whittington, the warden of the March and that he is willing to put his seal to whatever Morys sets down in writing with regard to Whittington. John knew, states the author, that Fouke had full claim to Blancheville, but he recalled the blow given to him by Fouke during the chess game (p. 24, ll. 4–8). This, we are told, is John's chance of revenge (*'se pensa qu'il se vengereit par yleqe'*, p. 24, ll. 5–6).[19] Although fully aware of the course of action dictated by the custom of *'dreit heritage'*, John chooses to ignore it in order to exact revenge for something which happened during his childhood; thus, for personal reasons, he fails in his duty to administer justice equitably.[20] The author points out that John's action was a contravention of both reason and common law (*'resoun et commun[e] ley'*, p. 24, l. 30).[21] Because of this, Fouke's life is radically altered. But for the exceptional qualities Fouke possesses, and the determination and resourcefulness demonstrated in the outlaw episodes, John's unjust action would have destroyed an entire family.[22]

We have already been told that John had a great propensity for anger. When, after the rupture, Fouke eludes capture, John becomes extraordinarily angry (*'devynt si corocé qe a merveyle'*, p. 26, ll. 16–17) and orders a hundred knights to travel all over England to track Fouke down. His anger seemingly blinds him to the financial prudence which would be expected of a king; the pursuers, we are told, *'averount totes lur costages de[l] roy, e, s'il le puissent prendre, le roy les dorreit terres e riche feez'* ('All their expenses would be paid by the king, and if they could capture him he would give them lands and rich fiefs') (p. 26, ll. 19–20). Fouke, who is described by Painter as 'a simple knight of meagre landed power' (p. 52) was certainly not, in reality, of sufficient stature to warrant such lavish expenditure. The romance's figure of a hundred knights sent to capture Fouke would seem to reflect the fact that in June 1201 the real King John sent a hundred knights under the leadership of Hubert de Burgh to hold the Welsh Marches.[23]

In the romance the issue of the ownership of Whittington Castle causes John to reveal himself as a poor king in several respects. But another aspect of his personality emerges as the episodes succeed each other: he does not know when to accept defeat. His unceasing efforts to capture Fouke and his constant failure to do so turn him into a comic, frustrated figure.[24] Episode after episode demonstrates Fouke's superiority and cunning and John's weakness and inadequacy. In the first of these episodes, Fouke captures ten merchants who are on their way to court carrying magnificent cloths which they have purchased for the king and queen. Fouke suspects that this is an opportunity to score a victory over John, but he only acts after taking pains to determine that any loss not caused by lack of care on the merchants' part would be borne by the king. Then he measures out the cloth and clothes his men, each according to his rank. On their return to court the merchants, wounded and maimed, duly tell their tale. The king's reaction is predictable; he almost goes mad with rage ('*a poy qu'il ne enraga de ire*', p. 27, ll. 30–1). Yet again his response is to throw money at the problem: '*E fist fere une criee parmi le realme qe cely qe ly amerreit Fouke vyf ou mort, yl ly dorreit myl lyvres d'argent, e, estre ce, yl ly dorreit totes lé terres qe a Fouke furent en Engleterre*' (p. 27, ll. 31–4).[25] Again, the sum of one thousand pounds in silver which John offers for Fouke's capture is far in excess of what would have been appropriate in this instance. By reacting in this way, the king continues to demonstrate the childishness and irrationality he showed in the chessboard incident.

There then follows a couple of episodes in which Fouke and his men elude the best efforts of the king's men to capture them. After this, the author turns to yet another side of John's character: his lustful behaviour. Fouke receives a visit from the Archbishop of Canterbury, Hubert Walter (here called Hubert le Botiler), who tells Fouke that his brother, Theobald le Botiler, is dead. His beautiful widow, Lady Matilda de Caus, is being pursued by John: '*Le roy Johan la desire taunt pur sa bealté qe a peyne ele se puet garder de ly*' (p. 30, ll. 16–18). In spite of the unsatisfactory nature of his circumstances, Fouke agrees to the Archbishop's request to marry Matilda. Ironically, John's lust for a vulnerable woman provides his enemy Fouke with a wealthy wife and, moreover, with one who in remarkably quick time produces for him what every nobleman desires: sons. Thus John has unwittingly helped to secure Fouke's future. A further irony is that Hubert Walter, the instigator of Fouke's marriage to Matilda, was in reality one of John's closest friends and supporters.[26] In contrast to the licentious, socially disruptive, John, Fouke is dedicated to the all-important values of family, land and dynasty. His wife proves a loyal supporter, even giving birth while sharing his outlawed state.

When John is next mentioned, the author stresses his inability to put into practice another of his responsibilities as king: to maintain good relations with allies or potential allies. Fouke succeeds in alliances with the rulers of both Wales and France. Fouke goes to Rhuddlan to meet with the Prince of Wales, Llywelyn the Great, and the prince asks him what sort of agreement there has been between himself and the king. Fouke replies that there has been no agreement, because he had found it impossible to secure peace with John under any circumstances; indeed, that was the reason why he had come to seek peace with Llywelyn. Fouke receives the reply he desires: '*Certes, fet le prince, ma pees je vous grant e doynz, e de moy bon resut averez. Le roy d'Engletere ne pees ou vous ne moy ne autre siet aver*' ('Certainly, said the prince, I grant and give you my peace and you will receive a good welcome from me. The King of England is incapable of having peace with you or me or anyone else') (p. 33, ll. 34–6). This blanket condemnation of King John is put into the mouth of one of John's most powerful and dangerous rivals.[27] The point being made is that John's character and behaviour are such that he is not only unable to reach a peaceful agreement with an outlaw, but also with men of much greater political importance. He is thus incapable of bringing peace and harmony to his kingdom and is therefore an inadequate ruler.

So determined is the author to make the most of the enmity between Fouke and John that he takes us right into the king's mind. Frustrated by his failure to capture Fouke and thus to restore his own honour and pride, John goes as far as to call into question his entire status as king and duke:

> Then news came to him that Fouke had killed Morys Fitz Roger and that he was staying with Llywelyn, the prince who had married his

sister Joan. He became very thoughtful and for a long time said nothing. Then he said: 'Ah, Virgin Mary! I am king and I govern England. I am Duke of Anjou and of Normandy and all Ireland is in my power.[28] Yet I cannot find or get in all my domain, whatever I may give, anyone who is willing to avenge me for the damage and shame which Fouke has inflicted on me' (p. 34, ll. 26–34).

This admission of total failure when faced with a seemingly minor threat to his authority both undermines John's status as King of England and boosts Fouke's importance as the hero of the narrative; he has reduced the king to impotence. If at times John's frustration makes him comic, here he becomes a poignant figure, overcome by self-pity and fully conscious of the gulf separating status from performance. Fouke's successful rebellion and the '*damage e hontage*' ('damage and humiliation') he has inflicted on John have reduced the king to rock bottom. The reader cannot but wonder what will happen next; how will John cope with this crisis? At this point the author exploits another of John's weaknesses, that of taking his own failure out on others. His response is to avenge himself on Llywelyn (his brother-in-law): '*Je ne lerroy qe je ne me vengeroy de le prince*' ('I shall not cease until I am revenged on the prince') (p. 34, ll. 34–5). This leads to a '*grant guere*' against Llywelyn. Surely now, with all his resources, John will restore his battered pride. But, sadly for John, this war becomes yet another example of his failure to succeed in an objective. After a fierce struggle, in which many of his men are killed and wounded, he is forced to retreat to Shrewsbury in a state of grief (*dolent*, p. 35, l. 32). He had been out-manoeuvred by men who could have been his allies, had he not been foolish enough to alienate them.

The author goes on to exploit another aspect of the relationship between John and Llywelyn: the latter's marriage to John's sister Joan.[29] When Fouke reveals that he has killed Morys de Powys (p. 32, l. 39), Joan helps to make peace between her husband and Fouke; Morys was Llywelyn's cousin and he would like to have had Fouke hanged and drawn. Had this happened, John would, of course, have been rid of his enemy, and ironically it is John's own sister who prevents this. Joan later plays an even more crucial role. Realizing that his efforts to capture Fouke have failed, and knowing that his brother-in-law is harbouring him, John writes to Llywelyn asking him to rid his household of *'son mortel enymy e son feloun'* and to let him have the body (p. 39, ll. 15–21). So keen is John to get his hands on Fouke that he offers Llywelyn peace and the return of all his lands. But Joan discovers this and informs Fouke of what John has in mind. Fearing treason, Fouke leaves for Paris in spite of Llywelyn's protestations that he will not act treacherously towards him (pp. 39, ll. 22–39 – 40, ll. 1–5). The fact that on two occasions John's sister supports Fouke and not her brother serves to tarnish John's image even further.[30]

The most damning comment made by the author concerning John occurs at the moment when John and what remains of his army are forced to retreat to Shrewsbury (p. 35, ll. 31–3):

> King John was a man without a conscience, wicked, quarrelsome, hated by all good people and lecherous. If he ever heard of any beautiful maiden or lady, wife of an earl or a baron or anyone else, he wanted to have his way with her, either by tricking her with promises or gifts or by taking her by force. For this he was most hated, and this is why so many great English lords renounced their homage (pp. 35, 34–8 – 36, ll. 1–3).

Here the author combines what he had said earlier about John's personality (*'maveys e contrarious e envyous'*, p. 22, ll. 29–30) with the lecherous behaviour displayed in his treatment of Matilda de Caus. John's treatment of Fouke's just claim to Whittington is an example of his lack of conscience, and his hounding of a beautiful widow, both before and after her marriage to Fouke, is an illustration of both wickedness and lust.[31] It is interesting to note that the author presents John's lust as the prime reason he was hated; his lust is therefore seen as more important than the disinheriting of magnates.[32] We also note that Fouke's renunciation of his homage is associated with that of 'many great lords'. Writing thirty to forty years after John's death, the author of the verse romance would have known of the loss of Normandy in 1204, an event which occurred after Fouke's outlawry and which damaged John's reputation irredeemably in the eyes of his contemporaries, and also of the loss of baronial support which led to Magna Carta in 1215.[33] The author's general statement concerning John's character serves both as an overall judgement on him, i.e. on his suitability as monarch, and as a justification of Fouke's actions. John was a bad king and other magnates thought the same, so Fouke's treasonable behaviour was fully warranted.

A humorous note is introduced into the narrative when John de Rampaigne disguises himself as a *jongleur* and makes his way to Shrewsbury, where the king is staying. He kneels before the king and tells him that he is a minstrel from Ethiopia. The king asks him what people were saying about him in foreign realms (p. 37, l. 35). The reply was: '*Vous estez le plus renomee roy de tote la cristieneté, e pur grant vostre renoun vous su je venu vere*' (p. 37, ll. 36–7). This pleases John, but the author then comments wryly that John de Rampaigne adds that he was famous more for his wickedness (*mavesté*) than for his goodness, but the king did not hear him (pp. 37, ll. 38–9 – 38, I.1). This reference to John's *mavesté* recalls the earlier uses of the adjective *mavois* (pp. 22, l. 29; 22, l. 39; 35, l. 34). John de Rampaigne's remark makes the king an ambivalent figure; he is certainly famous (*renomee*, p. 37, l. 38), but not in the way he himself interpreted the word. Like his inability to catch Fouke, the king's inability to catch John de Rampaigne's remark turns him once more into a figure of fun.

By this stage, the author's presentation of John is in danger of becoming repetitive. When Fouke's cousin, Sir Audulf de Bracy, captured in the fight between Fouke and Morys de Powys, succeeds in escaping thanks to John de Rampaigne, the king is predictably '*mout corocee*' (p. 38, l. 23), and this anger swiftly leads to a further, predictable demonstration of vindictiveness. He turns his attention to Lady Matilda de Caus, who is now married to Fouke but still desired by the king, who '*la voleit fere ravyr*'. John inflicts great losses ('*molt grant damage*') on the lady and also on the archbishop who had recommended the marriage (p. 38, ll. 32–5). Thus John shows that, when thwarted, he not only fails to respect married women, but also ignores his duty to protect the Church and its property.[34] Again, in attacking a friend and powerful ally, John was oblivious to both his own interests and those of his kingdom.

The narrative moves forward when Fouke, fearing capture, takes refuge with King Philip Augustus in France. When John learns of this, in a repeat performance of the letter he wrote to

Llywelyn, he writes to Philip telling him that he is harbouring Fouke Fitz Waryn, his *'enymy mortel'* (p. 41, ll. 14–17). Philip's treatment of Fouke provides a neat contrast to that of his counterpart in England. On seeing Fouke for the first time at a joust, he spots that he will be a redoubtable opponent for the arrogant French knight Sir Druz de Montbener: *'Avyseez vous bien'*, says the king to Druz, *'quar cely chevaler engleys est molt pruz e vaylant, e ce piert bien'* ('Take care, for it is clear that this English knight is very brave and valiant') (p. 40, ll. 19–20). In the ensuing fight Fouke throws Sir Druz flat on the ground, then unhorses a second opponent; at this point the king calls a halt to the proceedings and asks Fouke to remain at court as long as he wishes. Fouke is welcomed at court and esteemed by all those he meets. In France his fine characteristics, boldness, chivalry, prowess and excellence, are fully recognized and lauded; he is loved and honoured by both the king and the queen. Fouke has used a false name, 'Amys del Bois', but Philip rightly suspects that he is the knight referred to in John's letter. Knowing that Fouke is 'valiant', Philip questions him about his identity. But, on learning the truth, not only does Philip refuse to hand Fouke over to John, he actually offers him the opportunity to remain in France, with a gift of *'plus riches terres'* than he had ever had in England (p. 41, ll. 27–9). The vindictive John has driven Fouke into the arms of his enemy, the King of France, who, unlike John, shows that he knows how to treat a distinguished knight.[35]

It is clear that the author devotes a large amount of space to John's behaviour because the existence of an effective opponent for the outlaw is as important as that of the outlaw himself. The opponent needs to be obsessed with capturing the outlaw, to be vulnerable because of personal weaknesses, to have only lukewarm support from his own men, to fall into every trap and to turn himself into a figure of fun. Within the personage of King John the author encapsulates everything which good citizens did not want in their king. He shows him constantly committing acts which isolate himself from his subjects. This is conveyed with great clarity in the statements that Fouke and his men had no wish to harm anyone other than King John and those who were openly their enemies (pp. 30, ll. 29–31; 43, ll. 6–7). Fouke was no robber, but taking money from the king himself gave him particular pleasure: '*Sovent prist son aver e quant qu'il poeit del suen*' (p. 43, ll. 7–8). John's obsessive desire to capture Fouke is paralleled by the reader's enjoyment of Fouke's equally obsessive desire to defeat him.

After Fouke has undergone several adventures abroad, he returns to England with the intention of capturing King John. This he succeeds in doing, disguised as a charcoal-burner. In this episode the tables are turned on John in a remarkable fashion; the pursuer becomes the one who ends up being captured. His capture reveals John's vulnerability to cunning, his lack of heroism ('*Le roy trembla de pour*', p. 49, l. 38) and his willingness to perjure himself to save his own skin.[36] For John swears that he will grant Fouke peace for the rest of his life, but later refuses to keep his word. Knowing that John would have put him to death, Fouke's initial reaction on having him in his power is to punish him similarly, a course of action which would reflect the injustice and great losses sustained not only by himself but also by a large number of *prodhome*: '*Fouke jura qu'il morreit pur le grant damage e la desheritesoun qu'il avoit fet a ly e a meint prodhome d'Engleterre*' ('Fouke swore that he would die because of the way he had damaged and disinherited him and many worthy men in England') (pp. 49, l. 39 – 50, ll. 1–2). Again the author stresses that the king's injustices extended beyond those relating to Fouke. Begging for mercy, the king agrees to offer such surety as Fouke himself would devise, and Fouke grants the king all he asked for. But once freed, John returns to his palace, where he tells the tale and claims that he had sworn his oath under duress and would therefore not keep it; he orders all his men to attempt to capture the criminals (*felons*) concerned.

In the next episode, the king is deceived yet again. Sir James of Normandy alleges a certain reluctance to capture Fouke on the part of all the nobles including the king, the reason being that they are all cousins of Fouke; in Sir James's view this laxity amounts to treachery ('*pur ce sunt treitours al roy*', p. 50, ll. 17–18). Attempting to put things right himself, Sir James attacks Fouke but merely ends up being captured and despatched to the king in Fouke's armour; convinced that he has captured Fouke, John orders him to be hanged (p. 51, ll. 19-20). On discovering the truth, the king is very distressed ('*molt dolent*', p. 51, l. 27) and swears that he will never remove his hauberk until he has captured Fouke and his companions (p. 51, ll. 27-9). Once more, the king's frustration leads him to make immoderate claims and he sets himself up for another failure. In the succeeding fight between the king's men and the outlaws, the former are forced to take flight. The Earl of Chester's men in particular suffer severe losses at the hands of Fouke and his men. Although the latter are pursued by the king as they ride away, the king does not of course manage to catch them: '*Le roy e sa meyné les pursiwyrent, mes prendre ne les purreynt*' (p. 52, ll. 28-9).

We have already seen how Fouke's outlawry caused a rift to develop between John and both the Prince of Wales and the Archbishop of Canterbury. This happens again when Fouke's brother William is injured in the battle against the king's men. The Earl of Chester does not want to hand him over to John, so he sends him to be cared for in an abbey. On discovering this, John has William brought to him and thrown into a dungeon; he is angry with the earl for concealing him. Again the king had become so obsessed with catching Fouke that he has allowed it to affect his relationship with his most powerful baron (pp. 52, ll. 34-9 - 53, ll. 1-5).[37] In due course Fouke and his men hatch a plan to rescue William. In order to prepare the ground for his rescue, John de Rampaigne goes to the king disguised as a merchant. Predictably, the king is taken in by John de Rampaigne's disguise and also by his gift of a handsome white palfrey; he gives him permission to bring his men ashore (p. 56, ll. 24-5). William is duly rescued, and when the king discovers that he has been tricked by the merchant he considers himself to be ill-treated ('*mal bayly*', p. 57, l. 18); Fouke has thus reduced John yet again to self-pity. John interprets what has happened as misfortune rather than mismanagement.

The outlaws escape to Brittany by boat, but the next time they return to England they succeed once more in capturing King John. The king is out hunting in the New Forest and he and his men are captured and taken to Fouke's boat. The king is very frightened ('*molt esbays*', p. 57, l. 26), but after much discussion he puts aside his anger and agrees to restore Fouke's inheritance to him, promising that he will proclaim peace for him and his men throughout England. This time his intentions are confirmed by hostages and honoured. The king makes his way to Westminster and there tells the assembled earls, barons and clergy that he is granting peace to Fouke and his men. Fouke is received and he and his followers are granted their entire inheritance. John even goes as far as to order them to remain at court in Westminster, which they do for a month (p. 58, ll. 5–7).[38]

As the narrative draws to a close, we discover that early in the text there had been a veiled reference to King John, before he was mentioned by name. The Devil, driven out of Geomagog's body by Payn Peverel, predicts that 'the leopard will chase the wolf and threaten it with its tail . . . [The wolf] will cross the sea and circle this entire island. Finally he will overcome the leopard with his cunning and his skill' (p. 6, ll. 27–8, 33–4). Merlin prophesied that a wolf will come out of Blanche Lande and chase the leopard from it. The wolf, which comes from the Blanche Lande, is, we are now told, Fouke, and the leopard is King John.

> *Par le leopart puet estre conuz*
> *Le roy Johan e bien entenduz,*
> *Quar il porta en sun escu*
> *Les leopartz de or batu.* (p. 61, ll. 4–7)[39]

By the leopard is represented and symbolized King John, because he bore on his shield leopards of beaten gold.

The leopard is an appropriate symbol for John. Beryl Rowland describes this animal 'as the destroyer and as a thoroughly evil beast'.[40] The ambivalent nature of the wolf also seems appropriate for Fouke: it is 'a murderous beast of prey', but 'its fierceness and swift movement also caused it to be identified with the sun, the life-giver, and with life' (Rowland, p. 161). The wolf, adds Rowland, 'was also used as a symbol to denounce any person who misused his power, whether religious or secular' (p. 163). The term 'wolfshead' for an outlaw provides a further reason for its aptness.

The author of the prose version clearly attached great importance to the Devil's prophecy and its elucidation, as these are conveyed in the two verse passages retained from the original. The two passages contain both the first and last references to King John and the first and last references to the conflict between John and Fouke. Also contained within the second verse section (pp. 60, ll. 1–39 – 61, ll. 1–7) is the first allusion to the king who outstrips all others, King Arthur. The latter, we are told, had lost his chivalry and power, but recovered them in the chapel of St Augustine when Yvain's son Cahuz had a dream and shouted out so loudly that he awoke King Arthur; this, we are told, took place in Blanche Lande. Fouke is clearly being presented as a new Arthur-style figure, a true king in comparison with the substandard King John. In the course of the narrative Fouke overcomes a variety of adversaries including Morys de Powys who denied him his '*dreit heritage*', chess-playing villains who dress '*come nul roy*' (p. 43, l. 32) and are thus reflections of John himself, and a dragon which represents John's lust and depredations.[41] Just as Arthur regains his lost chivalry and power, Fouke's victory over King John allows him to regains his property and his rightful place in society and become thereafter a force for good.[42]

As the editors of the ANTS edition point out, monastic chroniclers painted a 'displeasing picture' of John in the aftermath of Magna Carta and during the minority of John's son, Henry III (p. xxix). As the romance author considered it to be the main reason why John was hated, the accusation of lust is of particular interest. Matthew Paris, in a damning passage, states that 'John was a tyrant not a king . . . he was envious of many of his barons and kinsfolk, and seduced their more attractive daughters and sisters'.[43] The Waverley chronicler also criticizes John on a number of grounds, including lust: 'He [John] disinherited some without judgment of their peers, and he condemned others to a dire death; he violated their wives and daughters – his only law was his despotic will.'[44] The chroniclers' comments are supported by the *Histoire des ducs de Normandie et des rois d'Angleterre*, one of the few vernacular texts to contain comments on John: '*Mol[t] mal homme ot el roi Jehan: crueus estoit sor toz homes; de bieles femes estoit trop couvoiteus; mainte honte en fist as haus homes de la tierre: par coi il fu moult haïs*' ('King John was a very evil man; he was crueller than any man; he was very covetous of beautiful women; he caused much shame to the noblemen in the land: as a result of this, he was greatly hated').[45] Another vernacular author to mention John's behaviour towards women is the Minstrel of Reims, who writes of the *'mauvais roi Jehan d'Engleterre, qui honnissoit ses barons, et gisoit avec leur fammes et avec leur filles à force, et leur toloit leur terres, et faisoit tant que Dieus et touz li mondes le devoit haïr'* ('evil King John of England, who humiliated his lords and lay with their wives and daughters by force, took their lands, and acted so excessively that God and all the people must hate him').[46] It is not certain, however, whether these views of John's behaviour towards women correspond to reality: 'The peculiar rub of John's lustfulness . . . seems to have been that it went out after the wives and daughters of his barons. So, at least, barely veiled accusations suggest, but none of them is substantiated' (Warren, p. 189). John was, of course, not the only king against whom such an accusation could be levelled; he merely seems to have lacked the compensating virtues of his more charismatic counterparts: 'The only characteristics that John shared with his father and brother were licentiousness and intelligence' (Painter, p. 19).[47]

The overall picture of John found in the Latin and vernacular chronicles differs little from that found in *Fouke le Fitz Waryn*.[48] *Fouke*, the *Histoire* and the *Récits d'un menéstrel de Reims* state that John was hated: *'hay de tote bone gent'* (*Fouke*, p. 35, l. 35); *'moult haïs'* (*Histoire*, p. 105); *'faisoit tant que Dieus et touz li mondes le devoit haïr'* (*Récits*, para. 292). The *Histoire* associates John's lust with wickedness, cruelty and shameful treatment of the nobility; the author adds that he was a man of generally bad character: *'Trop estoit plains de males teces'* (p. 105).[49] Matthew Paris (p. 563) and the *Histoire* (p. 105) both mention John's envious character. Turner comments on John's 'suspicion and dislike, even contempt for his barons' (p. 260). But although the barons experienced 'fearful uncertainty for their families and lands in the face of his [John's] arbitrary oppressions', Warren emphasizes that John's principal motive was his 'nagging fear of traitors and rebels' (p. 257). On the question of John's treatment of his barons, Painter concludes that 'it is extremely difficult to form a coherent picture of his [John's] relations with the English baronage as a whole' (p. 47).[50] Warren's overall judgement of John is that 'he had the mental abilities of a great king, but the inclinations of a petty tyrant' (p. 259). For Painter John 'lacked the attributes most admired in a feudal monarch' (p. 19).[51]

To gain maximum dramatic effect for his account of Fouke's outlawry, the author of *Fouke le Fitz Waryn* has exploited to the full John's many deficiencies; indeed, John was perfect for the role as an outlaw's adversary. The author was doubly fortunate in that John replaced Richard I, who was widely regarded as the model king: 'If we wish to know how a king was to behave if he was to satisfy contemporary ideals of kingship then Richard the Lionheart is our man' (Gillingham, p. 95).[52] The effectiveness of the entire narrative depends to a great extent on the actions of King John and the contrast they offer to those of his predecessors. His unjust decision to accept Morys's offer for Whittington triggers the outlawry, and his obsession with catching and punishing Fouke gives rise to the episodic structure of the forest section. Presenting him from the start as a wicked, quarrelsome and envious man, the author constantly illustrates John's flaws, including the one he regards as the worst of all: his lust. Within the range of kings offered to us, John contrasts badly with all of them with the exception of the giant Geomagog, whose body is said to have been taken over by a spirit of the Devil (*'un espirit del deble'*, p. 4, l. 36).[53] But in the closing stages of the narrative, once Fouke's outlawry has been pardoned, John's *mavesté* is forgotten and replaced by a celebration of Fouke's *'grant renoun de prowesse e de bounté'* (p. 59, l. 18) and commitment to a standard of courtliness and hospitality (*'Fouke fust bon viaundour e large'*, p. 59, l. 36) of which King Arthur himself would have been proud.

NOTES

1   See Jacques Le Goff, 'Le Roi dans l'Occident médiéval', in *Kings and Kingship in Medieval Europe*, Anne J. Duggan (ed.) (London: King's College London Centre for Late Antique and Medieval Studies, 1993), pp. 1–40. See also J. Dickinson, 'The Mediaeval Concept of Kingship and some of its Limitations as Developed in the *Policraticus* of John of Salisbury', *Speculum*, 1 (1926), 308–37. A full discussion of the person, function and responsibilities of the king would involve issues such as the meaning of the terms *rex*, *roi*, *king*, etc., the relationship

between kingship and divinity (*rex christianus, vicarius dei*) and that between kingship and nobility (*rex nobilis*). For the coronation oaths and charters of English kings see Percy E. Schramm, *A History of the English Coronation*, L. G. Wickham Legg (trans.) (Oxford: Clarendon Press, 1937), esp. pp. 186–96.

2   Many kings paid only lip service to their role as protector of the Church, an exception being Richard I, who considered that he had a responsibility not only to the Christian community in his own realm but also to the Holy Land (see John Gillingham, 'The Art of Kingship: Richard I, 1189–99', *History Today*, April 1985, 17–23, reprinted in Gillingham, *Richard Coeur de Lion: Kingship, Chivalry and War in the Twelfth Century* (London: Hambledon, 1994), pp. 95–103 (p. 96).

3   See Edward Peters, *The Shadow King: rex inutilis in Medieval Law and Literature 751–1327* (New Haven and London: Yale University Press, 1970). The expression *rex inutilis* covered various forms of royal inadequacy including the loss of power or the inability to wield power because of mental incapacity or political misjudgement (p. 2). J. C. Holt states that: 'A king was more likely to suffer disaster through kindness than through cruelty' (*King John* (London: Historical Association, 1963), p. 26).

4   From among the many studies of kingship in literary texts see for example Jane E. Burns, 'Portraits of Kingship in the *Pèlerinage de Charlemagne*', *Olifant*, 10 (1982–5), 161–81, Pierre Jonin, 'Le Roi dans les *Lais* de Marie de France: l'homme sous le personnage', in *Essays in Early French Literature Presented to Barbara M. Craig* (York, SC: French Literature Publications, 1982), pp. 25–41, and Wolfgang Van Emden, 'Kingship in the Old French Epic of Revolt', in Duggan, *Kings and Kingship*, pp. 305–50.

5   *Fouke le Fitz Waryn*, E. J. Hathaway, P. T. Ricketts, C. A. Robson and A. D. Wiltshire (eds), Anglo-Norman Text Society (Oxford: Blackwell, 1975). References are to page and line numbers in this edition. The kings are Harold, William the Conqueror, William Rufus, Henry I, Henry II, Richard I, John and Philip Augustus. There is also a brief allusion to the coronation of Henry II's son, Henry the Younger, who was crowned in 1170 and died in 1183: 'Henri fust coronee vivant son pere, mes il mourust avant le piere' (p. 22, ll. 27–8). In addition, several other kings are mentioned: Geomagog (p. 4, l. 27ff.), Bran Fitz Donwal (p. 5, l. 1), Aunflor (King of Orkanye, p. 44, l. 19), the King of Yberye (p. 46, l. 13), Messobryn (King of Barbarie, p. 53, l. 20ff.) and Arthur (p. 60, l. 12ff.). When Messobryn is introduced, he is said to have four kings with him (p. 55, l. 21).

6   On the question of the date of the prose version see Carter Revard, 'Scribe and Provenance', in *Studies in the Harley Manuscript: The Scribes, Contents and Social Contexts of British Library MS Harley 2253*, Susanna Fein (ed.) (Kalamazoo: Western Michigan University Press, 2000), pp. 21–109 (esp. pp. 26–9, 69–72).

7   Although the text as we have it is a fourteenth-century prose reworking, I am assuming that what we read concerning King John and his struggle with Fouke III can be attributed to the original author.
8   The references to Henry's elder brother, William Rufus, are very brief (pp. 4, l. 2; 7, l. 30).
9   When Richard came to the throne in 1189, Fouke II was still alive (he died in 1198). Fouke III would have been around 20 years of age at the time. Surprisingly, there is no allusion to the decision of Richard's *curia regis* in 1195 to support Fouke II's claim to Whittington. In that year Fouke II fined forty marks 'for having the castle of Whittington as it was adjudged to him in the king's court' (Pipe Roll 7 *Richard I*, p. 246). Richard set off for the Holy Land in 1199, so there was just time for Richard to invest Fouke II with his father's lands in person, but there is no evidence that he did so or that Fouke III was made warden of the entire March.
10 See the chapter entitled 'The Succession' in Sydney Painter, *The Reign of King John* (Baltimore: Johns Hopkins Press, 1949), pp. 1–16.
11 The term *envie* derives from Latin *invidia*, which was often regarded in the Middle Ages as the worst of all the vices; it embraced a variety of emotions including ill-will, resentment and hatred.
12 The verb *contecker* is defined by the *Anglo-Norman Dictionary* as 'to quarrel, brawl, contend, dispute'; a *contecour* is a 'brawler, ruffian'.
13 On the question of kings with a cry-baby image, see Albrecht Classen, 'The Cry-baby Kings in Courtly Romances: what is Wrong with Medieval Kingship?', *Studi Medievali*, 3rd series, 39 (1998), 833–63.
14 Robert Bartlett, who cites this game as an example, states that such disputes 'could be fatal' (*England under the Norman and Angevin Kings 1075–1225* (Oxford: Oxford University Press, 2000), p. 237). On the game of chess as an image of rivalry or struggle see Maria A. Rebbert, 'The Celtic Origins of the Chess Symbolism in *Milun* and *Eliduc*', in *In Quest of Marie de France: A Twelfth-Century Poet*, Chantal A. Maréchal (ed.) (Lewison, Queenston and Lampeter: Edwin Mellon, 1992), pp. 148–60; chess can act as a commentary on the action and as 'a figure of the action in which it has little or no explicit role' (p. 158). For chess as a prelude to fighting, with the chessboard as weapon, and the themes of a game of chess which causes the loser to seek compensation in other ways, see Pierre Jonin, 'La Partie d'échecs dans l'épopée médiévale', in *Mélanges de langue et de littérature du Moyen Age et de la Renaissance offerts à Jean Frappier*, 2 vols (Geneva: Droz, 1970), II, pp. 483–97 (pp. 488 ff.).
15 W. L. Warren, *King John* (London: Eyre and Spottiswood, 1961), pp. 26–7. There is no evidence in the text for Warren's statement that Fouke 'frequently quarrelled' with John (p. 26).
16 Janet Meisel, *Barons of the Welsh Frontier: The Corbet, Pantulf, and Fitz Warin Families, 1066–1272* (Lincoln, Nebraska and London: University of Nebraska Press, 1980), p. 135. Meisel adds that: 'Fulk and John may not have come to blows over a chess game, but that there was some sort of personal animosity between them that stemmed from

17   their childhood is entirely consistent with John's strange behavior regarding Whittington' (p. 135).

17   Richard Eales, 'The Game of Chess: An Aspect of Medieval Knightly Culture', in *The Ideals and Practice of Medieval Knighthood: Papers from the First and Second Strawberry Hill Conferences*, C. Harper-Bill and R. Harvey (eds) (Woodbridge: Boydell and Brewer, 1986), pp. 12–34 (p. 30).

18   See Alan Lloyd, *King John* (Newton Abbot: David Charles, 1973), pp. 6, 14. John was the only one of Henry's four sons to remain at home after the rebellion (p. 14).

19   For the verb *venger* see also pp. 34, l. 33; 34, l. 35; 39, l. 15.

20   See Roger Pensom, 'Inside and Outside: Fact and Fiction in *Fouke le Fitz Waryn*', *Medium Aevum*, 63 (1994), 53–60 (p. 55). Fouke will later reject an offer of lands from Philip Augustus on the grounds that it is unworthy to accept another's lands if one cannot rightfully hold one's own *'dreit heritage'* (p. 41, ll. 29–31).

21   Henry II had earlier offered Joce de Dynan *'ley e resoun'* (p. 21, l. 23). This reference to common law would seem to indicate that John was acting arbitrarily when he should have referred the matter to one of the common law courts established by Henry II. With respect to the real King John's handling of justice Bryce Lyon writes: 'Under him justice was swift and frequent but it suffered from his arbitrary and unscrupulous methods. He respected neither custom nor procedure and seemed to settle each plea upon the basis of his own whim' (*A Constitutional and Legal History of Medieval England* (New York: Harper, 1960), p. 281). For the administration of the *curia regis* under John see Ralph V. Turner, *The King and his Courts: The Role of John and Henry III in the Administration of Justice, 1199–1240* (Ithaca: Cornell University Press, 1968). Turner comments that: '[John] sometimes managed to keep within the letter of the law while violating its spirit' (p. 274).

22   John was crowned king by Hubert Walter, Archbishop of Canterbury, on 27 May 1199, and Whittington was granted to Morys de Powys in April 1200. After his coronation John left for France on 20 June and spent much of his time in Normandy until the beginning of October 1200 when he returned to England. In that month he embarked on a tour of the Midlands; he left Westminster for Wiltshire and from there set out for Gloucester and the Welsh March, going as far as Bridgnorth in Shropshire (Warren, p. 70). On 1 August 1200 Morys's sons took possession of Whittington. It therefore seems unlikely that events happened precisely as described in the romance.

23   Roger of Hoveden, *Chronica*, W. Stubbs (ed.), 4 vols, Rolls Series 51 (London: Longmans, 1868–71), IV, p. 163. See also Clarence Ellis, *Hubert de Burgh: A Study in Constancy* (London: Phoenix House, 1952), p. 13, and Painter, pp. 48–9. Painter states that Fouke 'was the chief source of trouble in the Marches in early 1201' (p. 50). But the date of June 1201 is around eight months after the time the rupture is thought to have occurred.

24   One thinks of the eternal quest of King Mark to catch Tristan, and of

that of Renaud de Boulogne in the *Romans de Witasse le Moine*, who constantly fails to capture Eustace the Monk.

25 *Memoranda Roll, 1 John*, for 9 April 1201, indicates that by that date all Fouke's lands in Shropshire had reverted to the crown ('*Fulconis filii Warini cum terra ipsius que sunt in manu nostra*', p. 93).

26 When Richard died, Hubert Walter and William Marshal went to England to plead John's case (Warren, p. 50). Hubert later became John's chancellor and was an 'indispensable adviser' to the young king (ibid., p. 134). Gillingham describes Hubert Walter as 'a man who ranks as the supreme embodiment of the civil service prelate' (p. 96).

27 The text states in the opening lines that an earlier Prince of Wales was the man William the Conqueror feared most (p. 3, ll. 15–16).

28 At the time of Fouke's outlawry, John's statement is correct; only a year or two later he would lose Normandy and other continental possessions.

29 In reality, Llywelyn's wife, Joan, was the natural daughter of King John, not his sister. In addition, Joan, whose mother was Clementina, was not married to Llywelyn at the time of Fouke's outlawry; she was betrothed to him in 1204 and the marriage took place in 1206 or 1207. But it is true, as the text states (p. 22, l. 10), that Joan received the lordship of Ellesmere as her dower. See C. Given-Wilson and A. Curteis, *The Royal Bastards of Medieval England* (London: Routledge and Kegan Paul, 1984), pp. 128–30.

30 On Joan's role within the text, and that of other female characters, see my 'Women in the *Fouke le Fitz Waryn*', in '*Por le soie amisté*': *Essays in Honor of Norris J. Lacy*, K. Busby and C. Jones (eds) (Amsterdam: Rodopi, 2000), pp. 75–93.

31 We are told that John used promises or gifts to seduce women; it was presumably when these failed that he used force (p. 35, ll. 37–8). We can thus conclude that, when thwarted by man or woman, he had no compunction in using whatever means were at his disposal to get his way.

32 As Fouke's marriage to Matilda le Vavasor (not Matilda de Caus as stated in the text) did not take place until 1207, the circumstances described in the romance cannot correspond to reality.

33 Fouke became an outlaw only a few months after John assumed the throne, so his poor reputation was not fully formed by that time (see below, note 48). Moreover, John spent very little time in England until the loss of Normandy.

34 Although pregnant, Matilda is forced to take refuge in the church in Canterbury, where she gives birth to a daughter who is baptized by the archbishop (p. 38, ll. 35–7). Even though Fouke takes Matilda to Alberbury, she is still not safe from the king, who has her spied upon. Pregnant, she travels to Shrewsbury and is spied on there too. She gives birth to a daughter in Shrewsbury Abbey. Again she is forced to flee and gives birth to a son, two months prematurely, on a mountain in Wales. Matilda's plight adds to the drama of the text, but by portraying the relentless nature of John's hounding of Matilda, the author was

clearly intent on painting John as a man who abused his power and would stop at nothing to get what he wanted. The text makes it clear that John wanted not only to capture Matilda but also to dishonour her (*honyr*, p. 39, l. 16).

35 Another king who treats Fouke well is the King of Barbary, Messobryn, who gives orders that he should be '*bien servy*', allows his sister to spend time with him and finally loads up the boat in which he and his brother depart with all the '*or, argent, chivals, armes e totes richesses que il voderount aver ou coveyter*' (p. 56, ll. 6–7). Because he treats Fouke well, Messobryn is able to harness Fouke's courage and skill to his own benefit, and Fouke in his turn puts an end to Messobryn's hostile behaviour towards Ydoyne de Cartage, which is reminiscent of John's treatment of Matilda de Caus, and helps to unite two communities and even to effect Messobryn's conversion to Christianity. In this case chivalry comes to the aid of monarchy and society, as it had done so earlier when Fouke restored King Aunflor's daughter to him and was received '*a grant honour*' and given '*riche douns*' (p. 45, ll. 14–15).

36 Fouke ensnares John with the story of an amazing stag, as Robin Hood does later with the Sheriff in the *Gest*.

37 At the time of the death of Richard I the most powerful baron in England was John himself; after him came Earl Ranulf of Chester (Painter, pp. 19–20).

38 John pardoned Fouke in November 1203. The romance states that the pardon was issued in Westminster, but in fact Fouke and his men travelled to Normandy to meet with the king. The pardon opens with the words: 'The king, etc., to his justiciars, viscounts, etc. You are informed that we offer our grace and favour to Fouke Fitz Waryn . . .' (see my *Two Medieval Outlaws: Eustace the Monk and Fouke Fitz Waryn* (Cambridge: D. S. Brewer, 1997), pp. 102–3).

39 When John came to the throne, his arms were two lions passant, but after his coronation he adopted the arms of his brother Richard: three lions passant guardant. The lions have often been referred to as leopards, because in the thirteenth century it was thought that a lion drawn with the head in profile and with its head full face was a leopard. See Adrian Ailes, *The Origins of the Royal Arms of England: Their Development to 1199* (Reading: University of Reading Graduate Centre for Medieval Studies, 1982), pp. 16–17, 73, 75.

40 *Animals with Human Faces: A Guide to Animal Symbolism* (Knoxville: University of Tennessee Press, 1973), p. 116. The leopard's spots are said to be 'indicative of its evil nature' (p. 117). For Rabanus Maurus the leopard was the Antichrist (p. 116).

41 Pensom considers the dragon-slaying episode as a restatement in mythic terms of King John's 'identity as a corrupter and destroyer of ordered succession and lineage' (p. 56).

42 The reference to King Arthur also seems to be the culmination of a series of attempts on the part of the author to inscribe his work within the authoritative tradition of historiography, beginning with the story of Geomagog, which recalls the account of Gogmagog in Geoffrey of

Monmouth's *Historia regum Britanniae*. See Timothy Jones, 'Geoffrey of Monmouth, *Fouke le Fitz Waryn*, and National Mythology', *Studies in Philology*, 91 (1994), 233–49, esp. p. 235.

43 *Chronica Majora*, H. R. Luard (ed.), 7 vols, Rolls Series 57 (London, 1872–84), II, pp. 562–633. Roger of Wendover also tells us, in Warren's words (p. 11), how John 'made free with the wives and daughters of his barons'.

44 *Annales monastici*, H. R. Luard (ed.), 5 vols, Rolls Series 36 (London, 1864–9), II, p. 282.

45 Francisque Michel (ed.) (Paris: J. Renouard, 1840, repr. London and New York, 1965), p. 105. The author adds that: '*Ses barons melloit ensemble quanques il pooit; moult estoit liés quant il veoit haine entre els. Toz les preudomes haoit par envie; moult li desplaisoit quant il veoit nullui bien faire*' (p. 105).

46 *Récits d'un ménestrel de Reims au treizième siècle*, Natalis de Wailly (ed.) (Paris: Sheed and Ward, 1876), para. 292. After *leur filles* MS F adds '*quant elles estoient jouenes et belles*' (for the manuscript tradition see the Introduction, pp. xvii-xviii).

47 Comparing John to his brother Richard, Painter comments (p. 19) that John lacked both his brother's prowess ('Richard was without doubt the ablest captain of his day') and his charming manner ('Richard was frank and open in manner and when well disposed, hearty, friendly, and jovial').

48 The author, writing around 1260, had the advantage of knowing what happened between the end of Fouke's outlawry and John's death. Holt informs us that during the early years of John's reign the chroniclers dealt with him 'reasonably'; it was from his middle years and especially after his death that they became hostile (Holt, p. 27).

49 No specific examples of cruelty or torture are mentioned in *Fouke*, but Roger of Wendover recounts John's treatment of the clergy. John is said to have imprisoned Geoffrey, archdeacon of Norwich, in chains, kept him in a cope of lead and deprived him of food, so that he died an agonizing death (Warren, p. 12). Ralph Turner comments that 'we cannot doubt his capacity for cruelty' (*King John*, London and New York: Longman, 1994, p. 13).

50 It is in his chapter 'The King and the Magnates' (pp. 17–56) that Painter includes several pages on one of the nobles who rebelled against John: Fouke Fitz Waryn III (pp. 48–52). Holt states that 'John's failure to control and lead the aristocracy was the crucial failure' (p. 27). The author of *Fouke* provides an interesting depiction of the relationship between John and his most powerful baron, Ranulf of Chester. In the narrative Ranulf remains loyal to John, as he did in reality, but he was not hostile towards Fouke; early in his reign John suspected Ranulf of what Warren calls 'treasonable designs' (p. 109, see also see Painter, pp. 25–9, 54).

51 We should note that the author of the *Histoire des ducs de Normandie* felt able to praise John's generosity: '*De grant despens estoit: moult donoit à mangier et larghement et volentiers; jà sa porte ne li huis de sa*

sale ne furent gardé au mangier: tout chil mangeoient à sa court qui mangier i voloient. As .iii. nataus donnoit volentiers grant plenté de reubes as chevaliers: de chou fu-il bien entechiés' (p. 105). 'Contrary to myth', says Lloyd, 'John had a "more endearing character" than his predecessors' (p. 390). Turner expresses the view that John's moral flaws, although real, were exaggerated by the chroniclers (*King John*, p. 261); he emphasizes John's tireless activity in hearing pleas and goes as far as to describe John as 'an administrative genius' (p. 263), adding that in warfare 'he was a capable enough strategist and skilled in siegecraft' (p. 258).

52 For a comparison between Henry II and Richard I, see Gillingham's chapter entitled 'Conquering Kings: Some Twelfth-Century Reflections on Henry II and Richard I' (pp. 105–18). Ironically, modern scholars have turned against Richard: 'There can have been few kings who have been so lavishly praised by contemporary writers and so fiercely criticised by modern ones' (Gillingham, p. 95).

53 The Plantagenets were, of course, known as the Devil's brood. See Lloyd, pp. 3–18, and the titles of books such as Alfred L. Duggan's *Devil's Brood: The Angevin Family* (London: Faber and Faber, 1957) and Richard Barber's *The Devil's Crown: Henry II, Richard I, John* (London: BBC, 1978).

Rabbie Hood: The Development of the English Outlaw Myth in Scotland

STEPHEN KNIGHT

Locating a hero

National heroes can have strange origins. If King Arthur, that doyen of English monarchs, had any historical reality it was as a Briton, speaking Welsh, fighting against the English. And quite possibly coming originally from Scotland and certainly coming late to the English language and his canonization as the strangely hybrid emblem of English kinghood.

Of course, cultural heroics can do more than reverse apparent conflicts as the Arthur story does. They can be quite exotic in origin: the late twentieth century saw the bizarre phenomenon of the Ninja Turtles, where Western child culture crossed both species and the globe to find comfort and delight in heroes displaced in both their eastern and chelonian kind.

The cultural mix I want to look at here stands somewhere between Arthur and the turtles, and I want to apply a mix of methodologies, in part sociopolitical and in part post-colonial to explore the development of the English hero Robin Hood in a Scottish context, as a figure who was in Scotland hybridized in various ways and then re-exported in a different and remarkably successful form.

Any survey of the influences and developments of the Robin Hood tradition over time must soon enough notice the recurrent element of Scottish involvement with the tradition – and yet there has been almost no analysis of this involvement, presumably because of the force of the identification of the hero as English. The Scottish interest has had two major periods, the fifteenth and sixteenth centuries and the time of Walter Scott – and the two are not unconnected. In both periods Scotland developed an interest in and a version of the English outlaw, and I will argue that it was in fact the Scottish version which lay behind major changes in the tradition of the allegedly English hero, changes which of themselves have helped make it still so popular today.

There is no birthright for continued fame for mythic heroes: it's just that some of them undergo crucial changes that reinvent them, while others die away. Whatever happened to Guy of Warwick and Bevis of Hampton? Those forgotten heroes remained in fully medieval English form, and only had archaic appeal in the early modern period, unchanged for a new era. Robin Hood changed a lot however, and so was able to present changing ideas of the meaning of resistance to authority, and still does. There is a Caledonian flavour to some of the most important of these changes, both the late medieval to renaissance one and the one led by Walter Scott. In this paper I will concentrate on the early period, as more work needs to be done on the nature and origin of Scott's reinvigoration of the Robin Hood tradition, but I will at least mention finally a few features of that second stage of 'Rabbie Hood'.

It has long been known that late medieval Scottish literary references to the English outlaw exist and that Robin Hood activities took place in Scottish towns in the late Middle Ages; the role of Scots chroniclers and writers in promulgating the English outlaw myth has been referred to by scholars. But these phenomena have not been looked at as a body, and not considered in terms of their wider implications, as I hope to do here. Lewis Spence's brief essay, 'Robin Hood in Scotland',[1] only deals with some of the material, though it did open up the idea interestingly – without, however, being pursued by other scholars. Apart from the intrinsic interest and relative neglect of the topic of Rabbie Hood, another good reason to return to it is that the whole phenomenon of a Scottish version of Robin Hood can now be looked at in the light of recently developed knowledge and theorization about how colonized cultures operate and, most interestingly for this paper, how they interact with native interests and how complex, even dialectic, are the forces involved. If Robin Hood in Scotland is one of the themes of this paper, then Rabbie Hood in England is another.

In this case, as in so many cases of colonialism and post-colonialism, the traffic was by no means one way. Scottish studies tend to resist post-colonialism on the grounds that Scotland was never a colony of England, just a negotiated ally and federate, but the complex and contributory role of Scotland to the Robin Hood myth may even in such a delicate context make post-colonial critical discourse conceivably acceptable.

To Aberdeen

The evidence of the inter-relationship in this outlaw myth between England and Scotland is clear. The Appendix to my 1994 book on the outlaw gathered together all the pre-1600 references that could be traced. There were 270 of them, and 53 are clearly related to Scotland or to Scottish authors. The quantity of the early Scottish references may of course be caused in part by the relatively sophisticated nature of lowland Scottish urban and mercantile life (which extends at least in this context up the east coast to Aberdeen), and also by both the detail and the relatively high survival ratio of their records.

About a fifth is still a large proportion, but it is also noticeable that this fifth contains a much larger proportion than one-fifth of the specific and amplified references – many of the English ones just refer to a Robin Hood play-game taking place, or to buying cloth for costumes. The Scots references tend to describe characters appearing in the streets with actions described, or they are literary references with some detail; or they are – and here the Scots have an exclusive – references to apparently real outlaws by chroniclers from Andrew of Wyntoun onwards.

No doubt more Robin Hood references will emerge from the present process of publishing the full records of early drama, but the relative weight and quality of the Scottish references is unlikely to be diminished. The extent, specificity and inherent importance of the early Scottish Robin Hood references clearly indicate that something was going on in this context in the north at that time. How are we to interpret this phenomenon?

Robin Hood is not the only British mythic figure to turn out to have strong early Scottish elements. King Arthur is the obvious candidate, and others are Myrddin/Merlin, Ywain, and Gawain (passing over on this occasion Sherlock Holmes's Edinburgh connection). The scholars who have pursued the northern King Arthur have seen it as a matter of origins, suggesting with some credibility that the real hero operated in the heroic British north and his tradition was preserved where the language of that area survived, namely Wales. But that does not seem to be a viable model for the dissemination of the Robin Hood myth, and in spite of neo-empiricist passions on the point, the concept of a historic Robin Hood is less persuasive even than that for a real King Arthur. An originary Scottish Robin Hood, disseminating south, is in any case not suggested by the evidence. Rather, Robin Hood is a figure of anti-authoritarian myth, who is widely located, through England and elsewhere, who may well be supportive of community when it is local and organic, but will become involved in opposition to authority when that community comes into conflict with external and intrusive authorities such as those of Abbot, Sheriff or indeed King.[2] His reality is like that of Santa Claus or Cinderella, a functional idea, and one that invites people not to identify him, but to identify with him.

In the case of Robin Hood, it is likely that the figure is traceable to the French *pastourelle* Robin des Bois, who sometimes loves and defends Marion but always celebrates with his rural friends, and that this French connection can explain the very curious early distribution of benign play-game Robin (as distinct from outlaw ballad Robin) in south-western England and south-eastern Scotland. These were sites of maritime contact with France which were not dominated by English aristocratic culture, and local celebration used this French figure intermittently as a model for a local summer celebrant and fund-raiser.[3] But while that would support a two-location origin, south and north, for Robin, that figure is in fact always called Robin Hood, a name which appears to have developed in England in the fourteenth century, and presumably through the drastic nature of that period distinctly enhanced his powers as a figure of resistance to authority. Whatever the origins and implications of the name Hood, by using it the Scottish events clearly show some cultural transmission through England. Hybridity is plain enough in the name of the ship *Le Robin Hude* which docked in Aberdeen in 1438 as well as some aura of criminality: we have the record because the master was accused, as if eponymously, of stealing goods in transit.[4]

However various the origins may be, the process of localization is clear in the Scottish play-game records. Aberdeen in 1508 has a requirement very like those from south-eastern England that *'all pepil that ar abill within this burghe . . . to pass with Robyne Hude and Litile Johnne'*. They are to be in costume (most of the English records of Robin Hood performances are notes of the cost of costumes): *'thair arrayment maid in grene and yellow, bowis, arrowis, brass and all uther convenient thingis according thairto'*.[5]

Robin Hood moves towards Rabbie Hood when both the date and the concept of the figure change. In the Aberdeen Municipal Statutes for that same year, 1508, under 17 November, it says that:

> all personiis, burges, nichtbouris, and inhabitaris, burges sonnys, habill to ryd, to decor and honor the towne in thar array conveinant therto, sall rid with Robert Huyid an Litile Johne, quilk was callit in yers bipast, Abbat and Prior of Bonacord, one every Sanct Nicholas day, throw the towne, as use and wont has bene . . .[6]

This is a communal fund-raising activity, as is indicated by the substantial fines to be paid by those required to ride but unwilling to do so – twenty shillings to St Nicholas 'werk' and eight shillings to the 'bailyeis'. That itself is an elaborate and prosperous – basically urban – version of the humble play-games in southern England where Robin and John walk through the woods to a nearby village and collect for their parish. But the time of year is unusual. The English play-games take place in May, usually late May at Whitsun. The presence of Robin Hood in May 1508 was a new phenomenon in Aberdeen: in the previous year this May festival was led by the 'Abbat and Prior of Bonacord'. But the greatest innovation is the date of this second Robin Hood event: 6 December. St Nicholas's Kirk is the main medieval church in Aberdeen. St Nicholas's guilds were associated with acting clerks in medieval England and December was the date of the 'Boy

Bishop' ceremonies, the monastic Feast of Fools with temporary reversal of ranks.

There are no English instances of a winter Robin Hood until his quite late inclusion in the Mummers' Play, which is eclectic beyond logic – he shares the stage with Lord Nelson and Beelzebub.[7] It looks as if the resettlement in Scotland of Robin Hood had also changed the figure significantly, detaching him in part from the strong natural symbolism of the English Whitsun practices – perhaps northern weather had an influence there – and making him more a figure of year-round urban harmony as implied in the title Bonacord, itself apparently a local cultural transmission from France.

It is already clear that Rabbie Hood is quite distinguishable from Robin Hood. It is not clear what leads to the change from one non-Scottish cultural reference – the Abbot of Bonacord – to another, but it may just be that fund-raising activities tend to be up with the latest imported crazes, as we see still in charity pageants. The year 1508 falls in a very active period in the Robin Hood tradition, and there are other signs of the name having cultural power in Scotland about this time, as we shall see. But the striking feature of this reference is the creation of a winter Robin, a distinctly northern transformation, it would seem. The Abbot of Bonacord had walked in both the summer and winter festivals, so, having replaced him in May, Robin served in the same role again in winter.

That hybridization of borrowed features with local elements, and even condensing them with other borrowed materials, is not uncommon: the development of Australian Rules football from English Rugby and Irish Gaelic football on the huge sports grounds available in Melbourne is another example. But not only is the Scottish culture creative with its received material: it can also disseminate its own parallels There is a clear knowledge in Wiltshire in 1432 of the border outlaws Adam Bell, William of Cloudesley and Clim of the Clough, seen in the Robin Hood context;[8] their story remained popular in ballad form in England throughout the fifteenth and sixteenth century.

But there seems to have been a more multiple and complex form of cross-border traffic concerning Robin Hood. Rabbie Hood is not simply a quaint kilt-wearing Robin Hood. He is a specialized and syncretic figure. The Scottish Robin Hood, like the nineteenth-century French Robin des Bois, the Hindu Ravi and, most relevantly, the English William of Cloudesley, is not a locally originated social bandit, like the French Thierry de la Fronde or the Indian Bandit Queen, or indeed the Scots William Wallace. Rabbie Hood, by virtue of being borrowed, fits into another worldwide model: the hero from another place who brings external and therefore specially credible values which are used to define a sense of local lack and need: as with Aeneas, Beowulf, John Wayne, Cristiano Ronaldo, a sense of local weakness (or in Robin's case disaccord) may be calmed by the special powers of the supra-local hero by virtue of his externality. Robin Hood in Scotland can mean more through his ability to be re-formed for special purposes, from Bonacord in November onwards.

The North writes back

There are Rabbie Hood formations beyond the Aberdeen winter street collector. A particularly striking phenomenon is the remarkable fact that the only chronicle references to Robin Hood before the dawn of English antiquarianism in the mid-sixteenth century come from a range of Scottish historians. The references deserve special and separate attention; they have some connections, but each introduces new features indicating that this is not just a sequence of chroniclers being faithful to each other: each generated a new type of Rabbie Hood.

Andrew of Wyntoun wrote his metrical history of Scotland in the 1420s and under the year 1283 he said:

Litil Iohun and Robert Hude
Waythemen war commendit gud;
In Ingilwode and Bernnysdaile
Thai oyssit al this tyme thar trawale.[9]

Little John and Robin Hood,
highwaymen, were praised highly;
in Inglewood and Barnsdale
they conducted their operations during the whole of this period.

The lines read a little oddly to a textual editor – not because John precedes Robin: in my view they were originally equal but John has been steadily downgraded to a strapping servant (see too Laura Blunk's essay on John in this volume). But there is a sense of padding about '*commendit gude*' and an awkward feel to the last line. Wyntoun is usually very brisk. A hypothesis worth putting forward is that there was previously a popular jingle:

> *Litil Iohun and Robert Hude*
> *Waythemen were in Ingilwode.*

The further hypothesis is that Andrew knew this couplet but, good scholar and chronicler as befits an Augustinian canon from a daughter house of St Andrews, he also knew of the Robin Hood of Barnesdale tradition (his source will be a subject of later speculation). So, it may be, he compiled the clumsily elaborated reference.

The date is of course intriguing: nothing in the surviving Robin Hood narratives can take us back to 1283, though 'real Robin Hood' historians in particular would like to think of a thirteenth-century origin for the tradition. There appears to be an implicit comparison between these noble outlaws and the near contemporary Wallace, that Scottish social bandit for whom Wyntoun has so much sympathy: Joseph Ritson noted this in his influential 1795 account of Robin Hood.[10] Certainly the implication is that Little John and Robin Hood are opponents of the English authorities under Edward I, and so have interests in common with similar figures to the north: the concept of an outlaw from a Scottish viewpoint entails a political and nationalist identity for the figure. Rabbie Hood is emerging.

Wyntoun has no doubt of their existence as real outlaws; he has nothing specific to say about their cultural popularity, though it can be assumed from the sense of '*commendit gud*'. The next Scottish chronicler to take up the theme had more to say about culture than politics. Walter Bower, writing only twenty years later, continued John of Fordun's *Scotichronicon* and dated his Robin Hood to 1266, the time of Simon de Montfort's rebellion against Henry III. He sums up more severely than Wyntoun:

Then arose the famous murderer, Robert Hood, as well as Little John, together with their accomplices from among the dispossessed, whom the foolish populace are so inordinately fond of celebrating both in tragedy and comedy.[11]

But Bower also tells a story of Robin's fidelity to the Church, insisting as he does on finishing mass deep in the forest before fighting off the sheriff. This might sound simply like a Christianized Robin Hood adventure, but the Latin suggests more: the sheriff is called 'viscount' and Robin is hiding from the '*iram regis et fremitum principis*' ('the wrath of the king and the roaring of the prince'), which seems in spite of Bower's dating in the time of Henry III to have a resonance of attacks on Scotland by Edward I and his son, and certainly sees Robin as an anti-royal noble on the Wallace pattern, a sense not found in the early English texts. Rabbie Hood is emerging more clearly.

As a Scot and a canon himself, Bower's story sophisticates Wyntoun's story and sets it in another time of resistance to an English king – Simon de Montfort's challenge to Henry III, an idea much liked in the nineteenth century, because it could associate this Robin with the alleged founder of the English parliament.

If Bower sophisticates the Scots chronicle tradition somewhat, and directs its idea of an anti-royal Robin back towards England, a third Scottish chronicler completes that process. Probably written in Paris, and published there in 1521, John Major's *Historia Majoris Britanniae*[12] not only gentrified Robin somewhat, but took him back into the time of bad King John, so his rebellion against royal rule can itself become fully legitimate. Major probably used the story of Fouke Fitz Waryn as a model for this distressed gentleman narrative. But in making Robin seem noble, as well as by making him resist a bad king, as is implied by the 1190s date, Major is closer to the Scots anti-royal war-leader model than the popular English hero, who was a plain man among men with no thoughts of nobility or politics beyond robbing a monk, shooting the sheriff and having fun with money in Nottingham.

Major makes Robin a 'most famous robber' and a war leader with a hundred ferocious bowmen – a warband fit for a resistant noble like Wallace, not a highwayman. He is famous all over Britain (not England); he is noble in manner and also in self – being the 'humanest and the chief' – and the Latin word '*dux*' here may well have inspired further chroniclers like Grafton who followed Major closely to state simply that he was a nobleman.

Commentators, including myself, have stressed the gentrification process in the history of the Robin Hood tradition: class remains an object of fascination, or obsession, for us all in Britain. But gentrification is also a different political model, shaping a man who moves on a national political stage, rather than lurking locally in a forest. Major's Robin of 1521 becomes very easily Anthony Munday's Earl of Huntington in the twin plays of 1598–9, *The Death* and *The Downfall of Robert, Earle of Huntington*: the resistance to a bad prince is already established in Major's dating of the hero to the 1190s. As the renaissance chroniclers like Grafton and Stow absorb this Robin back into the cultural bloodstream, it is as a respectable, aristocratic and national hero. This is a massive reconstruction of the myth that still reverberates throughout the tradition, and appears to derive from a distinctly Scottish reading of the figure – though not yet one that reads the figure as himself having national identity: that lies in the future and the hands of Walter Scott.

If Major himself was an example of that tedious phenomenon, the Anglophile Celt, the balance was, as usual in such colonial battles, redressed with interest, and Hector Boece and David Buchanan in their later sixteenth-century chronicles firmly restored a fully Scottish viewpoint, Boece even offering the view that Little John was a true giant and was buried in Moray.[13]

To theorize what happened in the case under examination, the destabilized character of the English Robin Hood in Scotland permitted developments which in England would have been blocked because Robin as social bandit was not so free-floating a figure. In the early English ballads he is empowered by stable and local organic values and is not as fluid a signifier as he became in transmitted and potentially hybrid form. It is in fact the non-local nature of the figure in Scotland, borrowed both in some way from England and in another way from France, which enabled him to be so labile there and so begin to form the structure that was to become the distressed gentleman in England. Studying the relationship with Wallace will both confirm and develop the sense of a striking Scottish influence on the Robin Hood tradition, but before looking at that it is relevant to look back at a previously unexplored channel of contact between England and Scotland in Robin Hood matters.

Lost in the forests

The surprising presence of 'Bernnysdaile' in Wyntoun's chronicle is worth considering. Robin Hood scholars have long speculated that the Yorkshire Barnsdale, mentioned in the *Gest of Robyn Hode*, is an early location of the myth, which became easily conflated with the Sherwood variant.[14] The existence of other apparent locations for Robin Hood around the country, including Inglewood, makes this only more probable. R. B. Dobson and John Taylor were a little uneasy about the Yorkshire Barnsdale, knowing it had never been a royal forest, was too sparse for serious outlaws, and so did not really fit the myth however much the compiler of the *Gest* (by definition a secondary process) might think that was the hero's address.[15]

But there was another forest called Barnsdale, and that originally a royal one, deep in the heart of Rutland. It had never been noticed by the empiricist historians, though if they had driven from Cambridge to Nottingham they would have gone through it on the A303, Stamford to Oakham. There are a number of local Robin Hood caves, stones and similar topographic affiliations.[16]

The major surprise is to find that this Rutland Barnsdale, right through the Middle Ages, had belonged to the Earl of Huntingdon, no less. And who was he? He was, no less again, usually a close male relative of the King of Scotland.[17] This was known to Spence and he speculated in 1928 that an estate near Huntingdon might have been a place for learning the Robin Hood ballads and taking them back to Scotland.[18] He did not seem to know the Rutland Barnsdale was part of the estate, and the presence of that name in Wyntoun is an intriguing link between the idea of Scottish aristocratic independence and the tradition of Robin Hood. Inglewood too was a royal Scottish forest, and Wyntoun's connection of the two, seen from north of the border, appears fully rational.

Less certain, but very tempting, is to speculate that perhaps Anthony Munday knew of the Barnsdale-Huntingdon connection. There has never been any explanation why Anthony Munday, when writing *The Downfall of Robert, Earle of Huntington* in 1589 chose that particular title for his newly gentrified hero. To speculate that the concept of hunting is the link seems an example of scholarly despair (especially as Robin never does any hunting), and Bevington's argument that the name comes from a pretender to the throne of the 1560s, while more specific, seems even more improbable.[19] Munday does firmly locate his forest exile in Barnsdale and I strongly suspect that John Stow, the all-knowing Elizabethan antiquarian, an acquaintance of Munday, knew about the Rutland Barnsdale and the Huntington connection and gave him the hint. But I cannot find any evidence of that in Stow's writing. A less likely link is the 1596 visit by Shakespeare's Chamberlain's Men (rivals to Munday's Admiral's Men) to the heart of Barnsdale at Christmas to play for Sir John Harington's 900 Christmas guests *Titus Andronicus* – obviously the *Christmas Carol* of its day. If Munday through Stow or the players did know somehow about the title and the forest, then that is another instance of the Scottish connection at the heart of gentrification.

A link with Munday remains speculation. The Wyntoun connection is stronger. It seems more than guesswork to suggest that he was influenced in discussing Robin Hood partly by the long-standing Scottish royal connection with the Rutland Barnsdale, and partly by the existence there of local Robin Hood connections – in 1354 a man who was arrested for deer-poaching named himself as Robin Hood in Rockingham forest only twenty miles away.[20]

But should this sound like a mere one-way colonial borrowing, albeit one where the Scots royal house was colonizing darkest Rutland, the actual situation appears more complicated, more multiple. If there was a Scottish presence and transmission deep in the East Midland Robin Hood area, there was apparently also an equally mysterious reflex, a soldierly nationalist Robin Hood far in the north. In David Laing's 1872 edition of Andrew of Wyntoun's *Chronicle*, the famous Inglewood and Barnsdale reference is not the only citation to the outlaw in the index. There is also a reference to a certain 'Hwde of Edname' who helped Sir Alexander Ramsay take Roxburgh by storm from the English in 1342. The reference is presumably to Ednam near Roxburgh (though tantalizingly there is also an Ednam in southern Lincolnshire, not far from Rutland).

If the Rockingham Robin is likely to be an auto-creation, a man taking the name because he did the appropriate deeds, then why, as Laing thought, should there not in Ednam be another example, though here it is a Rabbie Hood, a noble Robin Hood attached to the Scottish national cause.

Robin the Wallace

The previous argument does not only bear on the issue of how many Robin Hoods, how many Rabbie Hoods? It also stresses multiplicity: if there is a Hood of Inglewood, who can be linked with tales of faraway royal Scottish Barnsdale, there may as easily have been a more martial borderer from Ednam, who also used that name while fighting the soldiers of Edward III. More generally, though, what this implies is the fact that the Scottish reading of the outlaw figure is clearly not the same as the English, especially in terms of national significance. Rabbie and Robin were two different men. In England, Robin represents regularly the local against the national, the village against the sheriff, the people of the forest against the regulating mechanisms imposed by foresters, and the whole imagined rural organic community against the cash-oriented nexus of abbot and town business.[21] That is what the Rockingham man represents, while the Rabbie Hwde of Ednam is a nationally conscious freedom-fighter, at home among gentry, a leader of his people.

This notion of different heroes whose stories interrelate is best exemplified in the relationship between Robin Hood and the best-known Scottish national outlaw. It is clear from the epic Scots poem on William Wallace, apparently written by

'Blind Hary' or Henry the Minstrel, that there are close resemblances to events in a number of Robin Hood ballads. But these outlaw motifs in a fully Scotticized form have a powerful political thrust, now embodying resistance to English imperialism. In 'Robin Hood's Progress to Nottingham',[22] the hero is provoked when young into violence and outlawry by hostile opponents: in Wallace's case the cause is specified as an Englishman, young Selby, whereas for Robin Hood they are simply foresters. Both heroes later on save themselves from serious trouble by dressing as women with the help of a sympathetic old woman ('Robin Hood and the Bishop', Child no. 143), but where Wallace hides from Selby senior and his English soldiers, Robin escapes the Bishop, in a secular-clerical, not national conflict. Both outlaws rob and (very rarely in Robin's case) kill travellers (the *Gest of Robyn Hode*, Child no. 117; 'Robin Hood and the Monk', Child no. 119; 'Robin Hood's Golden Prize', Child no. 147), and both beat off a fierce ambush (the *Gest*), but again only Wallace's opponents have a national denomination. Both outlaws end by having a difficult encounter with the king, tragic and nationalist in Wallace's case, unsatisfactory but negotiated in the instance of Robin. Both share a noble death at the hands of their enemies, and leave an enduring and highly valued memory, but only Wallace's enemies and meaning belong in the domain of national and aristocratic politics.

The closest and most interesting of all the parallels is when both heroes play the part of a potter to enter a town, a strong suggestion of motif transference between the traditions ('Robin Hood and the Potter', Child no. 121). Wallace of course penetrates an essentially English borough in this way, but for Robin it is a journey to the heart of urban mercantilism.

The relation between the two traditions is also intriguing in terms of date. In almost all cases the Robin Hood survivals are a good deal later than that of Blind Hary's 'Wallace', and the two earliest Robin Hood ballads seem themselves almost a generation later. The manuscript of 'Robin Hood and the Potter' dates from 1500 at the earliest and while it contains scribal errors, it does not look as if it has had a long life in literary transmission. The manuscript version of 'Robin Hood and the Monk', which has usually been dated '*c*.1450' is now being pushed forward in time to after 1465:[23] it is still the only Robin Hood narrative which could, just, be thought to predate the 'Wallace' which is in manuscript by 1488, perhaps a little earlier.

The resemblance between Robin Hood and the Wallace was long ago noted, though not quite as long ago as Spence thought, relying as he did on a mistaken dating of the document written by a prior of Alnwick who calls Wallace *Scotico illi Robin Whood*, 'that Scottish Robin Hood'. Spence thought it had the sensational contemporaneity of 1304, but the modern opinion is 1504.[24] That later date, though, has its own relevance to this topic. It is quite clear that the two traditions are circulating more or less together – but only in Scotland. The 'Wallace' is printed in Scotland in 1508. This is the period when the *Gest of Robyn Hode* was widely printed: its first version may be as early as 1495, but then it appeared in four times between c.1505 and c.1515, and was constructed not very long before – post 1450, it would seem.[25] The *Gest* was being printed in the very period when Robin Hood newly walked in Aberdeen.

There are also literary references. As Dunbar's poetry was being printed in Edinburgh at just the same time as the *Gest* appeared (though not, as was once thought, by the same printer, Chepman and Myllar) it is hardly surprising that the poet refers to the English outlaw in 'Of Sir Thomas Norrey', as 'vyld Robeine under bewch' ('wild Robin under bough' – in the wood), but his knowledge there is a good deal wider than the *Gest* itself: he speaks of his opponent 'Guy of Gisburne' and 'Allan Belle' – presumably Adam – all in the context of archery.[26] At this time the ballad 'Robin Hood and Guy of Gisborne' (Child no. 118) was nearly 150 years away from its only recording in Percy's folio manuscript, though a play with some of the same action has survived from about 1475. Perhaps the early plays about the friar and the potter had travelled as far as Edinburgh? It is notable that another contemporary reference is theatrical, a simple mention of the Robin Hood processions in the poem formerly attributed to Dunbar and dated very early in the sixteenth century 'Ane Litill Interlude of the Droichis Part of the Play'. Gavin Douglas's *Pallice of Honur* dated before 1518 mentions Robin and

Gilbert with the White Hand – this makes it clear he knew the *Gest*, the only text where Robin appears, at the archery tournament, with this minor outlaw.

A Scottish poem recorded in the Hyndford manuscript in 1588 is usually dated between 1500 and 1510, and it says:

> Thair is no story that I of hier
> Of John nor Robene Hude
> Nor yit of Wallace wicht but weir
> That me thinkes half so gude.[27]

In this way it is clear that the English outlaw story is common knowledge in early sixteenth-century Scotland, and that Robin Hood and the Wallace are in some ways coterminous, though it is also clear that, for the latter, national identity is dominant. It seems that, in so far as Rabbie Hood exists, he may well, as the chroniclers suggest, be a hybrid of the Wallace and Robin Hood, a nationally conscious gentleman outlaw, royally mistreated by the King of England, noble, resistant, heroic in life and death – all of those features are not in the early Robin Hood story, but are in the Wallace story. Most commentators (most of them English) have assumed that the Robin Hood materials represent motifs that have long been in existence in the outlaw tradition, were used in the oral Robin Hood rhymes that Langland mentioned in the 1370s[28] and Bower in the 1440s, and so, by implication, were borrowed (in colonial style) into the Wallace narrative. However, the 'Wallace' lays down very specific versions of a number of major Robin Hood events which are remarkably like those found in English, mostly long afterwards. It is conceivable that Rabbie Hood may in fact in some important sense instigate Robin Hood: 'Robin Hood and the Monk', 'Robin Hood and the Potter' and the *Gest* represent a new literary realization of the English popular and orally known Robin Hood, and it is entirely credible that these texts were influenced by and textually structured on the model of an existing text about a heroic outlaw especially as both heroes were well known at the same time in Scotland.

Outlaw hybridization

My argument, then, is that in Scottish hands the figure of Robin Hood was reformulated. As in the English south-west there was probably a first stage where *Robin de Bois* was adapted as a figure of local festival, but even then he had gained his English surname by a form of cultural colonizing. In England he graduated to local good-outlaw violence, but in Scotland there were more urgent things for a popular hero to resist than a corrupt sheriff or abbot: natural justice there included a sense of national identity and resistance to a usurping king, neither of which had been central nor even of importance to the original Robin Hood. So Rabbie emerged, remodelled along the lines of Wallace and it may well be that some of the Wallace detail, such as the potter's disguise, was used back in England in the Robin Hood ballads. Certainly the greater nobility and greater political weight of the Scotticized figure was the mainspring of gentrification. This figure was returned to England, where he became highly valuable in Renaissance ideology, both to remove the unappealingly radical element of Robin Hood's resistance to kings and lords, and also to figure a nobleman under pressure from churchmen and bureaucrats, a central element of Munday's late sixteenth-century plays, through which gentrification of the outlaw was strongly disseminated.

This argument makes sense in itself, but may well seem unusual in its return function. Did the Geats get back an Anglicized Beowulf? Would the Portuguese revere a repatriated Ronaldo who loved chip butties? But there are models of this process in existence and I will suggest two, that relate to the topic here, one from each of the traditions of Scotland and Robin Hood. Robert Crawford describes how, to use his fine chapter title, there was in the eighteenth and especially the nineteenth century a 'Scottish invention of English Literature', which was then very influential in England outside the establishment circle of Oxbridge.[29] A parallel appropriation and replantation process has occurred within the Robin Hood tradition. Most people of advancing age, on hearing the name Robin Hood, smile and hum the tune of the 1950s television series. The essence of Englishness, surely, was Richard Greene playing the dapper officer-type Robin Hood who was feared by the bad and loved by the good. The tradition of the popular ballads seemed to have been handed down directly to the modern welfare state. Not so. The dynamic of these stories was American. The company for marketing reasons wanted a drama series, and no one in Britain knew how to do them. Through Hannah Weinstein, an American producer with left sympathies, they hired some good writers who would work cheap. The series was shaped by black-listed Americans, principally Ring Lardner Jr. and Ian McLellan Hunter. In distant New York, without passports, they created left-liberal greenwood idylls that were shot in England at Burnham Beeches, among a covey of American radicals, including the economist Bill Blake and his wife, the Australian novelist Christina Stead. The excellent film *Fellow Traveller* (1988), written by Michael Eaton, re-tells this story. English writers followed the lead set from the States as the hero was doubly re-localized . . . just as I am arguing happened in the late medieval period from Scotland.[30] Just as Edward I's mailed fist can be seen as the hand behind the Scottish-grounded gentrifying politicizations of the late medieval Rabbie Hood, so Joe McCarthy was the energizing daemon behind the ghost writers of Richard Greene as a newly socialist Robin Hood.

Though the late medieval process of Scottish-located hybridization did bring Robin Hood into the 1190s, it did not, as most people think, make him a Saxon. That was a later process, and one consistent with other changes to the hero which made him fit for a modern world. It too was guided from Scotland. Walter Scott in *Ivanhoe* made Locksley a Saxon – albeit a non-commissioned officer kind of Saxon, illiterate to boot. That in my view is because Scott knew all about and disliked the radical potential of Robin Hood, being familiar with the 1561 Edinburgh riot when, refused the right to a Robin Hood procession, the citizens rebelled, opened the Toll Booth, took the prisoners out and put the magistrates in. Scott refers to the events in his notes to *The Abbot*, and there is some resonance of them in his account of the Porteous Riots in *The Heart of Midlothian* (on Scott, *Ivanhoe*, and *The Abbot* see also Helen Phillips essay following this). The dynamism of the Scott reworking went further than vigorous nationalism, but to work out where he got the central idea of splitting the arrow and why so many people started writing about Robin Hood in 1818 is another paper, on the Scott, not the Scottish, influence on Robin Hood.

The point of this one has been to look at an earlier and rather more obscure period in which many Robin Hood roads led to Scotland – and, as I have argued, also back again, with considerable impact. As in so much of English culture, there is a significant deep-laid Scottish element in the construction and the continuing popularity of the tradition of Robin Hood.

NOTES

1. Lewis Spence, 'Robin Hood in Scotland', *Chambers Journal*, 18 (1928), pp. 94–6.
2. Stephen Knight, *Robin Hood: A Complete History of the English Outlaw* (Oxford: Blackwell, 1994), pp. 113–15.
3. Stephen Knight, 'Robin Hood: The Earliest Contexts', in *Images of Robin Hood*, Joshua Calhoun and Lois Potter (eds) (Newark: University of Delaware Press, 2008).
4. See Knight, 'Robin Hood: The Earliest Contexts' for details on this case.
5. Peter Hume Brown (ed.), *Scotland Before 1700 from Contemporary Documents* (Edinburgh: Douglas, 1893), p. 189.
6. Ibid., p. 190.
7. See R. J. E.Tiddy, *The Mummers' Play* (Oxford: Clarendon Press, 1923).
8. See J. C. Holt, *Robin Hood*, 2nd edn (London: Thames and Hudson, 1990), pp. 69–70.
9. See *The Orygynale Chronicle*, ed. D. Laing (Edinburgh: Edmonston and Douglas, 1903–14), vol. V, p. 135, lines 25–8. The text is reprinted and discussed in KO, pp. 24–6.
10. See *Robin Hood, A Collection of All the Ancient Poems, Songs and Ballads Now Extant Relative to the Celebrated English Outlaw* (London: Egerton and Johnson, 1795), p. ix.
11. Walter Bower, *Continuation of John of Fordun's Scotichronicon*, ed. T. Hearne (Oxford: Sheldonian Theatre, 1722); this translation is by Alex Jones, printed in KO, pp. 25–6.
12. *Historia Majoris Britanniae* (Paris: Josse Badius, 1521); extract in KO, pp. 26–7.
13. See Ritson, pp. cxxii–iii.
14. For a discussion of these issues see Holt, 'The Physical Setting', chapter 5.
15. DT, p. 20.

16 Knight 1994, pp. 29–32.
17 Medieval Inglewood also contained manors of the King of Scotland.
18 Spence, 'Robin Hood', p. 95.
19 *Tudor Drama and Politics: A Critical Approach to Topical Meaning* (Cambridge, MA: Harvard University Press, 1968), p. 295.
20 See DT, pp. 12–13.
21 For more detailed argument on this point see Knight 1994, pp. 112–14.
22 Francis James Child (ed.), *English and Scottish Popular Ballads*, 5 vols, reprint edn (New York: Dover, 1964), vol. 3, no. 119. Reference to other 'Child' ballads will be given in the text by their numbers in his edition.
23 See Thomas H. Ohlgren 'Date of the Manuscript', in *Robin Hood: The Early Poems, 1465–1560* (Newark: University of Delaware Press, 2007), pp. 39–40.
24 Spence, 'Robin Hood'.
25 On the date of the *Gest*'s early versions see Ohlgren, pp. 98–9.
26 William Dunbar, *Selected Poems*, ed. Priscilla Bawcutt, 2 vols (Glasgow: Association for Scottish Literary Studies, 1998), vol. 1, pp. 131–2.
27 Quoted by Spence, 'Robin Hood', p. 95.
28 *Piers Plowman*, B 5:395, C VII:11. Sloth does not know his paternoster despite knowing the 'rymes of Robyn Hode'.
29 See *Devolving English Literature* (Oxford: Clarendon Press, 1992), chapter 2.
30 On this see an article by Tom Dewe Mathews in *The Guardian*, 7 October 2006 (available at *http://books.guardian.co.uk*): he says Weinstein assembled twenty-two black-listed writers, and newly names Waldo Salt, Adrian Scott and Robert Lees among them: he promises a forthcoming book on the topic.

Scott and the Outlaws

HELEN PHILLIPS

Scott, outlaws and politics

Again and again Sir Walter Scott recreates the figure of the outlaw. The theme both attracts and repels this complex conservative. The bandit's obvious glamour for a writer in the Gothic era might seem to make further investigation unnecessary,[1] but idiosyncratic patterns recur in Scott's use of the outlaw, and these often relate more to his own political vision than to perspectives inherited from the long tradition of outlaw narratives. Stephen Knight (page 116) has pointed out that Scott, disliking the radical potential of the figure of Robin Hood, made his own Locksley/Robin Hood a nationalist, not a rebel: Scott created Robin the Saxon, a strongly enduring feature of the legend ever since. Scott, however, arguably had a more complex relationship to the subversive elements in the figure of the outlaw as well:

> I am a bad hand at depicting a hero, properly so called, and have an unfortunate propensity for the dubious character of borderers, buccaneers, Highland robber, and all others of a Robin Hood description. The rogue always, in despite of me, turns out my hero.[2]

Scott's comment is true yet evasive. 'Borderers' is a key word: outlaws inhabit a psychological territory on the margins of Scott's law-abiding heroes' minds as well as literally on the divisions between highland and lowland or Scottish and English worlds. Despite the attraction of his 'rogues', Scott never lets outlaws be heroes. His use of outlaws reveals deeply conflicting political approaches to power and order, not as simply and involuntarily as his wording, 'unfortunate propensity ... despite of me', claims.

An outlaw is a man outside the law, claiming his own territory: greenwood, mountains, the Bush. Perhaps the outlaw's attraction partly reflects Scott's situation in a nation with a still untamed rural landscape and two societies, highland and lowland. *Rob Roy* and *A Legend of the Wars of Montrose* identify the outlaw with the highlands. For Scott, a dedicated anti-radical and advocate of social progress through the retention of traditional hierarchy, the outlaw helps both to define and challenge his Tory vision. His outlaws are sites of complexity and contradiction in his political model. His sympathy with other outcasts, beggars and gypsies, seems not conflicted in the same way.[3]

Scott's outlaw does not just inhabit the lawful man's borders: at times he seems to be the borders of lawful men's experience. Knight and outlaw, leader and bandit, may change places or join forces temporarily, the outlaw appearing almost a shape-shifting form of legitimate leadership: a boundary easily crossed – though always by the leader. Scott confers strengths from outlaw tradition on leaders (*Ivanhoe* is the obvious example), but the leader's acquisition of imaginatively powerful outlaw attributes is not matched by any transitions in the opposite direction: outlaws never figure as heroes. Unlike authors of other outlaw tales, Scott never writes wholly from the outlaw's side. Whatever his historical setting, Scott's outlaw reflects political anxieties threatening early nineteenth-century political security: radicalism and popular unrest. Any identification with this political 'Other' of Scott's own world is complex and he often approaches the outlaw through a strange double perspective, presenting him as a play-actor or character in traditional minstrelsy – thus denuded of political substance – yet also as a serious threat of political violence.

Scott's ideal for outlaws is epitomized towards the end of *Ivanhoe*,

> Beneath a huge oak-tree the sylvan repast was hastily prepared for the King of England, surrounded by men outlaws to his government, but who now formed his court and his guard.[4]

Here an outlaw finds his true destiny as the willing servant of authority. Elsewhere Scott conceives this as the ideal role for the rebellious masses: remaining obstreperous only until a true leader is recognized, then happily recalled to feudal obedience. *Ivanhoe*'s subduing of the outlaw into harmony with his ruler, happens under 'a huge oak-tree'. An ancient tree is Scott's recurrent symbol of national well-being under traditional leadership.[5] Here those formerly outside the civil order return under its rule and protection, acknowledging legitimate authority: a New Tory model of a meritorious aristocracy reforming and restoring national order, obviating any need for radical reform. This sylvan oak-tree *agape* representing a social contract is a static image, briefly frozen in the novel's action. It is an untenable state for an outlaw to come in-law. *Ivanhoe*'s symbolic picture does not last. And awkwardly, but with an honesty found sometimes in Scott concerning unstable fissures in his political models, he has Locksley/Robin decide to keep the sylvan *rapprochement* brief: he apprehends danger but also a change in the royal mood (472–3).

Scott's age was one of revolution and political repression. Outlaws had been invoked by writers with an interest in reform: Thomas Holcroft's *Noble Peasant* (1784), Ritson's introduction to his edition of Robin Hood ballads (1795), and Keats's 'Robin Hood: To a Friend' (1818) are instances.[6] The outlaw, between 1780 and 1820, acquired a persona that was almost code for contemporary reformist ideals. Scott was a conservative, writing anti-radical Tory pamphlets as well as novels which celebrate legitimate and traditional authority. Yet the theme of outlawry recurs throughout his career. In Scottish history and popular imagination there was already a stronger link between national leaders and outlaws than in England. Chronicles describe Robert Bruce fleeing from the English into the mountains and moors, living rough, travelling clandestinely, while the usurping English Edward I attempts to rule as monarch in Dunfermline; the Scottish poem, *The Bruce*, celebrates Bruce's brave spirit whereas English chronicles satirize him, and their name for him, 'King Robin', perhaps links him – it would be an extremely early reference – to the outlaw Robin Hood.[7] Narratives about William Wallace assimilate him even more to the common treasury of tales about outlaws, with disguise, tricks, fierce loyalty from adherents, and courage against the odds. The motif of the 'king in the heather' continues with the story of Bonnie Prince Charlie.

Outlaws: aristocratic leaders versus harmless actors

As a ballad collector, Scott had deep knowledge of outlaw literature. His *Minstrelsy of the Scottish Border* (1801) includes, for example, the 'Sang of the Outlaw Murray': its aristocratic outlaw (never so far identified with any historical character) defies a monarch who tries to enforce homage on him. References to outlaws occur in Scott's novels in both their main narratives and various kinds of peritext: chapter mottoes, inset songs, or notes. Scott's use of such peritexts illustrates the importance – the centrality – of the marginal and of qualifications and equivocations in his world-view.[8]

Stephen Knight interprets Scott's decision to make Lord Ivanhoe, not Robin Hood, the hero of *Ivanhoe* as Scott's aversion to the associations between Robin and political subversiveness; he cites Scott's remarks in a note (a peritext) linking Robin Hood and misrule.[9] In containing Robin thus and giving his power to Ivanhoe, the unjustly exiled aristocrat, Scott reverses a tradition that since the sixteenth century had made Robin a dispossessed earl. Here Ivanhoe re-ascends to lordship, not Robin, who in Scott's version remains a yeoman ('stout yeoman Locksley', chapter 31, 335) from start to finish. He is 'good yeoman' and 'the woodsman', language that disregards his outlaw identity and formidable military might as a war-leader: words fitter for describing an industrious manorial peasant. Scott associates him with Chaucer's Yeoman, no outlaw but a knight's retainer, attributing to Locksley the devotion to St Christopher mentioned in Chaucer's portrait of this feudal tenant.[10] Scott's language divests Robin of as many taints of lawlessness or fecklessness as is consistent with his role as outlaw. This is not (see below) the only instance of Scott conceptualizing the outlaw in binary opposition to the industrious peasant. Locksley is the closest an outlaw can come to being a respectful retainer, serviceable and supportive to his leaders. Nor is Locksley's company anarchic or republican: even in sharing out booty, he distributes to the outlaws 'according to their rank and merit', showing 'men in a state so lawless' having nevertheless the benefit of being 'regularly and equitably governed . . . [by] the justice and judgment of their leader' (chapter 32, 356).[11] The king applauds such 'civil policy' ordering outlaw society. Locksley explains primly that, unlike some outlaws who actually enjoy the lawless state, he entered it reluctantly and 'exercise[s] its licence with some moderation' (chapter 33, 375).

Ivanhoe's Robin is divested of earldom and even his famous name, being 'Locksley' for most of the novel, besides the manorial names mentioned earlier. Scott is teasing his reader but also asserting his right to define his own outlaw. Denuded of his leadership role and the full, immediate popular acclaim of his audience to his name, Locksley/Robin is reformulated into a natural 'second-in-command', falling readily into subordination once he finds the leader he can respect, as in that climactic repast with his king under the oak.

The *Lady of the Lake* (1810) supports the hypothesis that Scott's agenda for Robin Hood is to show him subservient to a nobly born hero. He introduces Robin only to show him bettered by an aristocrat at his own skills. Lord Douglas wins at archery, wrestling and shot-putting, the medieval peasant sports at which early ballads and drama show Robin a master (Canto 5, xxii). Douglas wins the silver arrow, Robin's famous prize since the late medieval *Gest of Robyn Hode*, and usurps Robin's feat of splitting a wand, even splitting the arrow itself.[12]

The same stanza introduces Robin but then describes Douglas's triumphs at these sports (Canto 5, xii). Scott's style is confusing as to whether Robin here is a real outlaw or actor. This strange passage introduces a strategy that became common: Scott de-substantializes outlaws by making them literary or carnival figures. Robin, introduced with his merry men after a reference to morris dancers, challenges all comers to an archery contest. Presumably these are play-actors. Even so, the stanza juxtaposing them with Douglas's triumph pairs lord and outlaw in contrast, making the lord seem to take from Robin his famous archery feat as well as his traditional claim on a reader's admiration. Robin enters amid dancers: 'Their chequered bands, the joyous rout' (5. xxii). Scott's note underlines his unsubstantiality: 'The exhibition of this renowned outlaw and his band was a favourite frolic at such festivals . . .' Its tone changes from 'frolic' to civic disturbance: the Robin Hood games occasioned a 'rascal multitude', 'very serious tumult', 'disturbance', 'profane festivities'. The note's mixed message, like the text's 'chequered bands' and oxymoron 'joyous rout', conveys ambivalence. The political effect, however, is clear: characterizing an outlaw both as mere play-acting and serious civic unrest is a double denigration.

The conservative patterns in Scott's structuring of the sports are confirmed in its ending: the pageant-like atmosphere associated with outlaws ('morricers with bell at heel / And blade in hand', oddly phrased already) becomes a genuine riot. It starts over a perceived insult by the king's men to Douglas's dog (5 xxv–xxvi). The people revolt: 'tumult rose / And yeomen gan to bend their bows' (5 xxvi). How readily, Scott's sequencing implies, can the values represented by Robin Hood frolics become dangerous revolutionary aggression? There is 'uproar wild and misarray'. Royal horsemen turn against the crowd: a prefiguration of early nineteenth-century government repression of radical protest, culminating in Peterloo, 1819:

> With grief the noble Douglas saw
> The Commons rise against the law. (xxvii)

The noble's innate skill at controlling the people quietens the rebellious 'Commons', 'these misguided men' (xxvii). The 'rabble with disordered roar', whose 'wild fury' and 'misguided ire' are compared to mindless natural phenomena – their final contrite tears coming suddenly like rain after a storm (xxix) – are instantly stilled, glad to be restrained back into 'the bands of fealty' (xxviii). Older men 'Bless'd him who staid the civil strife'; mothers praise the aristocrat who restrained plebeian 'wrongs and ire' (xxix). Scott shows the people as instinctively imbued with feudal loyalty, happy to be directed by one of their natural leaders away from their equally instinctive tendency to riot. Scott depicts their anger itself as sprung from naturally feudal if misdirected loyalty, an attack on their lord's dog: the absurd pretext undermining any claims rebellion might have to serious respect. The people have the instinctive aggression and instinctive biddability (under the right master) of dogs. Scott puts into the king's mouth complaints, couched in patriarchal imagery, for the genetically unreliable instincts of these subhuman masses:

> This changeling crowd, this common fool . . .
> Who o'er the herd would wish to reign,
> Fantastic, fickle, fierce, and vain? . . .
> Fantastic as a woman's mood,
> And fierce as Frenzy's fever'd blood,
> Thou many-headed monster-thing,
> O who would wish to be thy king! (xxx)

Douglas is that early nineteenth-century Tory ideal, a dedicated aristocrat whose merits render democratic stirrings unnecessary and regain the mob's 'fealty'. His union of individual effort with inherited rank characterises other Scott heroes: Lovel in *The Antiquary* has the energy and responsibility of the protestant work ethic, winning respect by his own achievements, but also turns out to be the heir to a Catholic earldom. What is idiosyncratic in Scott's Tory vision of leadership is that he so often combines it with outlaw tradition. Douglas in the *Lady of the Lake* takes over from Robin Hood – and the modern radical agitator – the role of true people's hero. In endowing him with this function Scott turns him, like Ivanhoe, into an establishment hero with outlaw glamour. Douglas is at times both a woodland outlaw and an archer who can beat Robin Hood's feats with the people's own weapon, the longbow.

The sports/riot episode is followed by a sort of reprise: the King hears that another, real, outlaw, 'The outlaw'd chieftain, Roderick Ddu' and 'his rebellious crew', have joined his enemy. The revels are curtailed.

The poem introduces words associated with Robin Hood ballads while its worldview opposes that of the medieval ballads' humble yeoman outlaw. Both Douglas and Fitz-James (in 'hunting suit of Lincoln greens', 1 xxiii), spend time in the forest, and 'greenwood' and 'merrymen' recur.[13] A song repeats the phrase 'Merry it is in the good greenwood' (4 xii). This text is about outlaws but also about shape-changing: a virtuous knight can become an outlaw, a forest goblin turn back into a knight. Fairy green and outlaw green are paralleled – another Scottian way of neutralizing (into traditional minstrelsy) any political dynamics. A ballad sings of yearning to return to 'hunting the hart in forest green' (6 xxiv). Douglas's men are his 'merrymen' (4 iv) (erudite Scott knew this originally meant 'retainers', but for readers its primary resonance is inevitably of outlaws). Scott employs the romance topos of the king in disguise, but arrays his king like an outlaw: he reveals himself to Ellen thus:

> On him each courtier's eye was bent;
> Midst furs and silks, and jewels sheen,
> He stood, in simple Lincoln green.(6 xxvi)

Scott enjoys dressing up the establishment in romantic greenwood garb – shape-shifting in another form. Barczewski documents the early nineteenth-century passion for costume balls in her study of Robin Hood and Arthur in national consciousness.[14]

The outlaw role can be reduced to a glamorous wildness, a costume, performance or revels and sport. All these can enhance power and order, painting an image of leadership that can inspire popular support through adventurousness and social flexibility (like Richard I was sailing with the outlaw friar in *Ivanhoe*). *Rokeby* presents both Robin Hood and the King as actors.[15] The fancy-dress reappears in *Ivanhoe*. De Bracy exchanges 'his banqueting garments for a short green kirtle, with hose of the same cloth and colour, a leathern cap or headpiece, a short sword, a horn slung over his shoulder, a long-bow in his hand, and a bundle of arrows stuck in his belt'. While not exclusively outlaw garb, this inevitably recalls Robin Hood, underlined when John cries 'What mummery is this, De Bracy? . . . Is this a time for Christmas gambols and quaint maskings?' (chapter 14, 167). De Bracy has, though a Norman, complex and divided political views and Scott characteristically defines his costume change not in outlaw but nationalist terms: 'Norman knight in the dress of an English yeoman'. Soon after he disguises himself as an English outlaw for serous purposes.

Though *Ivanhoe* circumscribes Robin's role, the whole outlaw tradition clearly hovered in the background to composition. Small details illustrate this: the name 'Gandelyn' (128) from the ballad 'Robin and Gandelyn', and signs of inspiration from the Anglo-Norman romance of Fouke Fitz Waryn. This describes Fouke's outlawry and enmity toward King John. Fouke's legend resembles Robin Hood's and perhaps influenced its development.[16] Evidence for Scott's knowledge is his note on Brian de Bois-Gilbert's African squires, citing an episode in *Fouke* (unnamed by Scott).

> John of Rampayne, an excellent juggler and minstrel, [who] undertook to effect the escape of one Audulf de Bracy, by presenting himself in disguise at the court of the king, where he was confined. For this purpose, 'he stained his hair and his whole body entirely as black as jet, so that nothing was white but his teeth', and succeeded in imposing himself on the king as an Ethiopian minstrel.

The episode is one of several in *Fouke Fitz Waryn* whose hero is John of Rampaigne. A minstrel, resourceful fighter and trickster, like Little John he tricks enemies through disguise. Here Audulph de Bracy (perhaps inspiring Scott's use of the surname) is rescued by John of Rampaigne, penetrating Shrewsbury castle in minstrel disguise. This perhaps inspired the *Ivanhoe* episode where the jester Wamba disguises himself to rescue Cedric from Front-de-Boeuf's prison. Much in *Ivanhoe* suggests awareness of *Fouke*: the Norman setting; the delight in outlawry and disguise; the disguised hero winning at jousting, watched by his future bride; the outlaw and aristocrat opposing King John. The fictitious learned epistle attached to *Ivanhoe* claims its material came from an Anglo-Norman romance.[17]

Highlands and Wales

A Legend of the Wars of Montrose (1819) presents outlaws through contemporary cultural models of the Highlands. The topoi of the wild boy and the natural virtue of a savage people also contribute to its construction of the outlaw as, characteristically of Scott, a counterside to modern man. Modern man is represented more ambiguously in this novel than the outlaw, in the comic person of Dalgetty: pragmatic, materialistic and commercial, cynical, endowed with an absurd education, yet also brave and loyal – when he chooses individualistically his own allies. The novel shows Scott's fascination with the crossover between law-abiding man and outlaw: Allan McAuley becomes more savage than the outlaws.

The Betrothed (1825) revels in uncomplicated fashion in this stereotype of bandits as typical inhabitants of wild society and wild mountains. Its twelfth-century Norman heroine is abducted by 'Welsh banditti' in the Marches. The Italian word 'banditti' is symptomatic of the taste for romantic bandits in rugged scenery as part of the Romantic concept of sublime, wild landscape. The artist most associated with this taste was Salvator Rosa, but there are also examples from the early nineteenth century by Welsh painters or imagining such figures in Welsh landscapes, as the Welsh mountains, like the Lake District and Scotland, became British terrains that embodied the sublime for both tourists and artists. The Welsh, princes and banditti alike, are conceived in a style that mixes Salvator Rosa and the myth of the noble savage. The perils created by the bandits provide a Romantic backdrop for a meeting of star-crossed lovers. Perhaps once Scott left Scottish historical settings, where his personal familiarity and identification, even in antique scenarios, led to some acknowledgement of complexity in social binary oppositions, and he transferred his Romantic highland-outlaw paradigm to twelfth-century Wales, he found it easier to make the Celtic inhabitants of the British isles into representatives of the primitive 'Other', with naive virtues and naive weaknesses ('noise, fury, and devastation', 'engaged in private war with each other', 'peculiarly ardent in their temper', 'all the rude splendour and liberal indulgence of mountain hospitality', 'barbarous magnificence', a people vainglorious and delighting in bards' praise yet courteous amid their violence).[18] And these are the Welsh princes.

Scott's decision here to treat the Welsh, whether prince or outlaw, as 'Other', while his readers are guided towards sympathetic alignment with the Norman heroine and her associates, contrasts with Charles Kingsley's approach in one of the most popular Victorian novels about a medieval outlaw outside the oeuvre of Scott: *Hereward the Wake* (1877). Unlike Scott's readiness to treat national outlaws and rebels as 'Other', Kingsley re-imagines the medieval subversive's opposition to the (Norman) authorities of his own era as prefiguring a contemporary reader's sense of alienation from a past Catholic and feudal regime.

Rob Roy clearly constructs its outlaw hero within the cultural myths of the highlands and the noble savage: Rob is loyal and brave though tribal and primitive. Scott compares him to Robin Hood: 'a kind and gentle robber, and, while he took from the rich, was liberal in relieving the poor'; the last page calls him 'the Robin Hood of Scotland, the dread of the wealthy, but the friend of the poor'.[19] Rob Roy, like Locksley, has a circumscribed role and, despite appearing in the novel's name, is replaced as hero by a law-abiding protagonist destined to inherit an aristocratic title. Scott says Rob was a Jacobite, extending his 'operations against all whom he chose to consider as friendly to the revolutionary government'.[20] Bolton writes 'Scott loved "the gallant hero, Robin Hood . . . "', citing Lockhart.[21] But that love was apprehensive. As with other bellicose males – Denzil in *Rokeby* or Macintyre, the peppery highland soldier in *The Antiquary* – Scott limits Rob's power and his claims to serious respect. The most interesting of the male characters, the outlaws, do not star (the situation too of *Ivanhoe*'s female outsider, Rebecca). Scott uses various strategies to undermine the force of their very lawlessness: Locksley must be the most innately law-abiding outlaw in history; Rob Roy represents a primitive lifestyle, denizen of a different type of society from that of other characters, resembling an 'American Indian' and 'wild Arab chief'. He has the native American's 'wild virtues' and 'unrestrained license', like Scott's twelfth-century Welshmen.[22] Locksley belongs to the woods – though reluctantly. Rob Roy and the outlaws of *A Legend* belong to the Highlands: romantically wild but culturally colonized. Outlaws are politically less threatening the more they are figures of primitive morality: a strategy akin to that of presenting them as carnival actors. Tellingly Scott terms Rob's banditry 'pranks', like Robin Hood's.[23] Rob Roy is a mass of paradoxes: Scott knows historical facts about Rob Roy the bully, financial enforcer and blackmailer, but also presents him, as Ian Duncan observes, as 'half human' and 'half goblin', and resembling a bull or orang-utan.[24] He is described thus:

> mony a daft reik he has played—mair than wad fill a book, and a queer ane it wad be—as gude as Robin Hood, or William Wallace—a' fu' o' venturesome deeds and escapes, sic as folk tell ower at a winter-ingle in the daft days.

This is Scott's characteristic sliding, when dealing with outlaws, from full reality into ballad minstrelsy or carnival status. This passage's voice, significantly differentiated from Scott's own, expresses Scott's divided attitude to lawlessness:

> It's a queer thing o' me, gentlemen, that am a man o' peace mysell... it's a queer thing, I say, but I think the heiland blude o' me warms at thae daft tales, and while I like better to hear them than a word of profit, gude forgie me!—But they are vanities—sinfu' vanities—and, moreover, again the statute law—again the statute and gospel law.[25]

Rokeby's Bertram shows Scott enlisting the outlaw into his political theme of the necessity for hierarchy. The fugitive Bertram is invited to lead an outlaw band, perhaps reflecting the fourteenth-century romance *Gamelyn*, whose gently born fugitive hero is invited to become the outlaw king.[26] Outlaws seemingly prefer to defer to a member of the traditional ruling class, if lucky enough to encounter one in temporary woodland distress. *Gamelyn*'s structure is more amenable to Scott's worldview than medieval Robin Hood ballads: Gamelyn combines individualistic enterprise (and violent self-assertion) with gentle birth and an inheritance regained at the end. The notion that even outlaws need a leader and hierarchy, a favourite with Scott, runs counter to medieval ballads, where any attempt by Robin to impose conventional lordship is staunchly resisted. Scott prefaced chapter 32 of *Ivanhoe* with a verse of his own ('Old Play'), claiming:

> Trust me, each state must have its policies:
> Kingdoms have edicts, cities have their charters;
> Even the wild outlaw, in his forest walk,
> Yet keeps some touch of civil discipline...

Although willingly subordinate to his natural betters (Ivanhoe, King Richard), Scott's acceptable outlaw, Locksley, sits on a throne under the great oak, saying:

> in these glades I am monarch; they are my kingdom; and these my wild subjects would reck little of my power, were I, within my dominions, to yield place to mortal men. (chapter 32, 348)

He even uses the royal *we*. Scott envisages inevitable hierarchy repeated naturally through all levels of social order: a vision that would probably have aroused horror and contempt in authors of *Robin Hood and the Monk*, *Robin Hood and the Potter*, and *Robin Hood and Guy of Gisborne*, where Robin's men's loyalty is absolute but voluntary and a community of 'yeoman' is the political ideal.[27]

Rokeby demonstrates Scott's discomfort with outlaws. He is not in political sympathy and the writing chafes against even the traditional trope of greenwood merrymaking. These are men who have fled to the woods rather than submit to civil order: anarchic traitors, roundheads with no taste for religion allied with 'Cavaliers, whose souls . . . Spurn at the bonds of discipline' (Canto 3, xii). That disposes of any notion of outlawry representing alternative ideals. They betrayed their own causes because the associated duties were irksome.

Contrary to outlaw tradition, even their feasts are grim, the revelry of a 'desperate crew':

> There Guilt his anxious revel kept;
> There, on his sordid pallet, slept
> Guilt-born Excess, the goblet drain'd
> Still in his slumbering grasp retain'd. (Canto 3, xiv)

Greenwood conditions are not merry:

> Behold the group by the pale lamp,
> That struggles with the earthy damp. (Canto 3, xv)[28]

They lurk in a cavern: an image associated with revolutionary disorder in Scott's motto for the Robin Hood scene in *The Abbot*: 'the wild wind, escaping from its cavern' (see below).

They occasionally rally their spirits with outlaw song in something like the right spirit:

> But, hark! Our merry men so gay
> Troll forth another roundelay. (Canto 3, xxviii)

These songs rise briefly above Scott's bleak reformulation of outlaw life, being quite in the traditional register, with references to Lincoln green doublets and celebration of the humble lot of yeoman outlaws. As often, Scott uses inset songs, a stylistic substratum of popular culture, to present a worldview which potentially conflicts with the dominant ones of his text.[29] These greenwood songs occasionally voice something resembling the authentic spirit of that subversive celebration of freedom central to outlaw mythology.

The voice of freedom is not heard uncritically. Scott defines outlaw freedom as freedom from work, and a lifestyle that elevates the humble worker to the level of an aristocrat: overturning feudal order.

> Allan-a-Dale has no fagot for burning,
> Allan-a-Dale has no furrow for turning,
> Allan-a-Dale has no fleece for the spinning,
> Yet Allan-a-Dale has red gold for the winning . . .
> Allan-a-Dale was ne'er belted a knight,
> Though his spur be as sharp, and his blade be as bright,
> Allan-a-Dale is no baron or lord,
> Yet twenty tall yeomen will draw at his word;
> And the best of our nobles his bonnet will vail
> Who at Rere-cross on Stanmore meets Allan-a-Dale (Canto 3, xxx)

Outlawry here represents money-winning without work (the peasant's work being sentimentally pictured as his own acquisition of faggot, furrow, and fleece), and reversal of class, the outlaw rivalling the status of a 'belted knight'. Red gold suggests bloodstains on these profits. The noble doffs his hat to an erstwhile yeoman whose strong-arm tactics (spur, blade and army – mimicking a mounted knight) make him the terror of Stanmore. The outlaw's escape from work and rise in wealth, power and respect are not unequivocally approved by this ditty. Having allowed expression to a vision of radical improvement of the worker's lot, Scott calls the song (in case the ambivalences of its greenwood freedoms had escaped the reader) 'desperate merriment' and 'reckless glee', accompanied by drinking '[t]ill sense and sorrow both are drown'd' (Canto

3, xv). The key element underlying this disapproval is loosening of restraint, whether in revels, evasion of work or rebellion. Scott talks of 'idle hours' (xxix):

> When unemploy'd each fiery mate
> Is ripe for mutinous debate.[30]

It is the discourse of contemporary anti-radicalism. Later a young bandit, Edmund, suffers remorse: it was the attraction of 'minstrelsy' that turned a peasant into a bandit, when 'prank'd in garb of minstrelsy' he broke God's and Nature's laws, stirred on by his 'comrades' cheer': a life of 'powers misused, of passion's force, / Of guilt, of grief, and of remorse' (6, iii, v). Here is Scott's characteristic elision of 'minstrelsy' with unleashed anarchic violence and offences against divine and human law.

That motif of drunkenness removing any 'sense' from the rebel's demand for freedom is also used by Chaucer – another writer who, while celebrating conservative values, cannot resist depicting instabilities that threaten the myths on which they depend. Chaucer's Miller, a decade after the 1381 English Rising, is a fourteenth-century bolshie refusing to give deference to anyone and Chaucer neutralizes any claim of that subversive voice to be taken seriously by making the speaker drunk (as George Eliot makes farmer Dagley drunk in *Middlemarch*, chapter 37). Scott and Chaucer thus deny a rational basis to the desire for an easier lot by society's Allan-a-Dales, or to disrespect for established hierarchy. In the outlaw ballad of Alice Brand ('Merry it is in the good greenwood', Canto 4, xii–xv), a knight forced into outlawry spends his time in virtuous manual labour, cutting wood, building fences, bringing in firewood: a neat-handed Robinson Crusoe of the greenwood, while outlawed lady Alice makes cloaks from sheep's wool. Scott can apparently sympathize with outlaws only if disassociated from the spectre of discontent or disrespect.

Outlawry and anti-radicalism

Rokeby employs language associated with outlaw legend: 'greenwood' and 'merry men', yet portrays outlaws with suspicion. Denzil their leader is a coward and a crook who turns traitor and corrupts the young. His band consists of deluded Allan-a-Dales, simple men deflected into criminality from the profitable life of humble labour, together with selfish, dangerous ringleaders unworthy of respect. When treating it seriously, as historical political threat rather than pageant, Scott is as likely to associate outlaw life with treason as its traditional attribute of freedom.

An outright vision of the perils of misrule, linked with Robin Hood revelry, appears in *The Abbot* (1820). Unrest is here the mindless uproar of common people who, once they encounter skilful traditional authority, will respect it, be calmed and return to obedience. The historical setting is one of national disruption, the Dissolution. The change of political and ecclesiastical rule has overturned the status of monks. Scott describes monks electing their Abbot as now like outlaws, 'robbers who choose a leader'.[31] The bandit symbolizes hierarchy overturned. Correspondingly, the pageant erupting alarmingly into their conclave is one of dramatized outlaws and role-reversals, with a mocking jester as Abbot of Unreason and Monk of Misrule. In this context, political and theatrical, of traditional status reversed, the elected Abbot embodies Scott's political ideal: a leader who could reform mistakes from the previous administration and (like Douglas quelling the riot in *The Lady of the Lake*) command respectful submission of rebellious commons. Scott's Abbot presides in a Church of tyrannous superstition, but this makes it possible to isolate for praise his leadership qualities:

> Bold and enthusiastic, yet generous and forgiving – wise and skilful, yet zealous and prompt – he wanted but a better cause than the support of a decaying superstition . . . His brow was undeterred, and his step firm and solemn. (168)

His leadership is soon challenged: the Mass for his election is interrupted by tumult, an aggressive invasion by the lower

SCOTT AND THE OUTLAWS

orders, terrifying monks with 'dissonant clamour' (170), beating on the doors and demanding entrance (172). This riotous assault is defined characteristically: 'the shouts of the multitude, *now as in laughter, now as in anger* [emphasis added]', that combination seen in the mingling of Robin Hood games with aggression in *The Lady of the Lake*.

Scott builds up the awesomeness of the threatened invasion: loud roaring, hammering at the gates, fear of 'bloodletting'. The attackers reveal themselves:

> 'By whose authority do you require entrance?' said the Father.
>
> 'By authority of the right reverend Lord Abbot of Unreason', replied the voice from without. (103)

This is unexpected but reassuring though, in Scott's Tory paradigm, politically serious. Rebelliousness is 'unreason', the image employed for those drunken freedoms claimed by *Rokeby*'s outlaws – men lacking serious allegiance to political cause. The construction denies rationality to popular unrest.

'Masqueraders' enter, embodying normality overturned: men dressed as animals; characters from mumming plays; cross-dressed women and men; elders as children. They include 'a group of outlaws, with Robin Hood and Little John at their head' (105). The motives for rebellion are defined as an instinctive but unreasoned turbulence, whereas control is an effect of personality: a natural leader's psychological skill at controlling underlings, rather than any opposed political argument. The Abbot, in a canny political manoeuvre, redirects their mood and takes on himself the power to manipulate their obstreperousness. It works for a time, until they start demolishing the church fittings. This too is a 'freak', 'whim of the moment', 'indulgence', albeit a dangerous mood swing. The military arm of authority comes to the Abbot's aid: a mounted knight, Sir Halbert Glendinning quells the riot, telling the rioters that their actions are, themselves, analogous to popish superstition: a 'leprosy', a 'brutifying' licence that has 'misled' them. (115)

The political import is unmissable. One reveller, dressed as a dragon, shouts defiance at Sir Halbert, clearly designed by Scott as a St George, 'I hold myself as well born man as you'. (115) Without bothering to reply, the Knight simply fells the democrat with his lance's butt. Scott has already identified the crowd as the traditional unstable mob: '[t]he rabble, mutable as usual' alternate between obeying their new leader of 'unreason' and their traditional leader, the Abbot. Scott shows them, like children, suddenly cowed when their ringleader appears stabbed by one of the Abbot's entourage – a Wat Tyler moment – but they revive and are soon wrecking the church ('their wild caprice', 113). This scene, set in the sixteenth-century and complicated by the conflicting ecclesiastical sympathies, is a chillingly calculated political essay in the year after Peterloo. The people are 'wild and wilful', easily reduced to remorse, shame, even respect (190). They respond mindlessly to any leader, on any cause. Scott uses the image of a storm. Monks 'looked to their Abbot amid the tumult, with such looks as landsmen cast upon the pilot, when the storm is highest'(107). The chapter motto fuses natural, carnival and political wildness:

> Not the wild billow, when it breaks its barrier –
> Not the wild wind, escaping from its cavern –
> Not the wild fiend, that mingles both together,
> And pours their rage upon the ripening harvest,
> Can match the wild freaks of this mirthful meeting –
> Comic yet fearful – droll, and yet destructive. (*The Conspiracy*)

This extract, with telling (invented) title, mingles revelry, destructive Nature, and treason, prefacing a performance, with peasants playing Robin Hood and 'unreason', which personifies revolution, to the conservative imagination: 'comic yet fearful – droll, and yet destructive'. Scott's oxymorons, comic/fearful, droll/destructive, epitomize that familiar pattern in his writing of interchangeability between Robin Hood as cultural icon ('minstrelsy') and harbinger of serious political violence. In Scott's anti-Whig propaganda articles, published as *The Visionary* in 1819, radicals are a 'rabblement' of 'rascally banditti', led by Rob Radical, a Robin Hood avatar. Its Preface says that demands for universal male suffrage should be scorned because 'the bulk and mass of the population are rendered incapable of the due exercise of an elective franchise by their want of education and violence of passions'.[32]

Knight argues that Scott avoids allowing Robin Hood much scope in *Ivanhoe* through fear of his power, substituting the aristocratic Ivanhoe as a politically safer hero. Yet the power of the outlaw in a more diffused sense, is surprisingly dominant in *Ivanhoe*. Ivanhoe, even if invented to draw fire and glamour away from the radical outlaw tradition, is constructed on a Robin Hood model: that which developed during the seventeenth- and eighteenth-centuries, of the Earl of Huntington disposed and taking to the woods in the disguise of Robin Hood, just as Wilfred is disguised and joins with outlaws. The opening paragraph signals how strongly the Robin Hood tradition will haunt this text.

> In that pleasant district of merry England which is watered by the river Don, there extended in ancient times a wide forest, covering the greater part of the beautiful hills and valleys which lie between Sheffield and the pleasant town of Doncaster. The remains of this extensive wood are still to be seen at the noble seats of Wentworth, of Wharncliffe Park, and around Rotherham ... here were fought many of the desperate battles during the Civil Wars of the Roses, and here also flourished in ancient times those bands of gallant outlaws whose deeds have been rendered so popular in English song. (Chapter 1, 15)

Scott starts with 'merry England', forests and outlaws, and Sheffield and Doncaster – near the setting for the *Gest of Robyn Hode,* yet he uses this setting not to introduce outlaws but Norman tyranny against Saxons. It heralds a racial war not class war. His first scene brings on not outlaws walking through these forest glades but the loyal serfs Wamba and Gurth. Their discontent and social alienation are rendered justifiable, in a conservative nineteenth-century perspective, as those of an oppressed nation.[33] The outlaws of this society, Scott insists, are really Saxon yeomen loyal to their masters, forced outside the law by Norman forest laws: they 'respect the persons and property' of men like Cedric and Athelstane, their rightful leaders (chapter 19, 159).

These *Ivanhoe* serfs step onto a greenwood stage prepared for outlaws, and since the outlaw in Scott's fictions is often conceived in a problematic relationship to the spectre of plebeian discontent, we need to examine the novel's depiction of serfs. The representatives of non-outlaw peasants are, respectively, an ultra-loyal older feudal servant, Gurth, and a jester. Gurth, like the misguidedly loyal masses in *The Lady of the Lake*, mindlessly rioting about their master's dog (and therefore requiring natural aristocratic control), even becomes rebellious from a mistaken degree of loyalty to the Rotherwood ruling family. Like the underlings of *The Lady of the Lake,* his loyalty is linked with a dog, Fangs. Jester Wamba, 'son of Witless', plays a courageous, resourceful part in the war against the barons and has a rational mind and tongue of his own. He performs the part of a quasi-outlaw, being given by Scott the role, traditionally that of an outlaw in outlaw literature, of entering an enemy's stronghold in disguise, to spring a confederate from gaol. Making this capable but plebeian hero a jester Scott renders him safely insubstantial. Neither his heroism or criticism of his betters command the respect they might if Scott had not arrayed him in cap and bells. This considerable participant in guerrilla war against authority is neutralized by being a fool and performer. Unreason and carnival: we have seen it all before.

The first paragraph's language reclaims forest wilderness and outlaw territory for a later aristocracy. The outlaws are vaguely 'gallant' and the wild places have been, since their time, safely restrained, imparked in 'noble seats', the aristocratic re-ordering of the landscape (15). It is the same with *Ivanhoe*'s outlaws: their charisma and martial threat have been imparked. Robin Hood is subservient to king and lords; an aristocrat has appropriated much of his greenwood anti-establishment power. It is interesting to compare this landscape with the exploration of the vision of the mansion as source of order in landscape in Nigel Everett's study *The Tory View of Landscape*.[34]

Yet Scott's plot exploits the frissons created by scenarios familiar from outlaw tales: rich men who abuse authority ride through a forest bristling with hidden enemies and there is tension between two terrains, castle and forest – the law-officers' territory and that ruled by outlaws. In Scott's nationalistic reformulation the Saxon rulers resemble outlaws, dispossessed of position, opposing authority. Scott imbues the Saxon world with the forest-power of outlaw tradition: he prefaces our first experience of Saxons with a description of ancient oaks, that Scottian image of traditional political order, yet in this Saxon context absorbing the outlaw's forest as well. Cedric's manor, deep in the woods is, though a house, called 'Rotherwood': a fine wooden building, with wooden beams 'rough-hewn from the forest', and oaken furniture (chapter 3, 31). Cedric is even metaphorically an old tree: 'Let the old tree wither . . . so the stately hope of the forest be preserved', he says, sacrificing himself for his lord (chapter 26, 269). Note 'stately': for Scott the remedy for bad authority is never radicalism but righteous hierarchical rule.

Attraction and apprehension of the outlaw remain always in tension and without permanent resolution. Outlaws' willing submission to authority may be a desired ideal, in that symbolic picture under the oak in Locksley's forest. But that picture is not static. Locksley does not end as the King's courtier – any more than the Robin of the *Gest* could. Scott ends by returning Locksley to the ballad tradition:

> As for the rest of Robin Hood's career, as well as the tale of his treacherous death, they are to be found in those black-letter garlands, once sold at the low and easy rate of one halfpenny. (chapter 41, 475).

This is an evasive way of concluding Locksley's part in the novel. A generous view, however, might also interpret it as unevasive, acknowledging the recidivist power of outlawry. As legitimate authority is restored at the denouement, uniting warring nationalist tensions, and the Saxons' alternative hierarchy comes into willing subordination to rejuvenated legitimate rule, the outlaw is not resolved into lawfulness. He never could be, of course, but the impossibility of any other ending also acknowledges instabilities discernable in Scott's political model. That model often employs the outlaw to represent a triple theory about radicalism: first, the unserious and irrational basis of popular discontent; secondly, the dangerous threat it poses if not kept under control; thirdly, the innate proclivity of the people, if rightly handled, to accept traditional rulers when these show enough merit to deserve submission. Scott creates leaders: aristocrats who have the attributes of outlaws and outlaws who prefer ruling as greenwood kings to the communal 'fellowship' of medieval ballads.

Scott returns his Robin Hood, however, to 'minstrelsy' – to culture rather than political action – where, paradoxically, he may be dismissable as insubstantial but remains eternally subversive and alluring, playing what Scott terms his 'pranks'. It is an end that admits the presence and recalcitrance of conflicting elements in a conservative model, just as Scott's final decisions about Rebecca admit instabilities inherent in the order of marriage.

NOTES

1. See William Gaunt, *Bandits in a Landscape: A Study of Romantic Painting from Caravaggio to Delacroix* (London: The Studio, 1937); Hobsbawm; Renato Mammucari, *I Briganti* (Città di Castello, 2000). Eric G. Walker, *Scott's Fiction and the Picturesque, Salzburg Studies in English Literature, Romantic Reassessments* (Salzburg: Institut für Anglistik und Amerikanistik, 1982) discusses Scott's response to Salvator Rosa, citing Waverley's readiness to imagine himself in a Rosa landscape complete with 'banditti', p. 7.
2. Quoted in *Rob Roy*, ed. Arthur T. Flux (London: Black, 1903), p. x.
3. See Graham McMaster, *Scott and Society* (Cambridge: Cambridge University Press, 1981), pp. 155–65.
4. *Ivanhoe*, ed. Graham Tulloch, Edinburgh edition of the Waverley Novels (Edinburgh: Edinburgh University Press, 1998), ch. 41, p. 365.
5. See *The Visionary*, ed. Peter Garside, Regency Reprints 1 (Cardiff: Cardiff University, 1984), p. viii. On the radicals' Robin Hood see Knight 1994, pp. 153–70.
6. Knight 1994, pp. 154–70.
7. Helen Phillips, 'Remembering Edward I', in Anne Marie Darcy and Alan J. Fletcher (eds), *Studies in Late Medieval and Early Renaissance Texts in Honour of John Scattergood: 'The Key of all Good Remembrance'* (Dublin: Four Courts, 2005), pp. 270–86, 276–9.
8. On Scott's shifts between dualities see Marinella Salri, 'Ivanhoe's Middle Ages', in Piero Boitani and Anna Torti (eds), *Medieval and Pseudo-Medieval Literature*, The J. A. W. Bennett Mcmorial Lecture, Perugia, 1982-3 (Tübingen and Cambridge: D. S. Brewer, 1984), pp. 149–60.
9. Knight 1994, p. 176.
10. *Ivanhoe*, ed. Graham Tulloch; Locksley: 'the St Christopher at my baldric', (chapter 31, 259); Chaucer's Yeoman: 'A Christopher on his breast . . . A horn he bar, the bawdryk was of grene', *Canterbury Tales*, I 115–16.
11. Scott gets Little John ('my lieutenant') out of the story – sending him to Scotland (367) – perhaps fearing his obstreperous character would

12   strengthen the force of the outlaw world and give Robin an important alternative relationship to that with his superiors.

12   Scott established this motif for the later legend, though he must have known a now-lost ballad: the split-arrow motif only resurfaced for modern scholars with publication of the Forresters Manuscript, see Knight 2001, 59. In *Ivanhoe*, chap. 13, Locksley does it.

13   For James as hunter and hunted see Ralph Stewart, 'The Enchanted World of The Lady of the Lake', *Scottish Literary Journal*, 22:2 (1995), 5–13.

14   Stephanie Barczewski, *Myth and National Identity in Nineteenth-Century Britain: The Legends of King Arthur and Robin Hood* (Oxford: Clarendon Press, 2000).

15   See Philip Bolton, 'Playing Rob Roy as Robin Hood', in J. H. Alexander and David Hewitt (eds), *Scott in Carnival: Selected Papers from the Fourth International Scott Conference, Edinburgh, 1991* (Aberdeen: St Andrews University Press, 1993), pp. 478–90, p. 479.

16   *Fouke le Fitz Waryn*, ed. E. J. Hathaway, P. T. Ricketts, C. A. Robson, and A. D. Wilshere, Anglo-Norman Text Society (Oxford: Blackwell, 1975).

17   Dedicatory Epistle to the Rev. Dr Dryasdust, F.A.S., 531.

18   *The Betrothed and the Talisman*, ed. Andrew Lang, The Waverley Novels (London: Macmillan 1904), pp. 2, 10, 322–41.

19   *Rob Roy*, ed. Ian Duncan, World's Classics (Oxford: Oxford University Press, 1998), pp. 20, 452.

20   Ibid. p. 19.

21   Quoted in Bolton, 'Rob Roy', p. 479.

22   *Rob Roy*, Author's Introduction, pp. xxiv–xxv.

23   Ibid. p. 5, 31.

24   Ibid., pp. xxiv–xxv. On analogies between the highlands, Native Americans, and the 'instinctual life of man' in Scott, see Alexander Welsh, *The Hero of the Waverley Novels* (New York: Athenaeum, 1963), pp. 82–92.

25   Ibid., p. 304. Repeated 'queer' and 'daft' suggest irrationality in the material's attraction.

26   Scott calls it 'the Cokes Tale of Gamelyn ascribed to Chaucer', note on Canto 5 xxiii, *The Lady of the Lake*, which also cites the *Gest of Robyn Hode*.

27   See quarrels between Little John and Robin on the issue in *Robin Hood and the Monk* and *Robin Hood and Guy of Gisburne*. 'Yemanrey' and 'felischepe' apparently represent a new concept of fraternity between well-thinking men in *Robin Hood and the Potter*.

28   *Harold the Dauntless* begins Canto 2, 'Tis merry in greenwood . . . in the gladsome month of May' but 'Less merry, perchaunce, is the fading leaf'.

29   On songs as the deepest substratum in Scott's layered narratives see Kathryn Sutherland, 'Fictional Economies: Adam Smith, Walter Scott and the Nineteenth-Century Novel', *English Literary History*, 54 (1987), 97–127.

30 'But war had silenced rural trade', p. 3, xiv.
31 *The Abbot*, ed. Christopher Johnson, Edinburgh Edition of the Waverley Novels (Edinburgh: Edinburgh University Press, 2000).
32 *The Visionary*, pp. 25–30, 12.
33 Knight 1994, pp. 175–6.
34 Paul Mellon Centre for Studies in British Art (New Haven and London: Yale University Press, 1994), esp. pp. 91–122.

Sketches by a Green Crayon: Washington Irving, Robin Hood and the Emerging American Frontier

MARCUS A. J. SMITH AND †JULIAN N. WASSERMAN

Irving and the anxieties of a postcolonial America

Underlying the writings of Washington Irving are a pair of post-colonial anxieties which, though they reach out in two opposing directions, converge in the American author's interest in the Middle Ages and, more specifically, Robin Hood. To the east lay England and, therefore, a historical and political order rejected by the American Revolution. To the west lay America's future in a frontier full of promise but with no past to guide its exploration and colonization. For Irving's persona, Geoffrey Crayon, England is characterized by 'crumbling monuments of past ages' ('The Author' *BH*, p. 8).[1] By contrast, Crayon's America is a country where 'history was in a manner of speaking in anticipation . . . where everything pointed to the future rather than the past' ('The Author' *BH*, p. 8). Geographically expressed, these contrasting images of past and future to both the east and the west of America's Atlantic seaboard symbolize two conflicting desires of post-revolutionary America. But paradoxically beneath this desire for freedom and independence from the past is a contradictory desire for recognition by, approval of, and ultimately reconciliation with the 'parental' colonizing authority thrown off by the previous generation. Clearly, British approbation matters to Irving – and many of his contemporaries – even as he claims to be writing American works aimed at American audiences.

Pulled in these two directions, Irving mediates the antipathies between England and her former colonies by synthesizing an historical model for American development that combines Old World tradition with New World frontier vitality. In searching for what Henry Steele Commager would memorably label 'a usable past',[2] Irving chooses a pluperfect one – namely the British Middle Ages – in this case a politically 'safe' past beyond the immediate colonial order that had been rejected by the American Revolution. Moreover, in searching that medieval past for a figure to mediate between American frontier virtue and the noble traditions of England, Irving repeatedly turns to the rebellious Earl of Huntingdon, the noble-turned-outlaw living among common people in the forest. Indeed, for Irving's purposes (as his persona Geoffrey Crayon repeatedly laments), Robin Hood represents a particularly safe and acceptable past, the May Day traditions of Robin and Marian as well as the morris dancers, which to him seemed to be rapidly passing from the English consciousness, so that their cultural restoration in America might not seem a treasonous attachment to a past recently rejected.

Irving and the Robin Hood legend

Irving maintained a life-long interest in the greenwood outlaw. As a boy he was, according to George S. Hellman, deeply drawn to tales of the outlaw: 'the lure [of Pilgrim's Progress] centered for Irving in its adventurous quality. For the same reason, "Robin Hood", "Sinbad the Sailor", "Robinson Crusoe", and "Orlando Furioso" thrilled the Deacon's son'.[3] In 1832 (when Irving was 49-years-old) that interest had clearly not waned as he wrote to Charles R. Leslie: 'Behold me in the ancient hereditary mansion of Lord Byron, and in the very midst of the haunts of Robin Hood.'[4] The same enthusiasm is reflected in his letter to his sister, Catherine Paris as Irving makes repeated references to travelling to:

> the centre of Robin Hoods country, what once was merry Sherwood forest; though now it is an open country. There are some tracts of the forest, however, remaining in ancient wildness, with immense oaks, several hundred years old; mostly shattered and hollow, and inhabited by Jackdaws, I . . . rode through the green glades of these monumental forests and pictured to myself Robin Hood, and all his renowned band of outlaws; and have visited many points of the

neighborhood which still bear traces of him, such as Robin Hoods chair – Robin Hoods stable – His . . . &c &c. and I have a line of Robin Hood hills in view from the window of my apartment – I am thus in the midst of a poetical region.[5]

That such 'haunts' were the focus of his writing is seen in his letter of 20 January 1832 in which Irving wrote to his brother Peter:

> I have not altogether lost my time, however, for I have taken copious notes about the Abbey – the neighborhood – Lord Byron (&c) Robin Hood &c and have materials for a very popular little volume whenever I find leisure or inclination to turn them to account. I have in fact some scenes & anecdotes that will make exquisite little sketches.[6]

Indeed Irving is so familiar with the greenwood outlaw that his persona, Geoffrey Crayon might describe an 'Ancient Christmas costumed ball' in *Bracebridge Hall* by noting that a:

> young officer appeared as Robin Hood, in a sporting dress of Kendall green, and a foraging cap with a gold tassel. The costume, to be sure, did not bear testimony to deep research . . . The fair Julia hung on his arm in a pretty rustic dress, as 'Maid Marian'. ('The Christmas Dinner' *BH*, pp. 959–60)

Robin Hood in Irving's time: Scott, Ritson and Evans

Irving's own 'deep research' into the lore and legends of Robin Hood is evident throughout his work and was part of a fundamental turning back to the legends in Irving's lifetime. Robin Hood was in the air in a way he had never been before. Hellman notes Irving's childhood fascination with adventure narratives including Robin Hood. His adult interest may have been stimulated by his connection with Walter Scott. For example, Irving visited Sir Walter Scott in 1817. During this visit they became close friends,[7] and some twenty years later Irving turned this visit to Scott into what Lockhart terms 'a delightful essay' (*Journals*, III 180–90).

At the time of Irving's visit, Scott was hard at work on his own anti-English outlaw, Rob Roy, who as an historically based political model might be for the Scots what Robin Hood would be for Americans. Scott must have shared his interest in

Robin Hood with the younger American writer. Later, Irving was no doubt familiar with Scott's portrayal of the English bandit in *Ivanhoe,* which was in great part based on Joseph Ritson's monumental 1795 collection of Robin Hood ballads.[8]

To appreciate the importance of Ritson's collection for Irving and his age, consider Dobson and Taylor's assessment that: 'The rehabilitation of Robin Hood was essentially the work of one man, Joseph Ritson . . . [who] made Robin Hood intellectually as well as socially respectable for the first time in history' (54–5). Irving certainly must have known of Ritson. That Ritson's Robin Hood was particularly suitable for Irving's frontier America, is evident in Dobson and Taylor's further assertion that '[n]ot only did [Ritson] popularize and legitimize the study of Robin Hood, he also produced a highly influential interpretation of the hero', because Ritson was 'the first writer to convert Robin Hood into a thoroughly ideological hero', one who embodied the 'sentiments . . . of the French Revolution',[9] so that 'the long and still continuing interpretation of the forest outlaw as an apostle of popular liberty only seriously began with Joseph Ritson' (p. 56). Scott had a remarkable relationship with 'mad pedant' Ritson who put his marvellous learning at the complete disposal of Scott the northern balladwriter while Scott worked on *Minstrelsy*,[10] which Ritson termed 'the most valuable literary treasure in his possession' (*Journals*, I, pp. 323–4).[11]

Another immediate source of Robin Hood lore for Irving was Thomas Evans's influential 1777 volume, *Old Ballads, Historical and Narrative* (later editions 1784 and 1810),[12] which contains 28 ballads forming the core of the Robin Hood corpus. In fact, Irving cites 'Evans' Ballads' directly in the epigram to *Bracebridge Hall*'s essay, 'Bachelors'. Irving's introduction to Evans may have been through Scott whose enthusiasm for Evans is attested to in Lockhart by a 'schoolfellow' who 'recollects the eagerness with which [Scott] thus made himself master of Evans's Ballads, shortly after their publication' (I, p. 118). Or it might have been Evans himself who steered Irving to Ritson, referring in his headnote to 'The Pedigree Education and Marriage of Robin Hood . . .' to Ritson's volume as 'the most complete collection of everything that relates to [Robin Hood], a work evincing great research, and possessing considerable merit'.[13]

Irving's fascination with outlaw heroes

Irving's considerable knowledge of both Robin Hood and his place in English folkways was complemented by a similar life-long fascination with Robin Hood-like bandits. In his journals for 1823–4, Irving writes of being 'preoccupied with reading and writing "robber stories"' (April Wed. 7–Fri. 9, pp. 162–5 and May Thurs. 13–Tues. 18, pp. 184–5). Indeed, such robbers emerge throughout his works. For example, this vivid description of the Italian banditti in *Tales of a Traveler* is extraordinarily reminiscent of Robin Hood:

> The Italian robbers are a desperate class of men that have almost formed themselves into an order of society. They wear a kind of uniform, or rather costume, which openly designates their profession . . . They range over a great extent of wild country, along the chain of the Apennines bordering on difficult states; they know all the difficult passes, the short cuts for retreat, and the impracticable forests of the mountain summits, where no force dare follow them. They are secure of the good will of the inhabitants of those regions, a poor and semi-barbarous race, whom they never disturb and often enrich. Indeed, they are considered as a sort of illegitimate heroes among the mountain villages, and in certain frontier towns where they dispose of their booty. Thus countenanced, and sheltered and secure in the fastnesses of their mountains, the robbers have set the weak police of the Italian states at defiance. It is in vain that their names and descriptions are posted on the doors of country churches, and rewards offered for them alive or dead. ('The Inn at Terracina',' 'Part III: The Italian Banditi' *TT*, p. 571)

Irving's post-colonial tensions and literary anxieties

In order to understand Robin Hood's central place in Irving's imagination, we must revisit the dynamic well-spring of Irving's work, the antipathy, the disease between England and her former colonies. Both *The Sketch Book* and *Bracebridge Hall* begin with accounts of the chasm between the eastern and western shores of the Atlantic. The Preface to *The Sketch Book* begins with an account of 'the severity with which American productions had been treated by the British press' (p. 737). The antipathies between England and America clearly go far beyond matters of literary taste or even revolutionary politics. Irving at the outset of both *The Sketch Book* and *Bracebridge Hall* sets forth the essential differences between the two nations. In *The Sketch Book*'s 'The Author's Account of Himself', Irving's persona, Geoffrey Crayon, describes the manner in which he has personally felt the counterbalancing pull of these two polar nations:

> I visited various parts of my own country, and had I been merely a lover of fine scenery, I should have felt little desire to seek elsewhere its gratification, for on no other country have charms of nature been more prodigally lavished . . . no – never need an American look beyond his own country for sublime natural scenery.

But Europe held forth charms of stories and poetical association. There were to be seen the masterpieces of art, the refinements of highly cultivated society, the quaint peculiarities of ancient and local custom. My native country was full of useful promise; Europe was rich in accumulated treasures of age. Her very ruins told the history of times gone by, and every mouldering stone was a chronicle (pp. 743–4).

In *Bracebridge Hall*'s 'The Author', the same duality of attraction – to old and new, to art/high culture and nature, to the past and the future – is similarly set forth:

> But what more especially attracts his notice are those peculiarities which distinguish an old country and an old state of society from a new one. I have never yet grown familiar enough with the crumbling monuments of past ages, to blunt the intense interest with which I at first beheld them. Accustomed always to scenes where history was, in a manner, in anticipation; where every thing in art was new and progressive, and pointed to the future rather than the past . . . (p. 8)

Irving, in both instances above recasts the juxtaposition, not as an external clash of sovereign and separate nations but rather as a conflict of *experiential* emotions and attractions within an individual, a divided self. The disease between the two impulses is by definition an unnatural state. Hence the reconciliation must be made through a new synthesis generated by a new experience of the other, which in this formulation is not really an 'alien other' but an as yet unperceived 'missing' part. 'To a man from a young country', Irving can advise, 'all old things are in a manner new; and he may surely be excused in being a little curious about antiquities, whose native land, unfortunately, cannot boast of a single ruin' ('The Author' *BH*, p. 11). To the old, his own experience leads to a congruent although counter-directional claim:

> In traveling about our motley country, I am often reminded of Ariosto's account of the moon, in which the good paladin Astolpho found everything garnered up that had been lost on earth. So I am apt to imagine that many things lost in the Old World are treasured up in the new; having been handed down from generation to generation, since the early days of the colonies. A European antiquary, therefore, curious in his researches after the ancient and almost obliterated customs and usages of his country would do well to put himself upon the track of some early band of emigrants, follow them across the Atlantic, and rummage among their descendants on our shores. ('The Creole Village', p. 45)

In an early essay in *The Sketch Book*, 'English Writers on America', Irving notes the 'virulent national prejudices' (p. 792) only to plea that:

> Above all, let us not be influenced by any angry feelings so far as to shut our eyes to the perception of what is excellent and amiable in the English character. We are a young people, necessarily an imitative one, and must take our examples and models in great degree, from existing nations in Europe. There is no country more worthy of our study than England (p. 793).

The journey to reconciliation through appropriation

Indeed, the appropriation, the taking of models, in particular literary models, is the means by which Irving might affect reconciliation. His 'Preface' to his revised edition of *The Sketch Book* notes with great joy the reception that his work, although unintended for a British readership, has received abroad, demonstrating the ability of literature, and in particular, his own writing to bring together the two nations, despite their seeming antipathies. In *Bracebridge Hall*, Irving comments directly and effusively on the reception which the earlier *Sketch Book* received among British critics:

> When I first published my former writings, it was with no hope of gaining favor in English eyes, for I little thought they were to become current out of my own country; and had I merely sought popularity among my own country; and had I merely sought popularity among my own countrymen, I should have taken a more direct and obvious way, by gratifying rather than rebuking the angry feeling that were then prevalent against England.

And:

> And here let me acknowledge my warm, my thankful feelings, at the effect produced by one of my trivial lubrications. I allude to the essay in the Sketch-Book, on the subject of the literary feuds between England and America. I cannot express the heartfelt delight I have experienced, at the unexpected sympathy and approbation with which those remarks have been received on both sides of the Atlantic. ('Author's Farewell' *BH*, p. 373)

Such models then are, to Irving, most often literary. As he sets out on the voyage which is to produce *The Sketch Book*, Crayon casts the voyage in explicitly literary terms:

> As I saw the last blue line of my native land fade away like a cloud on the horizon, it seemed to me as if I had closed one volume of the world and its concerns, and had time for meditation before I opened another. ('The Voyage' *SB*, pp. 746–7)

Literature, by its nature, is for Irving the place where such reconciliation of old and new is affected. Nowhere is this made more clear than in *The Sketch Book*'s account of the British Library:

> I was, in fact, in the reading room of the great British library, an immense collection of volumes of all ages and languages, many of them now forgotten, and most of which are seldom read: one of these sequestered pools of obsolete literature, to which modern authors repair, and draw buckets full of classic lore, or 'pure English undefiled' wherewith to swell their own scanty rills of thought'. ('The Art of Bookmaking' *SB*, p. 809)

Taking this idea even further, Irving combines the old high culture of the European book with the natural process of the renewal of the American forest:

> After all, thought I, may not this pilfering disposition be implanted in authors for wise purposes; may it not be the way in which providence has taken care that the seeds of knowledge and wisdom shall be preserved from age to age, in spite of the inevitable decay of works in which they were first produced, birds which are 'nature's carriers to disperse and perpetuate her blessings. In like manner the beauties and fine thoughts of ancient and obsolete writers are caught up by these flights of predatory authors and cast forth to flourish and bear fruit in a remote and distant tract of time. Many of their works, also, undergo a kind of metempsychosis and spring up under new forms, What was formerly a ponderous history, revives in the shape of a romance – an old legend changes into a modern play, and a sober phylosophical treatise, furnishes the body for a whole series of sparkling essays. Thus it is in the clearing of our American woodlands; where we burn down a forest of stately pines, a progeny of dwarf oaks start up in their place; and we never see the prostrate trunk of a tree, mouldering into the soil, but it gives birth to a whole tribe of fungi'. ('The Art of Bookmaking' *SB*, pp. 810–11)

Pilfering, poaching and other post-colonial intertextualities

Extending the literary metaphor for such 'pilfering', for Irving, England again becomes a volume whose pages can provide the model needed to restore the divided (post-colonial) self by reconciling its divergent impulses:

> We may thus place England before us as a perpetual volume of reference, wherein are recorded sound deductions from ages of experience; and while we avoid the errors and absurdities which have crept into the page, we may draw from thence golden maxims of practical wisdom wherewith to strengthen and to embellish our national character. ('English Writers on America' *SB*, p. 794)

What model did Irving have in mind as a means 'to embellish [the American] national character'? The prototype is found in the writers busily at work in the reading room of the British Library. Recall that Irving describes these regenerators as 'pilfering'. Indeed, at the end of his stay at the library, he concludes his chapter on 'The Art of Bookmaking' by resorting to the same metaphor in order to describe his own activities:

> The librarian now stepped up to me and demanded whether I had a card of admission. At first I did not comprehend him, but soon found out that the library was a kind of literary 'preserve', subject to game laws, and that no one must presume to hunt there without special license and permission. In a word, I stood convicted of being an arrant poacher, and was glad to make a precipitate retreat, lest I should have a whole pack of authors let loose on me. ('The Art of Bookmaking' *SB*, p. 814)

Writers, Irving included, seem to share the common trait of poaching. In fact in his lifetime Irving was accused of 'plagiarism' and goes so far as to answer the charge in a footnote to 'The Historian' in *Bracebridge Hall*.[14] As a 'poacher' Irving sees himself in good company, no less than Shakespeare. In *The Sketch Book*'s 'Stratford-on Avon', Geoffrey Crayon goes in search of the Bard, only to find neither poet nor courtier, but rather the young Shakespeare who is caught poaching a deer from Sir Thomas Lucy. Of all the sights to be seen at Shakespeare's birthplace, 'the shattered stock of the matchlock with which Shakespeare shot the deer' is the one that catches the poet's eye. ('Stratford-on-Avon' *SB*, p. 984) This leads him to aver that such poaching was, no doubt, an early sign of the 'pilfering' nature of any maker of books:

> Various attempts have been made by his biographers to soften and explain away this early transgression of the poet; but I look upon it as one of those thoughtless exploits natural to his situation and turn of mind . . . It is often a turn up of a die, in the gambling freaks of fate, whether a natural genius shall turn out a great rogue or a great poet; and had not Shakespeare's mind fortunately taken a literary bias, he might have as daringly transcended all civil, as he has all dramatic laws . . . To him the poaching in Sir Thomas Lucy's park was doubtless like a foray to a Scottish Knight, and struck his eager, and yet untamed, imagination, as something delightfully adventurous. ('Stratford-on-Avon' *SB*, p. 990)

The next step is the author's imaginative reconstruction of Sir Thomas holding court over the young poacher who has just been brought in by the watchful gamekeeper who has apprehended him (p. 999).

Remarkably, *The Sketch Book*'s account of the imaginatively reconstructed trial of the young Shakespeare has its direct counterpart in the experiences of Master Crayon at Bracebridge Hall. There the poacher is a gypsy, one Starlight Tom, who is similarly apprehended by Old Christy and the gamekeeper (p. 207). For his part, the Squire has in the past 'wink[ed] at such deeds', because the poacher is 'expert at all kinds of games, a great shot with the cross-bow, and the best morrice dancer in the country' ('Gipsies' *BH*, p. 208), a fact repeated in a subsequent essay:

> 'The culprit . . . had found great favour in [the Squire's] eyes, as I have already observed, from the skill he had at various times displayed in archery, morrice dancing, and other obsolete accomplishments.' ('The Culprit' *BH*, p. 285)

Accused by one 'Ready Money Jack', the poacher is defended by 'poor Slingsby [who] spoke more from the heart than the head, and was evidently actuated merely by general sympathy for every poor devil in trouble, and a liberal toleration for all kinds of vagabond existence' (p. 286). In the end, Tom the poacher, is temporarily jailed in the upper loft of the tower of an 'out-house', yet despite the best efforts and watchful eyes of his nemesis the game-warder, Tom makes an escape, vanishing in trickster-like fashion.

This last poacher points to the model to which Irving ultimately resorts, the greatest poacher of them all, Robin Hood. Although, Starlight Tom, unlike Robin and Shakespeare, poaches a sheep rather than someone else's deer, the gypsy poacher is clearly an avatar of the greenwood outlaw. The basic elements are all there: the expert skill at archery, the gamekeeper nemesis, the trickster escape. There is even the sense of nature and freedom set against a growing and pernicious mercantilism in the person of his accuser, 'Ready Money Jack', along with the legal and ethical ambiguities generated by the 'social bandit' whose court defence is 'more from the heart than the head'. Most importantly, there is the repeated association of Starlight Tom with the morris dances and the May games, activities which Irving, through Crayon, explicitly linked with the Greenwood outlaw.

In fact, this link with the May Day festivities is what makes for Irving a Robin Hood who is a safe and usable model, one that can be imposed on emerging America without undue capitulation to the regime just cast off a generation before. In short, the morris dances hearken back to a lost pre-colonial 'Golden Age',[15] an England unlike the one thrown off in 1776, one in which there would be only minimal differences between itself and present-day America.

Rip Van Winkle: mediating between colonial past and post-colonial present

An immediate example of Irving's overt concern with such temporal mediation is *The Sketch Book*'s Rip Van Winkle, who is lured by gnomes who live in the wilderness (one is tempted to say diminutive Robin Goodfellows or little Merry Men)[16] into a 20-year sleep that carries him into a new era. Because Rip is a recent pre-revolutionary brought into a post revolutionary America, there is chaos upon his return.

A safe, usable past: Irving and the Middle Ages

What becomes clear is that a figure brought into and accepted by American culture must be a remote one. Here as elsewhere throughout his works and journals, Irving demonstrates a propensity for imaginatively translating himself into the Middle Ages, as in his earlier cited letter regarding his visit to 'the centre of Robin Hood's country'. For example, in Letter III of *The Letters of Jonathan Oldstyle, Gentleman*, Irving's persona describes his reaction to the play, *The Battle of Hexham, or, Days of Old*: 'Here, said I to myself, will be something grand – Days of Old – my fancy fired at the words. I pictured to myself all the gallantry of chivalry' (p. 10). Such temporal transpositions (and mediations) are, of course, central to Irving's project of providing a medieval model for developing America.

Within Bracebridge Hall, the attempt to bring the past into the future/present is cultural rather than personal. There it is the now antiquated morris dance which is transported into the present. Becoming one of the main topics of *Bracebridge Hall*, having two entire essays ('May Day Customs' and 'May Day') devoted to them, the morris dances are directly associated by Irving with Robin Hood[17] (as well as Robin Goodfellow) and are described as disappearing as England becomes increasingly urban, mercantile and less like verdant and 'natural' America. Moreover Robin Hood, like the morris dance, is threatened with a type of extinction.

In 'English Gravity', the Squire laments the 'New Middle class' (p. 203) and its effect on the countryside by evoking such a lost age with its symbol, Robin Hood:

> Our valleys smoking with steam-engines, and the din of the hammer and the loon scaring away all our rural delights. What's to become of merry old England, when all its manor houses are all turned into manufactories, and its sturdy peasantry into pin-makers and stocking-weavers? I have looked in vain for merry Sherwood, and all the greenwood haunts of Robin Hood; the whole country is covered with manufacturing towns. ('English Country Gentleman' *BH*, p. 203)

Crayon concurs, noting that the May games have declined 'in proportion as the peasantry has become expensive and artificial in their pleasures, and too knowing for simple enjoyment . . . chilled by habits of gain and traffic' ('May Day Customs' *BH*, p. 215). This observation of the disappearing of ancient custom is seconded not by any fictive character but by Irving himself in a letter from Newstead Abbey to his sister dated 20 January 1832:

> Many of the ancient Games and customs, obsolete in other parts of England, are still maintained in that part of the country and are encouraged by Mr. Rodes. We accordingly had Mummers, and Morris dancers, and glee singers from the neighboring villages.[18]

The Squire's attachment to the past and his dislike of the commercialized countryside ('English Country Gentleman' *BH*, p. 204) is exactly the reason that he repeatedly winks at the poaching of Starlight Tom, who we have been told finds favour in the Squire's eyes by excelling in archery and morris dancing. In fact, the squire, we are told, 'has something of old feudal feeling. He looks back with regret to the "good old times", when journeys were only made on horseback, and the extraordinary difficulties of travelling, owing to bad roads, bad accommodations, and highway robbers' ('Travelling' *BH*, p. 270). As part of that nostalgia – even as we would note for highway robbers, presumably of the greenwood sort – he explicitly tries to revive the May games, though alas, Robin and crew still remain absent:

> He manages to have every year a 'Queen of the May'; but as to Robin Hood, Friar Tuck, the Dragon, the Hobby Horse, and all the other motley crew that used to enliven the day and their mummery, he has not ventured to introduce them . . . Brought up, as I have been in a new country, I may appreciate too highly the faint vestiges of ancient customs which I now and then meet with, and the interest I express in them may provoke a smile from those who are negligently suffering them to pass away. But with whatever indifference they may be regarded by those 'to the manner born' yet in my mind the lingering flavour of them imparts a charm to rustic life, which nothing else could readily supply . . . I shall never forget the delight I felt on first seeing a May-pole . . . I had already been carried back into former days by the antiquities of that venerable place. ('May Day Customs' *BH*, pp. 213–14)

As the passage is constructed, Robin is the absent presence, attesting to the fact that he and the rest of the 'motley crew' are (1) not part of the present and are therefore free of associations with the rejected immediate past and (2) that the absence is a loss rather than a neutral omission, that something that should be there is missing.

That the Squire's attempt at poaching from the past, meets with Geoffrey's sympathies is seen when he states,

> One can readily imagine what a gay scene it must have been in jolly old London, when the doors were decorated with flowering branches, when every hat was decked with hawthorne, and Robin Hood, Friar Tuck, Maid Marian, the morrice dancers, and all the other fantastic masks and revelers, were performing their antics about the May-pole in every part of the city.
>
> I am not a bigoted admirer of old times and old customs merely because of their antiquity. But while I rejoice in the decline of many of the rude usages and coarse amusements of former days, I cannot but regret that this innocent and fanciful festival has fallen into

disuse. It seemed appropriate to this verdant and pastoral country
... ('May Day Customs' *BH*, pp. 214–15)

Indeed, what Irving wishes to preserve is exactly the kind of pre-mercantile Golden Age that the Squire laments losing. In a separate work 'The Creole Village,' Irving describes such a world where:

> The inhabitants, moreover, have none of that eagerness for gain, and rage for improvement, which keep our people continually on the move, and our country towns incessantly in a state of transition, There the magic phrases, 'town lots', 'water privileges', 'railroads', and other comprehensive and soul-stirring words from the speculator's vocabulary, are never heard. ('The Creole Village', p. 47)

Starlight Tom as Robin Hood avatar

Why might Starlight Tom as an avatar of Robin and master of the May games be a model for such revival? Besides the inherent anti-mercantile and anti-authoritarian nature of his actions, Starlight Tom's rootlessness links him explicitly to a truer poetic past which includes Robin Hood:

> Like all other vagabond beings, they have something to commend them to the fancy. They are among the last traces, in these matter-of-fact days, of the motley population of former times; and are whimsically associated in my mind with fairies and witches, Robin Good Fellow, Robin Hood, and the other fantastical personages of poetry. ('Gipsies' *BH*, pp. 210–11)

Tom represents the type of mediation, the past brought into the present, that the Squire embraces. Note that Tom like the medieval May games crew is described as 'motley'. And there may be an etymological pun here, the conversion of the medieval partly coloured patchwork cloth into the beggar's rags that parallels the diminishment of the medieval tradition into the present. Tom, in short, is outfitted in the clothes of yore, if in name only. More importantly, like Robin Hood, Tom represents the cultural mediation, especially as Robert of Locksley, the outlawed Earl of Huntingdon, the intersection of high culture in the form of nobility with the freedom of nature. Similarly, the locus of Edenic past, now lost to the English because of this mercantilism is explicitly a Creole – that is, by definition, mediated – village.

The ideal which Irving presents is the mediating figure who brings together both high and low, both the artificial or cultural and the natural together in his person. We have seen this in his admiration for Chaucer as a poet who could bring together the elegance and nobility of the Prioress with the natural crudeness of the Miller, as well as in the youthful Shakespeare whose poaching was a sign of frontier wildness and artistic sensibility. In the *Sketch Book*, the author devotes considerable attention to James I of Scotland, author of *The King's Quair*, who 'flourished nearly about the time of Chaucer and Gower, and was evidently an admirer and studier of their works' ('A Royal Poet' *SB*, p. 815). James is not merely another bookmaker but a 'pilferer' as well, for Irving turns scholarly source hunter, noting that '*The King's Quair* borrows much from the *Knight's Tale* by James' 'great prototype Chaucer' (p. 819). Irving imagines this Royal Poet as a mediating figure bringing high culture into the frontier, much like an aristocratic Loxley among the greenwood yeoman:

> I have delighted to view [James] merely as the companion of his fellow man, the benefactor of the human heart, stooping from his high estate to sow the sweet flowers of poetry and song in the paths of common life . . . He carried with him into the sterner regions of the north, all fertilizing arts of southern refinement. ('A Royal Poet' *SB*, p. 827)

Remarkably, one sees a parallel figure, a model as it were, in no less a person than Sir Walter Scott in John Buchanan's account of Irving's 1817 visit:

> [Scott] proposed to show Washington Irving 'some of our excellent plain Scotch people-not fine gentlemen and ladies, for such you can meet everywhere, and they are everywhere the same'. They were the stock that he most honored for they were the most idiomatic and enduring thing in the nation. It was this love of plain folk that made Crabbe his favorite reading. They are the true heroes and heroines of his novels, and they were his best friends in life. He respected them far too much to sentimentalize over them; indeed he had their own contempt for sensibility.[19]

We see the same mediating figure in another work by Irving, *Buckthorne, or the Young Man of Great Expectations* where Buckthorne begins by relating: 'My father was a country gentleman, the last of a very ancient and honorable but decayed family' (*Tales of A Traveler*, p. 499). Like James, Buckthorne 'mingled with lower classes' invoking yet another well-known man of two cultures: 'I was neither amused nor corrupted by their vices. In short, I mingled among them, as Prince Hal did among his graceless associates, merely to gratify my humour' (*Tales of A Traveler*, p. 312).

Finally, the inherent value of such mingling is seen in Simon Bracebridge, the nostalgic Squire of Bracebridge Hall whose aim like James was to 'render essential service to his country, by assisting in the disinterested administration of the laws; by watching over the opinions and principles of the lower orders around him, by diffusing among them those lights which may be important to their welfare; by mingling frankly among them' ('English Country Gentleman', pp. 192–3). Such mediation between the culture of the old world and the native vitality of the new is exactly the vision of Irving who, in *Traits of Indian Character,* makes repeated references to chivalrous knights as a way of bringing together old and new. Most telling are Irving's own journal entries recounting his own experiences in the American Frontier, where the writer describes 'Robin Hood, life and characters – Mr. E [The 'sophisticated Yankee Ellsworth'] – in half citizen half chasseur dress – embroidered leathern Indian Pouch. Powder horn with red delicate worsted band' (*Journals*, V 104). As Ross notes:

> Irving refers to Pierre Beatte in both the journals and the Tour, half breed, half-blood: 'Even though Beatte was the servant of Ellesworth and Washington Irving, Pourtales, in his journal, called him "'my interpreter" and "our intrepid half-blood" . . .' he spoke highly of Beatte's talents in finding a ford, searching for lost horses, killing a fat doe, and in capturing a wild horse with a lasso. Latrobe was most complimentary: 'Beatte was the son of a French Creole, by a Quopaw mother . . . there was something in his whole character and manner, which answered to the picture my fancy paints of Robin Hood . . .' (p. 110, n. 77)

That such mediated or Creole figures are associated with Robin Hood is perhaps a natural outgrowth of the figure presented in Ritson's 'Life' of the greenwood outlaw as a nobleman who mingled with the commons:

> Robin Hood was born at Locksley... His extraction was noble, and his true name was Robert Fitzooth, which vulgar pronunciation easily corrupted into Robin Hood. He is frequently styled, and commonly reputed to have been the Earl of Huntingdon; a title to which, in the latter part of his life at least, he actually appears to have had some sort of pretension'. (p. viii)

Indeed, the ability to combine two vastly different social worlds is embodied in Ritson's terming the outlawed Fitzooth as the 'prince of all robbers' (p. xiv).

Geoffrey Crayon's purloined purse

Where, then, in the midst of Irving's works do we find Robin Hood, not in the form of reference but made over as Irving claims writers do when they take models from the past? Irving does, in fact, make a habit of performing the literary 'metempsychosis' that he describes in his essay on 'The Art of Bookmaking'. In *Bracebridge Hall*, Geoffrey Crayon rhapsodizes with the Squire about an imaginary visit to the Tabard to meet the nine and twenty pilgrims whose portraits he summarizes and incorporates into his sketch. Indeed, he goes even farther, populating Bracebridge Hall with characters who are clearly pilfered from the Canterbury pilgrims, such as the title character of 'The Widow' whose dogs were 'pampered and fed with delicacies' (p. 44). In the *Sketch Book*'s 'The Mutability of Literature', Irving says of Chaucer:

> The setting may occasionally be antiquated, and require now and then to be renewed, as in the case of Chaucer; but the brilliancy and intrinsic value of the gems continue unaltered. (p. 863)

Irving closes *The Sketch Book* with 'The Legend of Sleepy Hollow', arguably his own attempt to 'renew' a Chaucerian fabliau which seems to share much with the *Miller's Tale*. But *Tales of a Traveler* also contains Irving's attempt at a comic Greenwood tale that ties together many of his themes.

As a writer searching for a theme, Geoffrey, like many an unsuspecting character in the Robin Hood ballads, finds himself in a tavern where he hits upon a remarkably appropriate topic for a post-revolutionary American writer:

> At an Inn, I had long wanted a theme and a hero; both suddenly broke upon my mind; I was determined to write a poem on the history of Jack Straw. I was so full of my subject that I was fearful of being anticipated; I wondered none of the poets of the day, in their search after ruffian heroes, had ever thought of Jack Straw. ('A Literary Dinner' *TT*, p. 486)

Yet also like such characters from the ballads, Geoffrey suddenly finds himself in the company of a jolly stranger, and in what has now become a debate about choosing literary models, albeit in an inn rather than a reading room, the green clad stranger declaims:

> 'our poets don't look at home. I don't see why we need to go out of old England for robbers and rebels to write about. I like your Jack Straw, sir. He's a home made hero. I like him, sir. I like him exceedingly. He's English to the back bone – damme – Give me honest old England after all; them's my sentiments, sir.'
>
> 'I honour your sentiment', cried I zealously, 'it is exactly my own. An English ruffian is as good a ruffian for poetry as any in Italy, or Germany, or the Archepelago; but it is hard to make our poets think so.' ('A Literary Dinner' *TT*, p. 487)

And of course, in a speech that mirror's the Squire's longing for the lost 'Golden Age', the talk of models turns – where else – to Robin Hood:

> 'Poets in old times had right notions on this subject', continued I; 'witness the fine old ballads about Robin Hood, Alan a' Dale and other staunch blades of yore'. 'Right, sir, right', interrupted he. 'Robin Hood! He was the lad to cry stand! to a man and never flinch'.
>
> 'Ah, sir!' said I, 'they had famous bands of robbers in the good old times. Those were glorious poetical days. The merry crew of Sherwood Forest, who led such a roving picturesque life, "under the greenwood tree". I have often wished to visit their haunts, and tread the scenes of the exploits of Friar Tuck, and Clym of the Clough, and Sir William of Cloudeslie.' ('A Literary Dinner' *TT*, p. 487)

In fact, mirroring the Squire's lament over the loss of the 'good old times, including highway robbers' ('Traveling' *BH*, p. 270), the unnamed gentleman in green likewise laments the passing of the highway robber:

> 'They were dashing, daring fellows; the last apologies that we had for the Knights errants of yore. Ah sir! the country has been sinking gradually into tameness and common place. We are losing the old English spirit. The bold Knights of the Past have all dwindled down into lurking footpads and sneaking pickpockets. There's no such thing as a dashing gentlemanlike robbery committed nowadays on the King's high way.' ('A Literary Dinner' *TT*, p. 488)

And the cause of such loss is, as in the Squire's view, the encroaching mercantilism of the rising middle class:

> 'that, sir. craving your pardon is not owing to any want of English pluck. It is the effect of this cursed system of banking. People do not travel with bags of gold, as they did formerly. They have post notes and drafts on Bankers.' ('A Literary Dinner' *TT*, p. 488–9)

Having fallen in with such a boon companion, Geoffrey leaves the inn, and while discussing the robberies Geoffrey sensibly observes: 'A man is an ideot to risk life, or even limb, to save a paltry purse of money' ('A Literary Dinner' *TT*, p. 490). To which the still unnamed man in green replies: 'Then hand me yours'. Like the purblind Sheriff of Nottingham, Geoffrey has failed to recognize that his travelling companion is the very green-clad bandit who is the subject of his own discourse, and like the sheriff, Geoffrey has fallen victim to the ambiguity of language which in the hands of the trickster is as potent a weapon as a longbow or sword. It doesn't even help that some months later Geoffrey later sees the same stranger being led away in chains, for by then he 'was cured of [his] poetical enthusiasm for rebels, robbers, and highwaymen' ('A Literary Dinner', *TT*, p. 490).[20] One cannot help recall the well-known proverb that 'Many a man speaks of Robin Hood who has not drawn his bow'. To which we might add, 'nor been his victim'.

It is extremely important to realize that what has taken place here is not, in fact, a simple robbery; that is, a unilateral act. In fact, what has occurred is a bilateral exchange. Master Crayon has, to be sure, divested himself of the contents of his purse, which in the context of his dialogue with the man in green, has become the embodiment of the mercantilism that characterizes contemporary England and possibly those parts of the new frontier, such as the Creole village. In return he has received the far more essential object of his desire/quest, the subject matter for the making of literature, the recounted (and now written) text. In this regard, the exchange mirrors the very peculiar framing of transactions between Robin Hood and his 'victims'. Traditionally, the greenwood outlaw does not simply seek to rob travellers but often frames his quest as a search for someone to feast his men. The victim, rather than simply being relieved of his money is ushered into the outlaws' lair where Robin Hood creates a ritual exchange, the victim's purse in exchange for the dinner which the contents of the purse are said to underwrite.

The contents of this literary exchange are worthy of commentary because they form a concrete microcosm of the submerged literary quest that underpins both *The Sketch Book* and *Bracebridge Hall*. The search is, straightforwardly a literary one, but it is clearly a search for a peculiarly American paradigm, in this case an individual. Significantly, the initial paradigms are all revolutionaries, and, in particular, historical figures, such as Wat Tyler and Jack Straw, whose insurgencies were directed against the English monarchy. Indeed Wat Tyler is a figure invoked by Tom Paine, who in his 'The Rights of Man' attests to the currency of Tyler in the revolutionary debates by noting that 'several newspapers of late [have] made frequent mention of Wat Tyler'.[21] In fact, in countering Burke's use of Tyler, Paine champions the medieval rebel by declaring that Tyler's 'fame will outlive [Burke & Co.'s] falsehood'.[22] Irving, as the editor of his journals notes, paraphrases Paine.[23]

While such considerations of Tyler and Bell are the launching points of Geoffrey Crayon's literary exchange with the Boar's Head Tavern's 'Man in Green', the bulk of the conversation's subject matter is not so much *who* should be the subject of Geoffrey's proposed text but rather from *where* – in particular, from which nation, foreign or domestic, this figure is to be drawn, which explains why the Robin Hood-like Italian *banditti* won't suffice. Finally, despite the initial impulse to choose a true revolutionary, the final choice, Robin Hood, is a negotiated choice, who while anti-authoritarian is more suitable for a second generation revolutionary than Tom Paine's Tyler or Bell.

Indeed, the later tradition of Robin Hood, certainly as he appears in Scott's *Ivanhoe,* is that of a mediated figure, one who rebels against abuse of the system but whose rebellion, far from being a radical attempt to replace the political system is actually a conservative action designed to reinforce the system by eliminating deviations (abuses) of fealty and the monarchical system. Robin is after all the most loyal of Richard's subjects, protecting his kingship not displacing it. Here Ritson's construction of Robin Hood is central to Irving's vision:

> It is not, at the same time, to be concluded that he must, in this opposition, have been guilty of manifest treason or rebellion, as he most certainly can be justly charged with neither . . . What better title King Richard could pretend to the territory and people of England, than Robin Hood had to the dominion of Barnsdale or Sherwood, is a question humbly submitted to the consideration of the political philosopher. (Ritson, pp. x–xi)

Ritson's Robin is 'a man who, in a barbarous age, and under a complicated tyranny, displayed a spirit of freedom and independence, which has endeared him to the common people, whose cause he maintained' (pp. vii–viii). In representing Robin Hood in such a fashion, Ritson provides Irving with the perfect apologia for the American Revolution, turning the English outlaw into a loyal subject who takes up arms to conserve the system while at the same time defying its (now corrupt) authority, thereby making the greenwood outlaw both a revolutionary and a conservative and, hence, the ideal figure to mediate between the conflicting impulses, both East and West, that call Irving both to reject and to embrace the English past in choosing a model for the American future. Ritson's Robin Hood – 'a man who, in a barbarous age, and under a complicated tyranny, displayed a spirit of freedom and independence, which has endeared him to the common people, whose cause he maintained' (pp. vii–viii) – is the English embodiment of the American revolutionary who makes the American revolution not a break from English tradition but a reliving of it, a return to the Golden Age of 'merry old England' (p. 205) before the colonial past.

SKETCHES BY A GREEN CRAYON
NOTES

1. Quotations from primary texts are taken from the following editions: Washington Irving, *History, Tales and Sketches: Letters of Jonathan Oldstyle, Gent*; Salmagundi, *History of New York*; *The Sketch Book of Geoffrey Crayon, Gent*, Michael L. and Nancy B. Black (eds) (New York: Twayne, 1983); Washington Irving, *Bracebridge Hall, Tales of A Traveler, The Alhambra*, ed. Andrew B. Myers (New York: Literary Classics of the United States, 1991); 'The Creole Village', in *Irving's Works, Geoffrey Crayon Edition*, complete in 27 Volumes, vol. XVII, Wolfert's Roost and Other Papers (New York, 1865); *The Complete Works of Washington Irving, Journals and NoteBooks*, vol. 1 (1803–6), ed. Nathalia Wright (Madison: University of Wisconsin, 1969); vol. 2 (1807–22), ed. Walter A. Reichart and Lillian Schlissel (Boston: Twayne, 1981); vol. 3 (1819–27), ed. Walter A. Reichart (Madison, 1970); vol. 4 (1826–9), ed. Wayne, R. Kime and Andrew B. Myers (Boston: Twayne, 1984); vol. 5 (1832–1959), ed. Sue Fields Ross (Boston: Twayne, 1986). The following abbreviations are used: *SB*: *The Sketch Book*; *BH*: *Bracebridge Hall*; *TT*: *Tales of A Traveler*.
2. Henry Steele Commager, *The Search for a Usable Past, and Other Essays in Historiography* (New York: Knopf, 1967).
3. George S. Hellman, *Washington Irving Esquire: Ambassador at Large from the New World to the Old* (New York: Knopf, 1925), p. 14.
4. Letter 980, to Charles R. Leslie 9 January 1832 in Washington Irving, *Letters*, vol. II, 1823–1838, ed. Ralph M. Aderman, Herbert L. Kleinfield, and Jenifer S. Banks (Boston: Twayne, 1979), p. 677.
5. Letter 983, to Catherine Paris, 20 January 1832, *Letters*, vol. II, p. 685.
6. Letter 982, to Peter Irving, 20 January 1832, *Letters*, vol. II, p. 681.
7. See John Gibson Lockhart, *Memoirs of the Life of Sir Walter Scott* (Boston and New York: Houghton, Mifflin, 1902), vol. 3, pp. 67–8, IV, 88–95. Lockhart refers to 'Scott's high estimation of Irving's genius' (vol. 3, p. 181).
8. Joseph Ritson, *Robin Hood: A Collection of all the Ancient Poems, Songs, and Ballads, Now Extant, Relative to that Celebrated English Outlaw* (London: T. Egerton and J. Johnson, 1795).
9. DT, p. 55. By way of capturing the radical nature of Ritson's political thought, Dobson and Taylor note that Ritson, eccentric in so many ways, was one of the few Englishmen to adopt the French revolutionary calendar (p. 55).
10. See *Journals*, vol. 1, pp. 322, 333, 334, 337, 344, 371.
11. Also see *Journals*, vol. 1, pp. 218 and 307.
12. The last two were revised into four volumes. The 1810 volume was revised by Evans's son, R. H. Evans. The Robin Hood ballads comprise ballads 15–43 in volume 1.
13. Of course, Evans goes on to add that the volume is 'disgraced by the petulance and impiety that pervade the biographical memoir and notes'. (vol. 2, p. 87) In the prefatory 'Advertisement' to the revised

1810 edition, R. H. Evans, expands on this academic animosity in describing the always querulous Ritson's treatment of Percy's famous Reliques: '[Percy's] work has been attacked with unusual acrimony by Ritson; the editor has been branded with ignorance, imposition, and every species of reproach which malignity could suggest; and every fault which learned petulance could discover, has been pointed out with a curious and offensive officiousness' (vol. 1, pp. ii–iii).

14 'I find that the tale of Rip Van Winkle, given in the Sketch Book, has been discovered by diverse writers in magazines, to have been founded on a little German tradition, and the matter has been revealed to the world as if it were a foul instance of plagiarism marvellously brought to light ... I had considered the popular traditions of the kind as fair foundations of authors of fiction to build upon, and had made use of the one in question accordingly' (pp. 298–9).

15 Robin Hood is linked to a Golden Age in *As You Like It* (I: i): 'They say [the old Duke] is already in the forest of Arden, and a many merry men with him; and there they live like old Robin Hood of England; . . . and fleet the time carelessly as they did in the golden world' (quoted in Ritson, p. xi).

16 Robin Goodfellow described by Irving as 'one of [his] favorites'. See Washington Irving, *Miscellaneous writings 1803–1859*, vol. 2, ed. Wayne R. Kime (Boston: Twayne, 1981), p. 332.

17 '[T]hough not actually canonized, he has obtained the principle distinction of sainthood in having a festival allotted to him, and solemn games institutes in honour of his memory, which were celebrated until the latter end of the sixteenth century' (Ritson, p. xvii). Note the past tense here, indicating, as Irving often does, that the games died out and did so with the coming of the new English colonialism.

18 Letter 983, to Catherine Paris, 20 January 1832, *Letters*, vol. II, p. 684.

19 John Buchan, *Sir Walter Scott* (New York: Coward-McCann, 1932), p. 368. Irving's account of 'Laird' Scott's relationship with the common men of his estates is recounted by Lockhart, *Life*, vol. 3, pp. 67–8.

20 We are currently engaged in a longer study of the image of Robin Hood in America in which we attempt to explain this seeming disillusionment or pulling back from Robin Hood on Irving's part.

21 *The Writings of Thomas Paine*, ed. Moncure Daniel Conway, 4 vols (New York: G. P. Putman's Sons, 1967), vol. 2, p. 476.

22 Dobson and Taylor compare Paine's conversion of Wat Tyler to Ritson's similar political conversion of Robin Hood, DT, p. 55.

23 *Journals*, vol. 3, p. 291, note 519 letter of 17 February 1824.

Robin Hood, King Arthur and Cold War Chivalry

JEFFREY RICHARDS

In a fascinating and thought-provoking recent book, Stephanie Barczewski has argued that in the nineteenth-century the myths of Robin Hood and King Arthur came to stand for opposing constructions of British national identity, with Arthur representing authority, conformity, conservatism and imperialism and Robin Hood representing rebellion, subversion, radicalism and anti-imperialism. While Robin remained exclusively English, Arthur stood for Britain as a whole. Celtic elements played an important part in the shaping of the Arthurian myth, but Barczewski argues that the myth of Arthur was increasingly annexed to England and Englishness as a part of an imperial takeover.[1]

How far her interpretation is valid for the nineteenth century is open to debate, but she does not take her analysis forward into the age of the cinema, the mass medium that most powerfully disseminated the myths of Robin Hood and King Arthur in the twentieth century. In cinema, Robin Hood and King Arthur became shared myths between Britain and the United States. Hollywood in particular became for both Britain and America a prime means of instructing audiences in national identity, social values and masculine role models.

It is a singular fact that in the heyday of Hollywood before 1945 there were only two significant Robin Hood films, *Robin Hood* (1922) starring Douglas Fairbanks and *The Adventures of Robin Hood* (1938) starring Errol Flynn. The only significant Arthurian films were the regular retellings of Mark Twain's *A Connecticut Yankee at King Arthur's Court*, which was filmed in 1921 and 1931 and again in 1948 and which satirized the conventions of chivalry and demonstrated the superiority of modernity to antiquity. But between 1945 and 1970 there were some ten Robin Hood films and six Arthurian epics.[2]

Both sets of films have to be seen in the context of a major film cycle in the post-war American cinema. A series of expensively mounted medieval chivalric epics was produced by Hollywood companies, many of them shot in whole or in part in Britain. Almost every studio contributed to the cycle: MGM (*Ivanhoe* (1952), *Knights of the Round Table* (1954), *The Adventures of Quentin Durward* (1955)), Warner Bros (*King Richard and the Crusaders* (1954)), Universal (*The Black Shield of Falworth* (1954)), Columbia (*The Black Knight* (1954)), Twentieth Century-Fox (*Prince Valiant* (1954)), and Allied Artists (*The Warriors* (1955)). In addition there was a new version of the Robin Hood myth *The Story of Robin Hood* (1952), shot in Britain by Walt Disney. There were three films centred on the idea of the son of Robin Hood (*Bandit of Sherwood Forest* (1946), *Rogues of Sherwood Forest* (1950) and *Son of Robin Hood* (1958)), there were two low-budget films (*Prince of Thieves* (1948) and *Tales of Robin Hood* (1952)) and there were three films from the British company Hammer (*Men of Sherwood Forest* (1954), *Sword of Sherwood Forest* (1961) and *A Challenge for Robin Hood* (1967)).

What all these films had in common was the adherence of their heroes to the code of chivalry. This was an ethic shared by both Britain and America, for in the nineteenth century gallantry, honour and *noblesse oblige* became and remained deeply embedded in the national psyche of both countries. As John Fraser has written in his masterly study of this phenomenon:

> The family of chivalric heroes has been by far the largest and most popular one in twentieth-century American culture, and its members, in whole or in part, have entered into virtually everyone's consciousness. They include, naturally, the legion of knightly Westerners in print and celluloid sired by Owen Wister's The Virginian and their Indian counterparts. They include Robin Hood and the Scarlet Pimpernel, and gentleman buccaneers like Rafael Sabatini's Captain Blood . . . They include the officers and gentlemen of *Lives of a Bengal Lancer*, and the gentleman rankers of *Beau Geste* and the First World War aviators of *The Dawn Patrol* . . . They include

honest cops like Dick Tracy, and fearless investigative reporters and incorruptible district attorneys, and upstanding young doctors like Doctor Kildare. They include battered but romantic private eyes like Raymond Chandler's Philip Marlowe . . . They include gentleman knights like Prince Valiant and Nature's gentlemen like Tarzan . . . They include Superman and Buck Rogers. They include men about town like Philo Vance, the Saint, and Dashiell Hammett's Nick Charles, and the figures played by Fred Astaire . . . They include gentlemanly English actors like Ronald Colman and George Sanders and gentlemanly American ones like Douglas Fairbanks Jr. and William Powell, and those immortals Gary Cooper, Spencer Tracy and the rest who have epitomised native American gallantry and grace.[3]

These figures were as popular in Britain as in America and helped to maintain the idea of the chivalric gentleman as the dominant masculine ideal in the culture of both those countries.

But why the great upsurge of medieval chivalric epics in the 1950s? One reason is economic. The first big chivalric epic, *Ivanhoe* (1952) was an enormous box office success, taking nearly eleven million dollars worldwide on its initial release.[4] It was MGM's top-grossing film of the year and was nominated for an Oscar for best picture. In the way of Hollywood, every other studio sought to emulate its success and MGM itself reteamed the star and director of *Ivanhoe* in two further chivalric epics. Linked to this was the fact that many of the films were shot in Britain because of legislation which prevented Hollywood companies removing their profits from the country. These so-called 'frozen funds' were deployed by the companies in making films in Britain and given the existence of ready-made castles and pastoral landscapes historical dramas were an appropriate genre.

But there is more to it than that. The 1950s were the era of the Cold War when the world was divided between the two great super-powers and their spheres of influence. On the one hand there was democratic Christian America and on the other the totalitarian godless Soviet Union. Hollywood responded to this with straightforward anti-Soviet propaganda in spy films but more subtly and allegorically in a series of Biblical and Roman epics (*Quo Vadis?*, *The Robe*, *Ben-Hur*, *The Ten*

Commandments, Salome) in which evil totalitarian empires (Rome, Egypt) are defied by devout and democratic Christians or Jews. The chivalric epics and the Robin Hood adventures can be seen fulfilling the same function as they played to the anti-Communist paranoia that spawned the infamous House UnAmerican Activities Committee (HUAC) and the McCarthyite witch-hunt of leftists in American society and in the mass media. A major theme of the Arthurian films is the threat of barbarian invasion from across the seas; and of the Robin Hood films the overthrow of legitimately constituted and genuinely popular authority by subversive cabals in the higher echelons of society.

But there was another domestic preoccupation in 1950s America – juvenile delinquency. This first surfaced in 1942–3 when rising crime rates among the young were reported and were attributed to the dislocation of families by the war. It became a major preoccupation after the war, the Gallup Poll indicating peaks of concern about juvenile delinquency in 1945 and in 1953–8. There was a flood of articles, books, and reports on the phenomenon. Hollywood made sixty films dealing with juvenile delinquency, some of which while moralizing about the subject actually succeeded in creating identification figures for rebellious youth in the delinquent heroes of films like *The Wild One* (1953) (with Marlon Brando), *East of Eden* (1954) and *Rebel Without a Cause* (1955) (both with James Dean). The concern about juvenile crime coincided in the 1950s with the emergence of a distinct teenage culture in America as youngsters with money to spend fashioned a distinctive youth culture around a youth uniform (jeans, T-shirts, D. A. haircuts), rock music, gang membership, motor bikes and hot rods, all of which featured in the films which while preaching against the lifestyle also imbued it with glamour. Much blame for this development was attributed to the mass media. A Senate Sub-Committee on Juvenile Delinquency under Senator Estes Kefauver investigated and called for greater responsibility and self-regulation by the media. At the same time Dr Frederic Wertham's enormously influential *The Seduction of the Innocent* (1954) denounced crime and horror comic books for imbuing the young with false values. Films which re-emphasized the basic values of chivalry could be seen as a useful corrective to a culture of disrespect, hedonism, violence and self-indulgence, promoting and endorsing acceptable male role models.[5]

Robin Hood and his Merrie Men and King Arthur and his Knights thus became Cold War warriors, promoting wholesome values at home and abroad and combating at the same time Communist totalitarianism, atheism and juvenile delinquency. The film which dictated the look and feel of the immediate post-war Robin Hood films was Warner Bros's *The Adventures of Robin Hood* (1938), directed by Michael Curtiz and William Keighley. It is still regarded today as the definitive Robin Hood film with its perfect cast headed by Errol Flynn as Robin, its glowing Technicolor, its surging Korngold score and its joyous, free-wheeling action sequences. It was very different in emphasis from Douglas Fairbanks's 1922 *Robin Hood*. Fairbanks's film was a large-scale chivalric epic, over half of its two-hour length devoted to the knightly prowess and *noblesse oblige* of Robert, Earl of Huntingdon (Fairbanks), depicted as the closest friend of King Richard the Lionheart (Wallace Beery). There is a full-scale tournament, a banquet, the spectacular departure of the crusaders and the romantic courtship of Lady Marian Fitzwalter (Enid Bennett) by Robert before he turns outlaw. Alerted by Marian to the reign of terror unleashed by Prince John in the King's absence, Robert returns and believing her dead, takes to the forest as Robin Hood and organizes resistance to Prince John and his men. Robin is eventually captured and sentenced to death but the timely return of the King and the intervention of the merrie men saves him. He is restored to his rank and marries Marian, who is not dead after all. It is a breathtaking spectacle but the outlaw high jinks in the forest and the recruitment of the merrie men are rather overshadowed by the earlier celebration of medieval chivalry.

In *The Adventures of Robin Hood* (1938), Robin is outlawed at the start of the film and remains an outlaw throughout until the King's providential return. Like Fairbanks's Robin, Flynn's Robin is an aristocrat, Sir Robin of Locksley, owner of a castle later confiscated by Prince John. But he is a Saxon aristocrat and this introduces a racial dimension absent from Fairbanks's film.

The context of the film established at the outset is the oppression of the Saxon peasantry by their Norman overlords during the regency of Prince John. Excessive taxes are squeezed from the peasantry and Norman rule enforced with a brutal regime of hangings, floggings, blindings, and house-burnings, which, it is made clear, contrasts with conditions during King Richard's reign when the peasants lived in peace and freedom. Sir Robin of Locksley, having defied Prince John and his henchmen, and taken to the woods, assembles the oppressed Saxons in the forest and administers to them as 'freeborn Englishmen' an oath to rob the rich and give to the poor, to fight to the death against oppression, to protect all women whether Saxon or Norman, rich or poor, to fight for a free England and guard her loyally until King Richard's return. It is emphasized throughout that Robin and the Saxons are loyal to the King and seeking only to resist illegitimate authority and oppression. In the context of the late 1930s, with militaristic Normans oppressing another race, the Saxons, in the same country, with the repeated contrast between freedom and dictatorship, this looks very much like a coded attack on fascism, not inappropriate for a studio which specialized in dramas about current burning social issues and was to produce the first explicitly anti-Nazi film *Confessions of a Nazi Spy* only a year later.

But the attack on Norman oppression is coupled with a plea for social inclusiveness. The Saxon Robin falls in love with the Norman Lady Marian Fitzwalter (Olivia de Havilland), the King's ward. Her initial hostility is melted when he shows her the victims of Norman oppression, the widows and orphans, the maimed and the oppressed, and talks passionately about poverty and deprivation. But Robin adds significantly: 'It's injustice I hate – not the Normans.' Marian comes to believe, thanks to Robin, that 'England is bigger than Norman and Saxon fighting and hating each other – it belongs to all of us to live peacefully together, loyal to Richard and to England.' This theme of reconciliation is consummated at the end when Richard returns and John's plans to assassinate him and have himself crowned are foiled. The King announces: 'All injustice and oppression is banished. Normans and Saxons alike will share the rights of Englishmen.' Robin is made Earl of Sherwood and Nottingham and united with Marian in a marriage that symbolizes the union of Saxons and Normans. Because of its stance on poverty and social inclusiveness, Ina Rae Hark has suggested that in King Richard and Robin and their programme we should see echoes of President Franklin Delano Roosevelt and the New Deal.[6] It is significant that Flynn's *Robin Hood* was reissued nationally in 1948 and achieved considerable success on its second outing. For its underlying political message was still relevant in the aftermath of war.

But like Douglas Fairbanks in 1922 and Errol Flynn in 1938, the Robin Hood of the Hollywood films of the late 1940s and 1950s, was no subversive or radical. He stood for the defence of the crown and the defeat of subversion. The first Robin Hood film after the war, Columbia Pictures's *The Bandit of Sherwood Forest* (1946), directed by George Sherman and Henry Levin, looked back to the anti-fascist message of A*dventures of Robin Hood* (1938). In personnel it also had direct links: cinematographer Tony Gaudio had worked on *Adventures*; composer Hugo Friedhofer had orchestrated Korngold's score for *Adventures*, and Anita Louise, cast as Lady Catherine Maitland, had been Warner's first choice for Maid Marian, a role eventually played by Olivia de Havilland.

In *Bandit*, King John is dead and his young son Henry III is on the throne. But the Regent, William of Pembroke (Henry Daniell), plans to seize the throne for himself. His first step is to announce to a gathering of nobles that he is abrogating Magna Carta, the fundamental charter of liberties which the nobles had forced King John to accept and which stands in the film as shorthand for the democratic American constitution. 'The people are not fit to rule themselves ... From now on the people will be taxed as they should be taxed and ruled as they should be ruled', says William. There was of course no democratic government in the historical medieval England but in Hollywood's medieval England there was and its spokesman is the Earl of Huntingdon (Russell Hicks), who as Robin Hood had opposed the tyranny of King John and now is the only noble to speak out against the regent. He declares that people have died to ensure the granting of the Magna Carta which ensured the right of the people to rule themselves and to live in freedom and dignity. For his pains he is banished and he retreats to Sherwood Forest where he reassembles his now elderly band and recruits others to resist the tyranny of the Regent. He is joined by his son, Robert (Cornel Wilde), who effectively takes on the mantle of Robin Hood and leads the outlaw band.

The actions of the Earl of Huntingdon and his son in this film recall those of the heroes of Second World War resistance movies, as they hide in the forest, and launch attacks on the tax collectors and 'storm troopers' of the black-clad proto-fascist Regent. Their legitimacy is underlined when the Queen Mother takes refuge with them in the forest. When they learn that William plans to murder Henry III, Robert and his band enter Nottingham in disguise. The boy king is spirited to safety but Robert and Lady Catherine Maitland, the Maid Marian figure who is a lady-in-waiting to the Queen but has joined forces with the outlaws, are both captured. In a final duel, in which Wilde, an Olympic standard swordsman, fences with both hands, Robert defeats and kills the regent, and Robin Hood and his outlaws, who have infiltrated the castle, overpower his supporters. At the end Henry III, restored to his throne, proclaims Robert Earl of Sutherland and marries him to Lady Catherine.

Robin Hood and his son are throughout supporters of the democratic constitution and the legitimate monarch against a coup d'état. The film thus endorses constitutional monarchy as opposed to dictatorship and the peerages of both Robin and his son confirm their membership of the legitimate establishment. The plot interestingly resembles that of the 1949 RKO Radio Pictures's film *At Sword's Point* (UK title: *Sons of the Musketeers*) in which Cornel Wilde as D'Artagnan Junior rallies the sons of the other musketeers to aid the embattled Queen Mother of France. Her ambitious Prime Minister the Duc de Lavalle (whose name echoes the wartime Vichy French Prime Minister Pierre Laval) seeks to gain power first by marrying Princess Henriette and then by eliminating the boy King Louis XIV. His plans are foiled by the musketeers and the king placed on his throne. Interestingly stock footage from Flynn's *Adventures of Robin Hood* was utilized to flesh out the action scenes. But this is another film essentially looking back to the war.

ROBIN HOOD, KING ARTHUR AND COLD WAR CHIVALRY

When Columbia Pictures returned to the theme of Robin Hood Junior in the rousing *Rogues of Sherwood Forest* (1950), directed by Gordon Douglas, which deftly incorporated chase sequences and outlaw gathering scenes from *Bandit*, the political situation had changed. The Cold War was now well under way. The emphasis this time is on the threat to democracy from without and within, and the implicit enemy is Communism.

The foreword to the film sets the context: 'The Bill of Rights and the liberty and justice we enjoy today stem from the Magna Carta, a great charter which the oppressed people of England forced from the tyrannical King John. In the year 1215 King John was secretly planning to crush all who stood in the way of his ruthless ambition.' Once again Magna Carta represents the American Constitution and its emergence in England links the two NATO allies in a commitment to democracy.

This time Robin Hood is dead by the time the film begins and his son, Robin Junior, already Earl of Huntingdon, returns from the Crusades with Little John (Alan Hale, resuming the role he played in both Fairbanks's *Robin Hood* and Flynn's *Adventures of Robin Hood*). This returned soldier finds that King John (George Macready) proposes to impose absolute rule. John declares to his council that, following the rule of his brother, King Richard I, when taxes were light and the people had rights, he proposes to rule dictatorially ('I'll break their stiff English necks with taxes. It's time I taught them who is the King of England'). So he imposes heavy taxes and cruel and arbitrary punishments, and Robin reassembles his father's old band and leads the resistance. When half a dozen leading barons are murdered and their lands seized, the rest of the barons with the support of the Archbishop of Canterbury, Stephen Langton, meet and decide to impose a Magna Carta, a charter to ensure 'the God-given rights to life, freedom and human dignity'. The King is seized and taken to Runnymede where he protests that he rules by divine right. The Archbishop tells him that he rules by the consent of his subjects and he reluctantly agrees to accept the Magna Carta which is sealed with his seal.

So Robin, already Earl of Huntingdon, is not subversive but is seeking to restore the democratic conditions that prevailed under Richard the Lionheart. In the context of 1950, the hero returning from the Crusades is the serviceman returning from the Second World War and finding his native land threatened from within by the subversion of the constitution but also by alien forces from outside. One of the reasons John has increased the taxes is to pay for Flemish mercenaries whom he proposes to import from across the Channel to help enforce his will. The narrative emphasis on the securing for the people of a charter of liberty (ancestor of the American Bill of Rights) is thus a rousing affirmation of American democracy against Communist totalitarianism. Robin is both aristocratic and democratic – the chivalric code being the link between the two. The blessing granted to the opponents by the church is also novel and reflects the cinema's deployment of Christianity in Cold War propaganda.

The third and least impressive of the three 'Son of Robin Hood' films was Twentieth Century-Fox's 1958 *Son of Robin Hood*, directed by George Sherman, who had co-directed *Bandit of Sherwood Forest*. It was energetic but badly written and cheaply mounted. The political situation recalls Sherman's earlier film. Duke Simon Des Roches (David Farrar) plots to seize the throne from the boy king Henry III. This time the Regent, Robert, Earl of Chester (Marius Goring), seeks to defend the King and rallies the outlaw band of the now dead Robin Hood to support him. Chester is captured by Des Roches but the outlaws send to Spain for Robin Hood's son. When he turns up, he is revealed as a daughter Deering (June Laverick). But although she proves adept with a sword, a son of Robin Hood is needed to lead the band and so Chester's brother, Jamie, newly returned from the crusades, is enlisted to fill the role. Eventually the plans of Des Roches are foiled. He is killed in a duel with Jamie, and Chester, freed from captivity, proclaims the coronation of Henry III. The theme is aristocratic subversion, the attempt to supplant the legitimate King and the defence of the King by Robin Hood's band. The only novelty is the presence of Robin Hood's daughter and this represents a trend in post-war swashbucklers, which in itself reflects the enhanced status attained by women during the war. This saw a succession of films in which women proved themselves as expert in swordplay and as daring as their male counterparts: Deering Hood's sword-wielding sisterhood included Binnie Barnes's Anne Bonney in *The Spanish Main* (1945), Jean Peters's Anne of the Indies in the film of the same name (1951), and Maureen O'Hara's Clare Athos in *Sons of the Musketeers* (1949) and 'Spitfire' Stevens in *Against All Flags* (1952).

In all three of the 'Son of Robin Hood' films an already established aristocrat revives the outlaw band to defend legitimacy and democracy. Interestingly absent from the films is the class conflict element coded as Saxon/Norman rivalry which was so prominent a part of *The Adventures of Robin Hood* in 1938. Class conflict had no part to play in Cold War propaganda where a united front of men and women of all classes was required for the battle against tyranny.

Two of the Hollywood Robin Hood films from this period were cheap and inconsequential. Columbia's *The Prince of Thieves* (1948) with Jon Hall as Robin, basically concentrated on the way in which Robin Hood and his band united three pairs of lovers. Hal Roach's *Tales of Robin Hood* (1952) was made for television as a pilot for a projected series which never materialized and was released to cinemas. It was an hour-long gloss on Flynn's version, with Robin (Robert Clarke) as the son of the Saxon Earl of Chester, who is murdered by the Normans. Robin then engages in conflict with Sir Guy de Clermont, Norman overlord of Nottingham.

The first retelling of the traditional Robin Hood story since the war came in the form of *The Story of Robin Hood* (1952), a Walt Disney production made in Britain to utilize 'frozen funds'. It was directed by Ken Annakin, with second unit direction by Alex Bryce. Anxious not to duplicate Flynn's 1938 *Robin Hood*, Annakin viewed it before embarking on his own and came up with a rather different product. This version with a sung ballad commentary on the action by wandering troubadour Alan-a-Dale (Elton Hayes) and with quasi-archaic dialogue (ye, thy, mayhap, nay) looked back to the medieval ballad origins of the mythos. It contained the familiar meetings with Little John and Friar Tuck and the archery contest, all also featured in the Flynn film. But it dispensed with the Saxon-Norman rivalry, Sir Guy ofGisbourne and the climactic sword duel that had also been features of Flynn's version.

This version begins with the departure of King Richard (Patrick Barr) for the Crusade, his venture blessed by the prayers of the Archbishop of Canterbury. He leaves his brother Prince John in charge of the midland shires, warning him: 'The strength of England stems from the well-being of the humblest peasant.' But once he has gone, John and his henchman, the Sheriff of Nottingham levy harsh taxes and impose dictatorial rule. The Robin Hood who resists them is no longer an aristocrat. He is Robin Fitzooth, son of the chief forester of the Earl of Huntingdon, though as played by Richard Todd he is certainly a gentleman. In this version it is Marian who is the daughter of the Earl of Huntingdon, in love with Robin, and joining his band disguised as a page. Robin takes to the woods and raises an outlaw band when his father is murdered by the Sherriff's champion archer. But after two years comes news that Richard is a prisoner in Austria; the Queen Mother Eleanor and the Archbishop of Canterbury arrive in the Midlands to raise his ransom. It is a theme derived from *Ivanhoe* rather than medieval myth. But it serves to underline the legitimism of Robin and the outlaws. They contribute to the ransom themselves, and raid the Sheriff's treasury to add his fortune to the ransom. Then when the Sheriff's men disguised as outlaws try to steal the ransom, the outlaws foil them and send the Queen Mother on her way with the money.

Eventually a mysterious Black Knight turns up in the forest who identifies himself as King Richard. The outlaws kneel before him and the King makes Robin Earl of Locksley and marries him to Marian. The outlaws thus remain loyal to the true King, who is a populist monarch and oppose only illegitimate and oppressive authority in the form of Prince John and the Sheriff. Robin's incorporation into the nobility at the end confirms his constitutional soundness. So the Disney version has Robin fighting domestic subversion rather than committing it.

The chivalric cycle proper began with MGM's lavish and stirring film of *Ivanhoe* (1952), shot in rich Technicolor on location in England and featuring one of the great cinematic action set-pieces, the intricately detailed and magnificently staged siege of Torquilstone. The background here is the conflict between the Saxons and the Normans but the solution to that divisive conflict is loyalty to the Crown, in the person of Richard I, for it is Richard who has inspired the loyalty of the leading character, the Saxon knight Wilfred of Ivanhoe (Robert Taylor). As in the Robin Hood films, a central theme is the plan of Prince John and the Norman knights to seize the throne by preventing the payment of the ransom, required by the Archduke Leopold of Austria, who holds Richard captive. Ivanhoe, who remains throughout devotedly loyal to Richard, sets about foiling John and raising the ransom. In this he is aided by Robin Hood and his Saxon outlaws. Robin Hood (Harold Warrender) is called Locksley throughout, reflecting Sir Walter Scott's practice. When Ivanhoe rides in the tournament at Ashby as the Black Knight and defeats the Normans, Locksley tells him: 'We are your men.' Later the outlaws take the injured Ivanhoe to the forest to recover, help to raise the ransom and lay siege to Torquilstone where most of the leading characters are held prisoner. The castle is taken and the captives freed.

But *Ivanhoe* is more than just a costume adventure. The product of the regime of the committed liberal Dore Schary at MGM, it is nothing less than a civil rights swashbuckler, for it includes two significant subjects on that theme. Wamba (Emlyn Williams), the jester of Cedric the Saxon, is freed from his serfdom and becomes Ivanhoe's Squire. The iron collar of serfdom is struck from his neck by Ivanhoe. Wamba says that he wishes all England could similarly be free and Ivanhoe says it will be when Richard returns. It is hard in the context of America not to see this as an oblique reference to the abolition of slavery and the struggle for civil rights for the ex-slaves.

Even more explicit is the role of the Jewish characters. Isaac of York (Felix Aylmer), the Jewish patriarch, who is despised by the Normans, is rescued by Ivanhoe from attack by men-at-arms and escorted to his home in Sheffield. Isaac's wife had been killed in Spain and he and his daughter had fled as refugees to England, only to find the Jews also being persecuted there. Ivanhoe asks for the Jews' help in raising the ransom for the King. Isaac replies that Richard had looted synagogues to pay for his crusade. Ivanhoe promises in Richard's name to end persecution of the Jews in return for ransom money. Isaac with enormous dignity replies: 'Let him promise justice for each man, be he Saxon or Norman or Jew', and Ivanhoe agrees. Throughout, Ivanhoe protects and supports the Jews and the Jews back the restoration of Richard in return for civil rights. This sympathy for the Jews and opposition to discrimination was briefly a trend in post-war Hollywood liberal films, such as *Gentleman's Agreement* (1947) and *Crossfire* (1947), the second of which films had been produced under Dore Schary's regime when he was at RKO Radio Pictures.

The plight of the Jews is linked in *Ivanhoe* with what can only be seen as a bold attack on McCarthyism. The Jewess Rebecca (Elizabeth Taylor) is accused of sorcery and witchcraft. She is put on trial not, as in the book, by the Grand Master of the Templars but by Prince John. It is made clear that this is a political trial. John's adviser, Waldemar FitzUrse, says that he does not believe in sorcery and witchcraft, but adds: 'But your people will.' Prince John makes a speech claiming that witchcraft (i.e. Communism in the contemporary context) is spreading through the land and must be stamped out. Richard has fallen into the hands of its practitioners the Jews: 'As the servant of the Jews, who would call Richard English?' John thus links false charges of subversion with anti-Semitism. John demands that Rebecca be burned, false witnesses give perjured testimony and Sir Brian de Bois Guilbert, who loves her, begs her to admit her guilt and renounce her faith in order to save her life. 'I would not live in the world you offer. It has no faith, no love, no honour', she replies. Ivanhoe appears to defend her in trial by combat, defeats the Prince's Champion Guilbert and saves her life. At this point, the ransomed and released King Richard (Norman Wooland) arrives at the head of his crusaders. John capitulates and Richard delivers the final message to the Saxons and Normans kneeling before him. 'Before me kneels a nation divided. Rise as one man and that one man – for England.' So the King confirms that he stands for a policy of reconciliation and integration. The trial scene was written by Communist Waldo Salt in an early draft of the script and, although he was later blacklisted for non-cooperation with HUAC, the scene remained in the final film.

In the context of 1952, *Ivanhoe* functions as historical allegory. Returned from the Crusades (Second World War), war hero Ivanhoe finds a nation whose racial divisions are exacerbated by anti-Semitism, the oppression of the poor and show trials of alleged subversives. He fights against all these wrongs and ensures the return of a King who will end discrimination and division. In all this, Ivanhoe is aided by Robin Hood.

The success of *Ivanhoe* was such that MGM immediately re-teamed star and director in *Knights of the Round Table* (1954), the first feature film to seek to dramatize the Arthurian epic of Sir Thomas Malory. But like all 1950s films, it is recast for the times. It becomes the story of the establishment of constitutional monarchy and an order of chivalry in England (rather than the more accurate Britain). It opens with civil war after the departure of the Romans and the crown of England contested by Arthur Pendragon (Mel Ferrer), Duke of Gwent, illegitimate son of Uther Pendragon, and Morgan Le Fay (Anne Crawford), the late King's legitimate daughter, and her champion, Modred (Stanley Baker), Lord of the Isles. (He is called Modred rather than the more usual form in English Arthurian tradition since Malory, Mordred.)

Arthur's adviser Merlin (Felix Aylmer) says that whoever can draw the sword Excalibur from the stone will be King: Modred fails, Arthur succeeds. He calls all the combatants to a conference at the ring of stones where Arthur preaches unity ('We have but one cause – England') and Merlin argues for constitutional rule ('The true ruler of England is her law'). But this view is opposed by Mar, King of the Picts, King Mark of Cornwall and Modred, who reject constitutional monarchy: 'He would make us serve the peasants who were born to serve us.' The civil war resumes and eventually Modred and his forces are defeated and Arthur is firmly established as King. The Round Table is created and the knights take an oath 'to fear God, honour the King and defend the realm with honour and might'. The King swears on his sword to do battle against all evildoers, to defend the helpless, to protect all women, to be merciful to all, to honour his word, to be true in friendship and faithful in love. All the knights repeat the oath. It establishes chivalry as the ethical code of the kingdom and the creed of the ruling elite.

Although Arthur has been reconciled with Morgan and Modred and they have taken up residence at Camelot, they continue to plot against Arthur. Arthur has married Princess Guinevere, who was rescued from captivity by Sir Lancelot and has fallen in love with him. Merlin detecting this love and fearing its disruptive potential, warns Lancelot that he must leave court. So he marries Elaine and goes to defend the Northern Marches against the Picts. He defeats the Picts, Elaine dies in childbirth and Lancelot returns to court. Morgan and Modred poison Merlin and now there is no one to stop them. Guinevere, jealous of the attentions paid by Lancelot to another woman, goes to his chamber at night and they are trapped there together by the knights sent to watch them by Morgan. They are charged with adultery and treason. In a departure from the assumptions of the medieval romances story but in line with the moralistic outlook of the 1950s, Lancelot claims that their love was never consummated physically: 'By denial and suffering, the heart is purified.' Arthur commutes the mandatory death sentences to banishment for Lancelot and a convent for Guinevere. Modred raises revolt, this time leading Englishmen as well as outlanders. In the final battle, Arthur is mortally wounded and Lancelot arrives in time to see him die. He gives Excalibur to Lancelot and orders him to throw it into the sea as it has been stained with English blood. Lancelot kills Modred and ends the civil war. The film culminates with Lancelot and Perceval in the Hall of the Round Table, where Perceval, but not Lancelot, sees a vision of the holy grail and hears the voice of God telling him he has been granted this vision 'so that faith in what is eternal may be renewed. Of fellowship and honour nought is lost.' Perceval is ordered to comfort Lancelot, tell him he is forgiven and his son Galahad will become the greatest knight of them all. 'Blessed be God who lives and moves in all things forever.'

This is a version of Malory cleaned up and reinterpreted for the 1950s. The love of Lancelot and Guinevere is pure and honourable; the objective of Arthur and Merlin is to establish constitutional monarchy and Arthur's enemies seek to overthrow both in favour of dictatorship. The Arthurian vision is blessed at the end by God.

It is instructive to compare this version with *Lancelot and Guinevere* (1962) (US title: *Sword of Lancelot*), which was directed by and starred Cornel Wilde, the erstwhile Robin

Hood Junior and D'Artagnan Junior. He plays Lancelot as a civilized French-accented knight by contrast with Robert Taylor's stolidly American Lancelot. This version still stresses the threat to King Arthur's throne from subversion (Sir Modred, in this version his illegitimate son, seeks the throne) and from invasion by the pagan Saxons. Modred murders Arthur and allies with the Saxons eventually and Lancelot has to take charge of the armies of Britain to defeat him. What is notable about this version, and shows that we are moving into the 1960s when there was to be profound social and cultural change, in the film's concentration on the love affair. In this version it is physically consummated, unlike in *Knights*, and it is Guinevere (Jean Wallace), sexy and sultry, who takes the lead, pressing Lancelot to sleep with her, and later urging him to kill Arthur and Gawain in single combat so that they can be free. But Lancelot is constantly tormented by the conflict of love and honour, just as Arthur is tormented when the adultery is discovered by his need to implement the death penalty which he himself introduced for treason and by his natural human desire to remit it. By the 1960s, the code is a cause for anguish rather than single-minded and unquestioning application. Also, with bodies transfixed by spears, heads cleaved open and arms shorn off, it is far more violent that previous chivalric epics and another harbinger of cinema to come.

But *Knights of the Round Table* was only one of three Arthurian epics to be released in 1954. Twentieth Century-Fox's *Prince Valiant*, directed by Henry Hathaway and based on the comic strip drawn by Harold R. Foster from 1937 to 1979, was almost a direct response to Dr Wertham's attack on comics. For far from being corrupting and depraving, the *Prince Valiant* strip was inspiring and instructive. For here was a hero, Prince Valiant (played by Robert Wagner, then twenty-four) who was the perfect chivalric identification figure for American teenagers and a cinematic corrective to the moody rebels played by Marlon Brando and James Dean in films released at the same time. Valiant is devoted to his parents and to the crown, learns and lives by the code of chivalry and chastely and devotedly loves a beautiful princess.

This film contains the twin threats of Cold War 1950s: the external threat from barbarians and the internal threat from subversion. The context is the conflict of Christianity and paganism. The Christian royal family of the Viking kingdom of Scandia have been overthrown by a pagan traitor Sligon who has occupied the throne. Prince Valiant, son of the exiled King Aguar, swears to restore the cross of Christ to Scandia and is sent to Camelot to train for knighthood under the tutelage of Sir Gawain. Valiant is eventually captured by the pagan Vikings and taken to Scandia with his family. Sligon plans to crucify all the Christians in his kingdom. But the Christian Vikings loyal to the old royal family rise in revolt, chanting: 'In this sign conquer' (the motto of the Christian Roman Emperor Constantine in his war against the pagans). They overthrow Sligon and restore the royal family. Intertwined with this threat to Christianity from paganism is the plotting of Sir Brack (James Mason), alias the Black Knight, who is in league with Sligon, plans to overthrow Arthur and seize the throne of Britain. He is exposed by Valiant, who kills him in a duel. Valiant is then admitted to 'the most Christian order of the Knights of the Round Table'. However, Liberal scriptwriter Dudley Nichols boldly inserted a direct comment on McCarthyism in a scene in which Prince Valiant resists the demands of Sligon's seneschal that he name the names of the members of the Christian opposition movement.

The Black Knight figured again but on the side of right this time in another piece of Arthurian apocrypha, *The Black Knight* (1954), directed by Tay Garnett. It was produced by Warwick Films for Columbia Pictures, with interiors shot at Pinewood Studios in England and exteriors shot in Spain and utilizing some very Spanish-looking castles. Warwick Films, the company set up by Americans Irving Allen and Albert R. Broccoli, specialized in British-made action adventure films with American stars in the lead and a transatlantic hard edge often lacking in the native British equivalent.

The ethos of the film is once again chivalry but chivalry democratized, an ethos available to all regardless of birth. The hero is John, a humble-born sword-smith who aspires to marry Lady Linnet, daughter of the Earl of Yeonil. John should really have been played by someone like the youthful Robert Wagner but in a piece of curious miscasting is played by forty-one-year-old Alan Ladd, tired, ageing, glum-looking and giving the impression he would sooner be anywhere else rather than Arthurian Britain. John is not wealthy or noble-born and needs to make his own way to prove himself. He has an older mentor, Sir Ontzlake (Andre Morell), who trains and advises him. Ontzlake encourages him to go for knighthood ('Nothing is impossible . . . knighthood is a flower to be plucked') and tells him to fight for it ('There comes a time in every man's life when he must fight for what he wants most'). Sir Ontzlake reveals that he was also of humble origin and won knighthood by his own efforts. The Round Table is thus defined as both democratic and meritocratic.

When 'Viking' raiders attack and sack Yeonil Castle and kill Lady Yeonil, John adopts the guise of the Black Knight to hunt them down. In a scene designed to demonstrate the values of knighthood, King Arthur (Anthony Bushell) knights Sir Hal. Hal promises to show valour and courtesy, defend the right, be loyal to the King, not to fight for worldly gain and 'to be in all things a Christian gentleman'. At the end, having like Hal proved himself worthy, John is knighted by the King and marries Linnet. So one theme of the film is the training and qualification for knighthood of the young humble-born hero.

Even more significant is the threat to King Arthur's land – called England throughout – from without and within. This results in *The Black Knight* being a prime example of Cold War paranoia. The external threat is represented by Sir Palamedes (Peter Cushing), the Saracen knight at King Arthur's court. He is plotting with King Mark of Cornwall to overthrow Arthur and take over England. The so-called Vikings are Mark's men in disguise. Mark, although baptized as a Christian to allay suspicion, is secretly a pagan (i.e. a Communist) and plots to overthrow Christianity and replace it with the worship of the Sun God. Sir Ontzlake observes darkly in the authentic tones of a Cold War warrior: 'There is treason all about us and it must be stamped out before all of us, yes, and King Arthur himself are overwhelmed by it.' The villains are the pagan Celts of Cornwall (Communist subversives) and the Saracens of Palamedes, waiting across the Channel to invade (the Soviet Union). It is made visually clear by the fact that where the Christian knights are clad in conservative blue, the Saracen forces are clad in red and symbolize therefore the Soviet 'reds'.

King Arthur endows a new monastery and inaugurates it with a speech about the spread of Christianity. 'All who defend not the faith are heretics who have already gone over to the enemy', says the King. In other words, all those who are not committed democrats and Christians are ipso facto Communists. The 'Vikings' under Palamedes attack the monastery, slaughter the monks and carry off captives to Stonehenge for human sacrifice to the Sun God. At Stonehenge while dancing girls gyrate and Vikings carouse, monks are burned in cages and the High Priest prepares to sacrifice the captured Linnet. King Arthur and his knights ride to the rescue in the nick of time and the King orders Stonehenge, the symbol of paganism, destroyed. John kills Palamedes in a duel and the Christians defeat the Saracen forces in a pitched battle.

The Black Knight is a recurrent trope in the chivalric films of the 1950s and although sometimes he is a force of evil, a plotter concealing his identity behind black armour, the better to accomplish his evil (Sir Brack in *Prince Valiant*, Sir Mordred in *Adventures of Sir Galahad*), he is more often an undercover force for good. John in *The Black Knight* is actively seeking the identity of the plotters against the King. Ivanhoe adopts the guise of the Black Knight to fight the Norman supporters of Prince John. King Richard adopts the guise in *The Story of Robin Hood* in order to make contact with the outlaws. The guise also figures notably in *The Warriors* (UK title: *The Dark Avenger*) (1955), which is set in France in 1359, where after years of war, Edward III, having conquered half of France, seeks peace and reconciliation with the French nobles; they, however, plot his overthrow. The hero, Edward, Prince of Wales (Errol Flynn) adopts the guise of the Black Knight to enter the French castle, rescue the captive Lady (Joan Holland) and learn the enemy plans. All this undercover activity for good and ill parallels a trope in contemporary anti-Communist film-making of figures acting undercover either to unmask Communist plots (*I Married a Communist, I Was a Communist for the FBI*) or to further Communist plots (*My Son John, Conspirator*).

But not all the chivalric epics were necessarily conservative. As we have seen, *Ivanhoe* was notably liberal. *King Richard and the Crusaders* (1954), directed by David Butler and based on Sir Walter Scott's *The Talisman*, was the only 1950s film actually to feature the Crusades and it proved remarkably sympathetic to the Saracens, in contrast to *The Black Knight*. The book also featured the person who was during the reign of Richard I the actual Earl of Huntingdon, the title frequently granted in films and books to Robin Hood. The title was held by David, Prince of Scotland, who was a character in the novel, going on crusade under the *nom de guerre* of Sir Kenneth, the Knight of the Leopard.[7] The film simplified matters by having the hero simply be Sir Kenneth of Huntingdon, younger son of the Earl of Huntingdon. But it never explains why he should be Scottish. The film takes a distinctly jaundiced view of the Western allies, notably France and Austria, who plot and squabble among themselves, seeking to undermine the leadership of King Richard I (George Sanders).

He is threatened more by his internal enemies than by the external enemies, the Saracens. The most guilty are the ruthlessly ambitious Sir Giles Amaury, Grand Master of the Knights of the Castle Refuge, and the scheming Venetian Marquis Conrad of Montferrat, who plan to assassinate the King and use the army to carve out a kingdom for themselves in the East. Richard is wounded by an archer in Giles's pay but healed when the Saracen Sultan Saladin sends his personal physician Ilderim of Kurdistan (Rex Harrison) to tend him. In fact Ilderim is Saladin in disguise. 'By our lady, this is chivalry indeed', declares Sir Kenneth of his actions. Scottish Knight Sir Kenneth of Huntingdon (Laurence Harvey) is pro-Moslem and denounced Amaury and his Castellans for persecuting defenceless Moslems. He admires Saladin who is the most civilized and attractive of the film's characters, and he declares: 'The warriors of Saladin and the knights of Richard have a goodly creed in common – chivalry.' When the King's banner is torn down, while Kenneth is on guard, he is disgraced, stripped of his knighthood and banished, to take refuge with Saladin. But when Saladin's peace envoys are murdered and Lady Edith Plantagenet (Virginia Mayo), cousin of Richard and sweetheart of Kenneth, is carried off by Amaury and his men, the Crusaders and the Saracens join forces to rescue her. Kenneth fights and kills Amaury, is restored to knighthood and marries Edith. True chivalry has triumphed over racial divisions between Westerners and Saracens and over the greed and ambition of false Christians.

The Robin Hood and King Arthur cycles came together in one of the last films of the cycle, *Siege of the Saxons* (1963). Produced for Columbia Pictures and directed by Nathan Juran, it was constructed around big action scenes lifted from earlier Columbia productions: the opening tournament and attack on the royal procession from *Rogues of Sherwood Forest*, the forest chases and outlaw gatherings from *Bandit of Sherwood Forest*, the attacks on Yeonil Castle and the monastery and the final pitched battle from *The Black Knight*.

The ailing King Arthur (Mark Dignam, who played Merlin in *Lancelot and Guinevere*) has a hitherto unknown daughter, Princess Katherine (Janette Scott). But his chief minister, Edmund of Cornwall, is plotting to seize the throne. He is in alliance with the Saxons, whose Prince ('England is ready to be conquered – weak after years of peace') promises him forces to help overthrow Arthur. Thus internal and external threats are linked. Arthur goes on a hunting trip and is held up in the forest by Robert Marshall (Ronald Lewis), a Robin Hood type outlaw opposed to the tyranny of Edmund on his estates. But Arthur recruits Robert to help him in his hunt. However, the Saxons attack Edmund's castle where the King is staying and Arthur is killed. Marshall rescues Katherine several times from Edmund's men and they seek Merlin, who is living in retirement in the forest of Chatham. Edmund proclaims himself Regent and prepares to ascend the throne. Marshall recruits a band of outlaws, rescues Merlin from Edmund's men and together they interrupt Edmund's coronation. Merlin produces Excalibur and insists that only the rightful ruler can draw it. Edmund fails and flees to Saxons who kill him for failing, and attack Camelot. Katherine succeeds, is proclaimed Queen and her loyal forces defeat the Saxons. She makes Robert Baron of Cornwall and Chatham and marries him. So the outlaws support the legitimate heir and ensure the defeat of the usurper and his barbarian allies.

While Hollywood was devoting its energies to Arthurian epics, the British company Hammer Films, more commonly associated with Frankenstein, Dracula and the Mummy, produced three lively low-budget Robin Hood films, *The Men of*

Sherwood Forest (1954), *Sword of Sherwood Forest* (1961) and *A Challenge for Robin Hood* (1967), each of which seemed to be striving for a different idiom. Val Guest's *The Men of Sherwood Forest* looked back to Flynn's *Robin Hood* for its style of non-stop action and the uncovering and foiling of a plot by Norman aristocrats, who support Prince John, to assassinate King Richard (Patrick Holt) on his return from captivity in Austria. Minor Hollywood star Don Taylor was cast as Robin and his beard, haircut and superficial resemblance to Flynn evoked immediate memories of the 1938 film, until he opened his mouth, when his gravelly American voice contrasted markedly with Flynn's pure English accent. In this version, Robin's chief henchman was Friar Tuck (Reginald Beckwith) and there was particular emphasis on both as quick-witted tricksters, Tuck pioneering roulette and strip poker and Robin posing as a troubadour to enter the enemy castle.

Sword of Sherwood Forest was the feature film culmination of the long-running television series *The Adventures of Robin Hood,* one of the most significant developments in the Robin Hood saga.[8] Sapphire Films's *The Adventures of Robin Hood* was shown on British and American television between 1955 and 1958 and starred Richard Greene, whose mature and wise Robin projected an avuncular image appropriate for teatime viewing for children. One hundred and forty-three half-hour episodes were made, many of them scripted pseudonymously by blacklisted American leftists. This may explain why one of the continuing themes of the series is the overriding concern with social justice and in particular the iniquities of the feudal and manorial systems. It also shows a recurrent preoccupation with informing and 'naming names' that can only reflect the experiences of McCarthyism. The immediate model for the television series was Disney's 1952 *Robin Hood* and like Richard Todd, Richard Greene is a commoner, the son of the chief forester of the King, but as the owner of Locksley manor and as played by Greene he is undoubtedly a gentleman. He is also inflexibly loyal to King Richard and opposes Prince John's schemes to displace him. But the reinstatement of the Saxon/Norman rivalry absent from the Disney film, and which should in this context be seen as shorthand for lower class/upper class conflict, underlines the social concerns of the scriptwriters. When Greene came to star in and co-produce the feature film, however, he dispensed with his television supporting cast and returned to a plot closer to Hammer's previous Robin Hood entry, *The Men of Sherwood Forest*. This time Robin and the outlaws foil a plot by dissident aristocrats to murder Hubert Walter, Archbishop of Canterbury, Chancellor of England, representative of the King and champion of the people's rights. But Greene retained the ballad introduction of the 1952 film and the television series. Here it was sung by Dennis Lotis, a popular singer of the day, cast as Alan-a-Dale.

A Challenge for Robin Hood proposed an entirely new version of Robin's outlawry. In this version uniquely Robin (Barrie Ingham) is a Norman, Robin de Courtenay. The context is inheritance disputes, when Robin is framed for the murder of his cousin Henry, by Henry's brother Roger who wishes to inherit the whole of the Courtenay property, divided by will between the three of them. Robin flees to the greenwood and becomes leader of a band of Saxon outlaws, led previously by Alan-a-Dale. The rest of the film is a battle between them and the Norman forces of Roger and his ally, the Sheriff of Nottingham. Although Robin and the outlaws are loyal to the absent King Richard and Roger is a supporter of Prince John, there is really no political dimension to this film. Its direct inspiration is in fact the English pantomime tradition, which Robin Hood had entered as a character in *Babes in the Wood*. This version has a Cinderella theme with Marian, daughter of murdered Saxon knight Sir Brian FitzWarren (a character from *Dick Whittington*), posing as a kitchen-maid until rescued by Prince Charming (Robin), who at the end she marries in the greenwood. One of the highlights of the film is a massive pie-fight which covers the rescue of Robin and Will Scarlet from the gallows, and confirms the pantomime inspiration.

The reduction of the Robin Hood saga to pantomime and domestic concerns confirms the end of a cycle which had begun in the immediate aftermath of the war, with precise political and ideological concerns. The conditions that had given it birth had themselves changed. The heyday of the HUAC hearings was 1947 to 1954. During that period Hollywood, anxious to demonstrate its political credentials, made some thirty-three anti-Communist films.[9] It is precisely the period of the major Arthurian epics and the majority of the Robin Hood films, but in 1954 McCarthy over-reached himself and was censured by the Senate after attacking the army and the President, and HUAC's operations ceased. McCarthy died in 1957 but the blacklist of leftists in Hollywood continued. It was overturned only in 1960 when Dalton Trumbo, one of the imprisoned Hollywood scriptwriters, was once again able to receive screen credits for his work (on *Exodus* and *Spartacus*), and thereafter the blacklist was abandoned.

In a wider context the first phase of the Cold War ended in 1965 and from then until it revived in 1973, the United States embarked on a policy of détente. The economies of both the super-powers were in trouble and it was in both their interests to de-escalate conflict. More significantly, America became embroiled in the Vietnam War and hoped to use the Soviet Union to put pressure on Ho Chi Minh. So the propaganda imperatives of the Cold War weakened and the need for Cold War warriors on film lessened.[10]

During the 1960s wider social and cultural changes in the Western world eclipsed the code of chivalry that was a central ingredient of the Robin Hood and King Arthur films. The old Hollywood studios, already weakened by the court decision which forced them to divest themselves of their cinema chains and further undermined by the rise of television, began to break up and instead a wider range of independent producers emerged. At the same time the nature of the audience changed. Increasingly from the 1960s the core audience for films was perceived to be largely under thirty. This had far-reaching ideological consequences. The old studio structure had by and large aimed at a cross-class, mixed gender and all age audience from six to sixty and had demonstrated in its films a commitment to the political, social and cultural status quo, dramatizing what it perceived to be widely held common values and seeking to avoid controversy. The new youthful cinema audience was assumed to be on the whole anti-Establishment and unsympathetic to the values and beliefs of the older generation, something given substance in 1960s America by, for instance, the rise in drug-taking, the decline in marriage and the widespread opposition to the Vietnam war. In both Britain and America chivalry was rejected: by the left as class-bound, by feminists as patriarchal and by individualists as inhibiting. Where chivalry had been based on the subordination of self to concepts of honour, duty, and service, the dominant philosophy of the 'Swinging Sixties' was a hedonistic individualism based on the assertion and fulfilment of the self and the slogan 'I want it now'.

In films, the chivalric hero was eclipsed by a new hero more in tune with that philosophy. His emergence can be dated precisely to 1958 and the enormous success of Richard Fleischer's film *The Vikings* in which the heroes were hard-fighting, hard-drinking, lusty, pagan Viking warriors, with a code of instant gratification, violence and self-assertion. This can properly be described as a seminal film as it had no precursors and was followed in the 1960s by a host of imitations: *The Last of the Vikings*, *The Fury of the Vikings*, *The Norseman*, *The Long Ships* and then in the 1980s by a cycle of films heroizing barbarian supermen, *Conan the Barbarian*, *Conan the Destroyer*, *Mad Max* (and its two sequels). So the very pagan barbarians whose philosophy was the antithesis of chivalry, and who had been a threat to the civilized Christian values of the Round Table and the knightly commitment of Robin Hood and his outlaws, themselves became the heroes of the next generation of cinemagoers.[11]

The dichotomy that Barczewski discerned between the Robin Hood and the King Arthur myths in nineteenth-century British culture does not hold true for the cinema, the most potent disseminator of the myths in either British or American culture for the first seventy years of the twentieth century. The two cycles have far more similarities than differences in their cinematic version. The heroes of both the Robin Hood and King Arthur films are usually, though not invariably, gentlemen. Even those heroes who are not gentlemen (John the swordsmith in *The Black Knight*, Robert Marshall in *Siege of the Saxons*) earn themselves knighthood and/or elevation to the peerage. This confirms the centrality of chivalry to the culture of both Britain and America. The heroes of both cycles are unalterably loyal to the crown, which functions as the symbol of legitimate authority and is seen as the guarantor of freedom, justice, equality before the law and civil rights for all. When they are in revolt, the heroes are seeking merely to restore legitimate authority and end an arbitrarily imposed tyranny. Legitimate authority always resides in the rightful king, be he Richard I, Henry III or King Arthur. The heroes of the Robin Hood and King Arthur films were always combating internal attempts to subvert the constitution and external threats from foreign, usually pagan invaders. They had come to stand not for different aspects of a British national identity but a shared Anglo-American identity, based on chivalry, Christianity and constitutional government.

The casting of these films confirms that they are a shared Anglo-American project. Robin Hood films are as likely to have American leads (Cornel Wilde, John Derek, Don Taylor) as British (Richard Todd, Richard Greene, Barrie Ingham). While the heroes of the chivalric epics are almost invariably American (Robert Taylor, Robert Wagner, Alan Ladd, Cornel Wilde), it is significant that King Arthur is almost always played by a British actor (Brian Aherne in both *Prince Valiant* and *Lancelot and Guinevere*, Anthony Bushell, Mark Dignam); as is King Richard I (George Sanders, Norman Wooland, Patrick Barr, Patrick Holt). The most notable exception to this is the casting of the American Mel Ferrer as Arthur in *Knights of the Round Table*. In general, royal authority has a British accent.

Almost totally absent from the narratives is magic, an integral element of the Arthurian legends. The only exception to the absence of magic is Columbia's 1950 production, *Adventures of Sir Galahad*, a cheaply made and on the whole badly acted fifteen-episode serial starring George Reeves, later to be the television *Superman*, as Galahad. It utilized the costumes, props and title music from the 1946 Robin Hood film *The Bandit of Sherwood Forest* and was shot on the Columbia ranch, familiar from a host of 'B' westerns. During the course of the serial, Merlin, Morgan Le Fay and the Lady of the Lake all performed magic. But beyond this, the film was structured around the three themes that were to be common in subsequent Arthurian epics: Galahad proving himself and gaining his knighthood by combating internal subversion (Sir Mordred aiming to dethrone

Arthur) and external threat (the invading Saxons). Where magic was to be an important feature of later Arthurian (*Excalibur*) and Robin Hood (*Robin of Sherwood*) ventures, reflecting the rise of alternatives to Christianity, it had no place in the 1950s and 1960s cycle where the concern was politics and ideology. When Merlin appeared (*Knights of the Round Table, Lancelot and Guinevere, Siege of the Saxons*), it was as wise man and adviser to the King rather than as magician.

Barczewski suggests that in the nineteenth century the myth of Arthur, which had strong Celtic roots, was taken over by the English and became increasingly English rather than British. In the cinema, it is true that, where Arthur's kingdom is correctly called Britain in *Prince Valiant* and *Lancelot and Guinevere*, it is called England in *Knights of the Round Table, The Black Knight, Siege of the Saxons* and the stodgy 1967 film version of the hit Lerner and Loewe Broadway musical *Camelot* (which retold the Arthur-Guinevere-Lancelot story with largely unmemorable songs). But this reflects not so much an English take-over as the fact that these were American films and Americans invariably refer to Britain as England.

Robin Hood and King Arthur would come back again after the 1960s both to cinema and television, but in guises very different from the ones examined here. There would be a peasant Robin (*Robin and Marian*), a socialist Robin (*Robin of Sherwood*) and a politically correct Robin (*Robin Hood-Prince of Thieves*); while in *First Knight*, the British King Arthur (Sean Connery) would hand over the Camelot project and Guinevere to the American Lancelot (Richard Gere). These eternal mythic figures were being refashioned to fit new political and social conditions, new value systems and new role models and gender images, very different from those which had prevailed in the Cold War and which had for some twenty years called on Robin Hood and King Arthur as Cold War warriors.

NOTES

[1] Stephanie L. Barczewski, *Myth and National Identity in Nineteenth Century Britain: the Legends of King Arthur and Robin Hood* (Oxford: Oxford University Press, 2000).

2   On the full corpus of Arthurian films, see Kevin J. Harty (ed.), *Cinema Arthuriana* (New York: Garland, 1991); Kevin J. Harty (ed.), *King Arthur on Film* (Jefferson, N.C.: McFarland, 1999); Rebecca Umland and Samuel Umland, *The Use of Arthurian Legend in Hollywood Film* (Westport, Connecticut: Greenwood, 1996). On the Robin Hood films, see Scott Allen Nollen, *Robin Hood: a Cinematic History of the English Outlaw and his Scottish Counterparts* (Jefferson, N. C. and London: McFarland, 1999); Kevin J. Harty, 'Robin Hood on Film: Moving beyond a Swashbuckling Stereotype', in Thomas Hahn (ed.), *Robin Hood in Popular Culture: Violence, Transgression and Justice* (Cambridge: D. S. Brewer, 2000) pp. 87–100; Stephen Knight, *Robin Hood: A Complete Study of the English Outlaw* (Oxford: Blackwell, 1994), pp. 218–61. On both Robin Hood and King Arthur films in the context of the swashbuckling genre see Jeffrey Richards, *Swordsmen of the Screen* (London: Routledge and Kegan Paul, 1977).

3   John Fraser, *America and the Patterns of Chivalry* (Cambridge: Cambridge University Press, 1982), pp. 12, 16.

4   *Ivanhoe* cost $3,842,000 to make and took $5,810,000 in America and $5,150,000 overseas ($10,960,000 overall). I owe these figures to H. Mark Glancy. Its follow up, *Knights of the Round Table*, took $8,230,000.

5   James Gilbert, *A Cycle of Outrage: America's Reaction to the Juvenile Delinquent in the 1950s* (Oxford: Oxford University Press, 1986).

6   Ina Rae Hark, 'The Visual Politics of The Adventures of Robin Hood', *Journal of Popular Film*, 5 (1976), 3–17.

7   David, Earl of Huntingdon, was the younger brother of King William the Lion of Scotland. He married in 1190 Maud, sister of Ranulf, Earl of Chester and not Scott's entirely fictional Lady Edith Plantagenet. A later medieval tradition claims he went on the Third Crusade. A gap of three-and-a-half years in his recorded career in the 1190s could plausibly be explained by his absence on crusade but it cannot be asserted unreservedly. He died in 1219. For his career see K. J. Stringer, *Earl David of Huntingdon* (Edinburgh: Edinburgh University Press, 1985).

8   Jeffrey Richards, 'Robin Hood on Film and Television since 1945', *Visual Culture in Britain*, 2 (2001), 65–80.

9   Terry Christensen, *Reel Politics: American Political Movies from 'Birth of a Nation' to 'Platoon'* (Oxford: Oxford University Press, 1987), p. 89.

10 Walter Lafeber, *America, Russia and the Cold War 1945–1980* (New York: McGraw Hill, 1980), pp. 258–79.

11 For a full discussion of this phenomenon, see Jeffrey Richards, 'From Christianity to Paganism: the New Middle Ages and the Values of "Medieval" Masculinity', *Cultural Values*, 3 (1999), 213–34.

'And for best supporting hero... Little John'

LAURA BLUNK

> Robyn stode in Bernesdale,
> And leyned him to a tre;
> And by hym stode Litell John,
> A good yeman was he.[1]

From his earliest mention in the legend 'Little John has always been the most important and inseparable of Robin Hood's companions'.[2] The *Gest of Robyn Hode* quotation above shows John linked to the formulaic 'Robin stode in Bernesdale'. He is placed by the author at the iconic heart of the myth, with the hero 'standing' – defying his enemies – in the forest and Little John *standing by* him. Singman suggests Robin's friendship with Little John is 'a relationship so prominent both in the stories and the external references to the legend that it is probably one of the oldest features of the legend'.[3] Two fifteenth-century chronicles pair the two as an outlaw duo already long famous and celebrated: Andrew of Wyntoun's *Orygynale Chronicle* (c.1420), in his entry for 1283, calls John and Robin 'Waythmen' who 'war commendit gude' ('were praised highly') and Walter Bower's *Continuation* of the *Scotichronicon* (c.1440) testifies to the fame and popularity of the two, placing them in 1266, as sympathizers with de Montfort's rebellion: 'the famous cut-throat Robin Hood, as well as Little John, together with their accomplices'.[4] The close relationship between the two is represented near the beginning in each of the early ballads. It is a suggestion by Little John that gets the action of the *Gest* started; Robin and John act together at the start of *Robin Hood and the Potter*; *Robin Hood and the Monk* begins with a near-fatal quarrel between John and Robin; and the two men set off together at the beginning of the adventure of *Robin Hood and Guy of Gisborne*. The earliest extant play (1475) includes John and Friar Tuck in a daring rescue of Robin from the Sheriff's jail.[5] In early modern Scotland, where annual festivities had earlier been led by a pair usually called the Abbot and Prior of Misrule or Unreason or Bonacord, or by the 'Summer King', these were gradually replaced (sometimes by direction of town councils) by Robin and John.

In ballad, drama, novel and film, Little John is never far from Robin's side. He appeared, standing by Robin's side, as soon as the tales of Robin Hood first came to the screen in the twentieth century. Like much in this protean cultural myth, however, the figure of John in film has not been static but changed in different eras in his social rank, confidence and the relationship with Robin as his leader. If the Robin Hood myth shows an outlaw defying authority, the relationship of John and Robin provides a further arena in which questions of leadership, rank, respect and rebellion can also be explored. His role as henchman among the outlaws or as Robin's closest companion and adviser gives rise to many different interpretations of the power relations between Robin and John and variations in John's own rank become as significant in the social dynamics of different versions as do differences in Robin's own rank.

Among the early ballads, we see an obedient, respectful John in the *Gest*'s opening stanzas not only the willing recipient of moral guidance from his master but actually asking to be given instructions about every aspect of conduct ('Tell us . . . what life we shall lede' (pp. 43–44)), whereas in the *Monk* he is fiercely resistant to any attempt by Robin to act as his master and pull rank on him.[6] The special relationship of these two outlaws is often the fulcrum out of which the beginning of the adventure comes, and it is clearly something the audience is assumed already to find familiar. In several early versions the story gets underway with a wager between Little John and Robin.[7] In others there is a difference of opinion.[8] The opening stanzas often show John offering conventional, or sometimes distinctly more sensible, advice where Robin is bolder, sometimes rash or headstrong.[9] It is curious that in the mysterious ballad 'Robyn and Gandelyn' the woodland companion of

Robin is 'his knawe Gandelyn', who avenges his master's death. There is no mention of Little John. The poem's Robin may not be Robin Hood, though the association with the forest, and the possibility that 'Gandelyn' is related to the name Gamlin which recurs in association the Robin Hood tradition, makes it hard not to feel here is a strand in the tradition that has otherwise been lost.[10]

The best known and most influential cinematic retellings of the legend in the English-speaking world have been the 1922 *Robin Hood*, starring Douglas Fairbanks, and the 1938 *Adventures of Robin Hood,* with Errol Flynn in the title role. Although the films are separated by sixteen years, Alan Hale played John in both of them, setting his mark on the screen image of the character.

Reinforcing the traditional literary interpretation of Little John, Hale's outlaw is a large man.[11] Introduced into the 1922 film as 'the Earl of Huntingdon's faithful squire', he is taller, if only by inches, than Fairbanks's athletic Robin. He is brawny and strong as well. It takes four men to hold him down when he and Robin, falsely accused by Gisbourne of desertion from King Richard's army, are arrested. In prison he is strong enough to bend the bars in his cell door and reach through the opening, nearly strangling the guard and forcing him to unlock the door. Once free, he rescues Robin and easily carries him outside, where he tends to the wounds of his injured lord.

Although his square-cut wig and moustache make him, to later audiences, look like a figure escaped from an illustration in the Brothers Grimm, there is nothing ludicrous about his character. Robin's faith in him is indicated when, just before leaving for the crusade, he gives John the task of protecting Marian: 'I leave in your keeping my dearest treasure. Guard her with your life.' John proves worthy of the trust. Sent by Marian to tell Huntingdon of Prince John's villainies at home, John stands loyally by his master when he is falsely imprisoned and it is he who effects their escape. The squire returns with the Earl to England and follows him to Sherwood Forest, becoming the outlaw Little John. When Robin has an important task to be done it is entrusted to John. When, with Robin apparently about to be executed by Prince John, Marian attempts to kill herself, it is Little John, first of all the outlaws to sneak into

'AND FOR BEST SUPPORTING HERO ... LITTLE JOHN'

the great hall of Nottingham Castle who reaches out and stops her. Always the right man in the right place, suffering with his lord the debasement from court to outlawry in the forest, Little John is in this film a model of strength, compassion and, above all, loyalty. From the moment he is introduced as 'the Earl of Huntingdon's faithful squire' faithfulness is the keynote of the concept of this character. But his character is only superficially sketched; the film's makers show no interest in developing it beyond that of trusty sidekick.

In his 1938 portrayal of Little John, Hale gets to play a slightly more rounded – if still limited – character. Although clad in the ubiquitous tights and wearing a silly feathered cap, this film's new yeoman Little John is a strong capable man with a sure sense of his own worth. His strength, self-confidence and easygoing nature show in the scene recounting Little John's first meeting with Robin. Following mainstream tradition going back at least to the ballad 'Robin Hood and Little John' (*c*.1624), the two meet when crossing a stream. In contrast to the lord-squire relationship in the Fairbanks movie, the 1938 John, though a yeoman, and as such of lower social standing than Sir Robert of Locksley, shows no subservience to Robin. Ordered by Robin to step aside, he replies: 'Only to a better man than myself.'[12] A friendly quarter-staff fight ensues during which the two men exchange blows and banter before John wins the contest by knocking Robin into the water. In the early literature too we see this sort of sportive conflict, whether wagering or sparring – literally or metaphorically – between Robin and John as a parallel to Robin's really serious conflict, which is with authority.

In the 1938 film there is no real animosity behind their conflict, and fight and scene are both light-hearted. The way different films treat this traditional fight over the stream is instructive about different approaches to the character of John and the permutations in the meaning of the myth. Here all is comradeship. Laughing, the two men sit of the bank of the river and converse as equals. Learning that his defeated opponent is Robin Hood, John says: 'Right glad I am that I fell in with you. I want to join you.' Instead of being in service to the Earl from the start, this John joins him later, voluntarily and with proud independence, and out of his own desire for justice.

That John is an outlaw out of principle rather than greed or loyalty is further demonstrated later in the film by his response to Robin's query as to what should be done with the ransom money taken from Gisbourne. To Robin's suggestion that they keep it for themselves he shouts out: 'Hold it for Richard.'

As member of this band of the merry men, John does not have pride of place as Robin's closest friend. That belongs to Will Gamlin who, clad in scarlet and playing the lute, merges Will Scarlet and Alan-a-Dale into one character. But John is always by Robin's side. When Locksley delivers his impassioned speech to the people of Nottinghamshire, urging his listeners to fight for 'Richard and England', it is John – standing to the right and just a little below Robin, but above the crowd, who cries out: 'Robin's right!' Strong and principled, John is also capable and reliable. It is he who is sent to carry out the attack on Gisbourne's advance guard; it is he and Tuck whom Robin asks to escort Marian out of Sherwood; and it is he whom the outlaw leader first asks to search for Richard when news comes of the monarch's return to England. Right-hand man, then, rather than closest friend, John is characterized here by good humour and accepting, tolerant nature, within the band. When Tuck responds to his gibe about the friar's girth with 'It will take twice that to fill your empty head', he laughs heartily, taking no offence. Tuck's remark, however, implies that John is not the brightest bulb among Sherwood's lights. Acting often on instinct, this yeoman John is shown not always taking time to think a situation through, for example, when Marian comes to the Saracen's Head tavern, offering to help the outlaws rescue Robin, John does not want to trust her because she is a Norman. It is the more thoughtful Will Gamlin who gives her a hearing. Later films picked up this impulsive, unreflective, trait, often depicting a John who is brave, loyal and good in a fight, but not particularly thoughtful.

Hale took on the role of Little John once more, playing now an older mentor to Robin's son in the 1950 *Rogues of Sherwood Forest*, but added little but age to his earlier characterization, which became the classic cinematic Little John: a large man of even bigger heart, loyal, capable, principled but not over-bright.

'AND FOR BEST SUPPORTING HERO... LITTLE JOHN'

In addition to *Rogues of Sherwood Forest*, a number of other Robin Hood films appeared during the 1950s: the Disney live-action *The Story of Robin Hood and his Merry Men* in 1952, *Men of Sherwood Forest* 1956, and *Son of Robin Hood* 1959, but the most memorable retelling from these years was on the small screen, *The Adventures of Robin Hood*, starring Richard Greene, aired in both Britain and the United States during the late 1950s.[13] Famously this series, in a heyday of socialist reform in Britain and employing left-wing Americans fleeing from the McCarthyite strains of the US film industry, has among its themes a strong sense of communal interdependency, as well as a distinct interest in the motifs of spies, 'moles' and betrayals. When asked about the programme's popularity, Greene stated that: 'It's harmony. Once you lose harmony, you lose quality in the whole thing. Then you lose the viewers. But here, we've always worked together as a team.'[14] Serendipitously, the teamwork of the cast and crew also mirrored the legendary harmony of Robin Hood's band, creating a programme with Robin as leader as the focus, but in which the main members of his band are given their moments in the spotlight. The episodic structure of a TV series no doubt contributed to this tendency. In this respect the series returned to a characteristic of the ballads, which not only depicted a Robin whose success was often due at least as much to teamwork as to individual prowess, but which often depicted one outlaw in a discrete adventure: a seventeenth-century example featuring Little John is 'Little John a Begging'.[15] Television series, with a much longer total screen-time than a two-hour film, have the time for writers and actors to develop characters more fully and *The Adventures of Robin Hood*, like *Robin of Sherwood* after it, is peopled by more three-dimensional outlaws rather than the broadly sketched stereotypes of earlier films.

Played in all but ten of the episodes by Archie Duncan, the series' Little John is first introduced in the third episode, 'Dead or Alive'. Now conceived as a serf, who is ordered to carry logs to his lord's house, John is again a huge man, whose size is commented on in a mixture of admiring but contemptuous terms by his feudal master, a reminder of the fact that unfree serfs were legally properties on an estate analogous to the stock: 'Isn't that splendid? Look at the size of the neck and shoulders! I think I'll select the healthiest lass I can find on the estate and marry him to her. Ought to produce a remarkable litter. Flex your muscles, bend your arms . . .'[16] Understandably angered by this treatment, John lifts the diminutive lord off the floor and deposits him helplessly on a high window sill, visual imagery exposing the lord's superiority as empty and contingent. As the lord calls for his guards to come and arrest John, the serf runs away to Sherwood. There he meets Joan, a serving girl from the Blue Boar Inn. She invites him to the tavern for breakfast and pretends to the soldiers they encounter there that he is her cousin. But the soldiers know that he is the fugitive serf and offer him a bargain: if he can catch Robin Hood, he will receive his freedom for a year and a day, the time necessary to make him a free man for good.

Responding to this offer John says: 'If you could make me a free man with the right to go where I choose and live as I choose, there's nothing I wouldn't do.' This bondman Little John's love of freedom is established thus early in the series' presentation of him, and in the socio-legal context of medieval serfdom. In a less positive characterization, however, the programme perpetuates the image of John as a man lacking intelligence. Depicted as an ignorant man, this John does not even know what an outlaw is until the soldiers tell him (he acts as surrogate for the young TV audience, of course, receiving this information).

Returning to the forest to search for the outlaw, John meets Robin in the traditional scene, while crossing a stream. When Robin orders him to step aside the love of freedom the programme has already established, simmering below the servitude and deference required of a serf, comes to the fore: 'I'm a free man,' John replies, 'And I was on the bridge first.' The traditional quarter-staff fight follows. Although this initial encounter between the two men is more hostile in tone here than in the sportive fight in the Flynn movie, the banter is as spirited, the match as equal, and Little John just as clearly the victor. As he helps Robin out of the stream, however, the two men laugh, and Robin asks Little John to join the outlaw band.

John, a spy at this stage, persuades Robin to accompany him to the Blue Boar, where the soldiers are waiting to arrest him, but along the way, as he listens to his companion, John begins to have second thoughts: not as stupid as he appeared, though still characterized as slow to perceive things, John senses he has been used by the soldiers. Hesitating, he says: 'Maybe you shouldn't come in.' But Robin, who suspected the trap, has prepared for an ambush and insists upon entering the tavern. Inside they are both taken prisoner, the guards breaking their promise to John. Disillusioned and shocked, he joins Robin and the fortuitously arrived outlaw band in fighting off the soldiers. The theme of hidden betrayal in this episode reminds us that the TV series was written in the context of the McCarthy era. When the outlaws are victorious, John agrees to join the band for real.

All the essential elements of the series' Little John are evident in this episode. John is a huge man, a serf, of far humbler social origins than the 1922 squire or the 1938 independent yeoman, proud and freedom-loving, and possessing a native and developing intelligence masked by superficial dim-wittedness. John's supposed lack of intelligence and sensitivity concerning it are central episodes in one other episode: 'Good-bye Little John'. A newcomer, Will Scarlet, has joined the band. Bright, intelligent and self-confident, Will is quickly trusted by Robin and soon takes a leading role in plotting the band's activities. Jealous of Robin's friendship with Scarlet and convinced that he is not smart enough to compete with the newcomer's brains, John, who is confident only in his physical prowess, persuades Will to have a wrestling match with him. When, to his great humiliation, he loses that match, he storms angrily out of the camp. We have here an episode not only focusing on individual outlaws but also developing dramatic dynamics of emotion and personality between them. Still furious, John takes out his anger first at a bush then a luckless tinker who is passing by. Only the arrival of Durward, another member of the band, keeps him from inflicting major damage on the tinker. As Durward tries to persuade him back to camp, John announces he is finished with Robin Hood.

We have here essentially the same motif we find in early ballads, of a quarrel between John and Robin, men who actually love each other deeply, a quarrel which leads to peril from the outlaws' real enemies. Such a quarrel initiates the action of *Robin Hood and the Monk*. In both the TV series and the ballad the quarrel creates the plot motif of danger and also a deepened emotional verisimilitude of John's outraged sensitivities (and in the *Monk* Robin's insensitivities). In the TV episode the emotion is that of rivalry for Robin's esteem, complicated by the status of a freed serf given to the character Little John. In both the anomalous mix of unconventional hierarchy/authority and equality within the band creates an unstable situation for its members that can only be managed safely through magnanimity and group spirit.

In 'Good-bye Little John', soldiers approach, but Durward and John, familiar with the forest, slip away, while the unfortunate tinker is arrested for being in the company of outlaws. Taken to the deputy sheriff he gives him the pleasing news that Robin and John have fallen out. The deputy sees an opportunity to break up the outlaw band and sets his plans in motion. Meanwhile, John returns to camp and Robin warmly reassures him he is second in command and the very best of lieutenants: Will, says Robin, is better at planning but John is better at carrying things out. Only partly mollified, John presses for clarification, asking who would be in command if anything happened to Robin. Robin tells him the band would have to decide. John's temper and tendency to act first and think later, he warns John, are traits that will go against him. Understanding that a contest between him and Will will only split the band, John tells Robin that he has to leave: he will not be a cause of dissension. The issue of John's opportunities to betray Robin now raises its head again: as before in this series, the traditional theme of John's loyalty is developed into a drama of betrayal to a discredited authority. The deputy sheriff sends a message to John offering him a pardon. Suspicious, John meets with the Norman official, greeting him with a mock bow, and demands to know what the bureaucrat wants in return. The deputy sheriff replies: 'Nothing'. Tuck, who luckily for the plot is present, reads the pardon and assures John it is real. Still doubtful, however, and less impulsive than he was, John points out that it is not signed and needs to be witnessed. After this, John takes time to think about things. He returns to tell the deputy sheriff he refuses the pardon. The deputy replies that it is too late: the pardon has been given, John is no longer an outlaw. John, however, responds:

> The pardon proves that you want to break up Robin Hood's band. The pardon proves you want to shout out to the whole country that you're a merciful man and you're not! The pardon proves that any man who wants to leave Robin Hood's band and live under the law all the time can do so by toadying to you... Listen, I don't want your pardon. The freer it makes me, the less I want it. I want to be Robin Hood's best man. I want to be the biggest outlaw in Prince John's territory. I don't want your pardon![17]

In order to regain outlaw status he attacks the deputy sheriff. As he does so both the outlaws and the sheriff's guards arrive. The usual fight takes place with the usual victory for the outlaws. The themes of John's mingled naivety and growing intelligence, which is also a growing political intelligence about the treachery involved in corrupt legitimate authority, and of the over-riding importance of group-loyalty, dominate this unfolding plot.

At the close of the episode, John, Robin and Will stand together laughing. Symbolically, John unexpectedly flips Will over in a wrestling throw. More confident now in his intelligence and pleased he was able to overcome Will in a physical contest, John is once more content. As Will, defeated by his fellow outlaw, looks up, laughing back at John, the two men are reconciled and all is well with the merry men.

The 1973 Disney animated film, *Robin Hood*, accepted the stereotype of the large, brave, loyal and superficially simple sidekick. With Phil Harris giving voice to the character, John is depicted, in Stephen Knight's words, as 'a large and stupid bear'.[18] This John adds to his already-established role of loyal friend, the role of emotional confidant in Robin's love life. The film does have one highlight, as far as John is concerned, however: the light-hearted romp together through the forest of Robin and his best friend as the soundtrack plays 'Robin Hood and Little John'. The song and the film stress John's closeness and loyalty to Robin. Their friendship as a duo is a prominent feature here, rather then the dynamics of the band as a whole.

Closeness and loyalty to Robin are not, however, at first, qualities associated with John in the next major television adaptation, the BBC series *The Legend of Robin Hood*, first aired in 1975. When the audience first sees Little John, played by Conrad Asquith, he is a suspicious character, the leader of a rival outlaw band. It is a fight between one of his men and one of Robin's that leads to his encounter with Robin over the traditional stream. It is an encounter between established power and a new contender for power in the forest. After making a derogatory remark about John's size, Robin tells him he will take revenge if any of John's men attack his again: 'You can take your revenge now! Or are you like a lizard that disappears as quickly as its tongue?' replies John, in no mood to be ordered about by a newcomer to the forest.[19] When Robin answers he is unarmed, John throws him a staff – symbolizing his own control over hostilities in the forest up to now – and the fight commences. Unlike the 1938 contest, this is no friendly sparring match. Blows fall fast and heavy before John knocks Robin into the stream and Robin pulls John in after him. Having, however, formed a basic respect for each other, through conflict, the two men finally wade laughingly out of the water. Yet, though no longer openly hostile to each other, they do not trust each other: in contrast to earlier versions, John does not join Robin's merry men as the conclusion to the fight. John continues to be set up as an enemy. When Robin is betrayed to Gisbourne's men, his followers suspect John is responsible. Robin, having escaped, seeks out John's band, with his men, to exact revenge. John explains he is innocent but the culprit was one of his followers. Asquith's Little John is big, as in earlier film versions, but here his height is menacing as Robin and his men do not know whether he is friend or enemy. This John is impressive, not a friendly, unconfident simpleton. Handing Robin his dagger, John says, unarmed, 'I speak the truth.' Robin believes him and finally the two bands unite. A difficult period of adjustment follows as the two men, both proud and used to command, learn to share authority and become friends. This is a new variation on the recurrent theme, centred on John in several versions, that divisions between outlaws weaken them in their fight against their real enemies. More than in any earlier version, this series presents John and Robin as equals. When John finally accepts Robin as leader, he is still ready to question or disagree and

Robin, in turn, values John's knowledge and skills, trusting him as his lieutenant. John stands by him even refusing, when captured by the sheriff, to save his own life by betraying Robin. As in the Percy folio ballad 'The Death of Robin Hood', it is John alone, of all his band, who is with Robin when, poisoned by the prioress of Kirklees, he dies. The series creates a John who has adult dignity, self-confidence, and a past life of his own in which he has independent power.

Robert Lester's *Robin and Marian*, in the next year, 1976, expands this more complex and equal interpretation of Little John. Lester's Little John is traditional only in his humble social origins and fierce loyalty to Robin. He is a seasoned warrior of whom to be wary. As in the Disney cartoon *Robin Hood*, he also watches sympathetically over Robin's emotional life. Played physically against traditional type, Nicol Williamson's Little John is shorter and slighter than Sean Connery's Robin Hood, but he is also more thoughtful and intelligent than his friend. At the beginning of the film an older Robin and John, who have served in King Richard's armies, are in prison in Chalus for disobeying Richard's orders. While a rebellious Robin searches for a way out of his cell, John is more philosophical. Soft-spoken in contrast to Alan Hale's John, once described as 'roaring', Williamson's John is stoical, cautious and ironic.[20] Time, the sense of a long past for these two friends, and for their relationship with Marian, allows the film to create complex relationships and complex responses.

The film deals in retrospection, not least upon the tradition itself. Released from prison by Richard just before his own death, the two former outlaws return to England where they find Marian a nun, their fellow outlaws dead or aged, and King John's regime oppressing everyone – even their former nemesis, the Sheriff of Nottingham. Driven by his hatred of injustice – and tempted by the thought of one last, good, fight – Robin recreates the outlaw band and prepares to battle with the sheriff one more time. The retrospective perspective allows for John to be a man with unsuspected depths and complexities, hidden from his past. On the night before the battle Marian speaks to John:

Marian: Don't let them march out against the sheriff.

John: What?

Marian: Didn't he tell you?

John: Fight the sheriff? No, that's mad. They're fourteen to one against. We'd be slaughtered. What's he thinking? These are just boys we've got. Farmers.

Marian: Tell him. You're the only one he'll listen to.

John: Me? Say no to Rob?

Marian: Just this once.

John: We've always been together. I'd be nothing without him.

Marian: But I want him safe. It's all right that I leave. What more do you want of me?

John: I haven't asked for anything.

Marian: You never liked me.

John: You're Rob's lady . . . If . . . you'd been mine, I never would have left you.

Astounded by this revelation, but still terrified of losing Robin, Marian falls into John's arms. As he holds her tight, comforting her with the promise he will look after Robin, Williamson's John is a more thoughtful, mature and conflicted character than any previous screen Little John. The most obvious innovation is the triangle of sexual dynamics, involving both sexual attraction and long friendship between the three characters. Repressing his own attraction to Marian because she's his friend's love, he loyally follows Robin – knowing that in this war, as in his treatment of Marian, Robin is wrong – because Rob is his friend. The next day John frankly tells Robin the plan is mad but does not attempt to stop him, calmly preparing to enter the hopeless battle at his friend's side. Here the proof of Little John's traditional loyalty is that it over-rides even the non-traditional intelligence with which this film endows him. When Robin asks John what he said when Marian asked him to prevent Robin fighting, John says, with a conspiratorial wink between the men, 'that you'd be lost without me'. This is a remark as poised between superior capabilities and deferential loyalty within this John's character, as it is, in context, poised between heterosexual and homosocial loyalties.

Before the battle, realizing it is hopeless, Robin, to save his men, opts for a one-to-one duel with the sheriff. The screenplay continues with its paradoxes of loyalty. John offers the aging combatant the promise that he will kill the sheriff if he kills Robin, but Robin says 'No', knowing he can trust John: 'You'll keep my word.' When Robin kills the sheriff but is mortally wounded, it is John and Marian who carry him off to the convent, where Marian poisons herself and her lover, knowing Robin will never again have such a day as this. As these two members of the trio await death, Robin delivers his encomium of the third, his/their closest friend: 'He's something, John is. No one gentler in the world – or as terrible.' Another paradox here, expressive of this film's Little John, who is simultaneously independent, impressive and devoted, open-eyed and blindly loyal.

The BBC *Legend of Robin Hood* and *Robin and Marian* mark a major change: after them the most significant and influential film versions of the story have followed their lead, abandoning the simplistic sidekick for a more equal and complex comrade to Robin. The best of these more recent treatments, *Robin of Sherwood*, written by Richard Carpenter for Goldcrest and HTV in the mid-1980s, with twenty-six hours of screen time, created the most interesting characterization of Little John yet. Excellently played by Clive Mantle, the series' John at first appears to conform to a, by then, well-established stereotype. He is a very tall man, a serf by origin, loyal to Robin, and sometimes makes stupid decisions, such as endangering the people of Wickham by visiting his lover Meg there. But as the series progresses, John proves more than the traditional sidekick.

Carpenter introduces sorcery and magic into the story of Robin Hood and it is through sorcery that the character of John is developed. In the first episode, 'Robin Hood and the Sorcerer', a shepherd, John, has been bewitched by the evil baron Simon de Belleme, and is used by the Baron both as a mouthpiece for a demon and as a henchman.[21] He sends John into the forest to kill Robin who, as a protégé of Herne the

Hunter (the forest spirit used by Carpenter as a Merlin-like mentor for Robin), threatens his evil power. When John meets Robin in the traditional fight over the stream the episode's entire meaning is original: this time John intends to kill Robin, but when Robin (the victor in this version) knocks John into the water and sees the pentangle drawn on his chest, he washes it off and frees the shepherd from his enchantment. Now free, John's real character comes back to the fore: amiable, able to laugh at himself and grateful to Robin. The two splash about in the water, in a return to the sportive conclusion that usually characterizes this scene, and a lasting bond is formed.

This John has far more reason than most to differ from Robin's decisions: he is sceptical whether his new friend is really Herne's son and whether the upcoming battle with Belleme is really a battle of light against darkness, and he urges their companions to disobey orders and follow him out of the forest to Castle Belleme. When this leads to a massacre in which half the outlaws are killed, John is stricken with guilt. Seated, weeping, with the survivors – Robin, Marian, Much, Scarlet and Tuck – John draws comfort from Robin's impassioned statement, in which 1970s New Age mysticism and confidence in democracy unite, that their comrades against oppression did not die in vain and their spirits are free in Sherwood. For John as for Robin freedom becomes something worth fighting and dying for. John's commitment to freedom and distrust of England's rulers comes to the fore in 'The King's Fool'. Here, as in well-established tradition, an unrecognized King Richard visits the outlaws' camp and enjoys a meal with them. He refuses to pay for the meal with his horse, offering to wrestle, instead, with one of the band. John's strength and prowess are almost equal to the king's but the king wins and haughtily turns on the outlaws. He informs them of his identity and the fact that he came to the forest hunting for them He invites them, using all his charm, to dine with him in Nottingham. In this version of the myth even the traditionally respected Richard is cast as a malign ruler.

Whereas a dazzled Robin accepts, a sceptical Scarlet refuses to go. At the Castle, John desperately tries to open Robin's eyes to the monarch's untrustworthiness:

'AND FOR BEST SUPPORTING HERO ... LITTLE JOHN'

John: Look, we're his pets, the wolves clever King Richard trapped and tamed ...

Robin: That's enough, John.

John: You're dazzled by him, aren't you? He's but to snap his fingers, and you're running round his legs like a little dog. Say something funny, Robin. Show us some sword play, let's see your skill with the longbow. Tell us how to run the country! Do you think he listens?

Robin: I know he listens.[22]

Here John, once literally freed from enchantment, and now metaphorically disenchanted with government which seems to respect the people but merely hoodwinks and exploits them, tries to pass his message onto a Robin who believes in the promise of good intentions from traditional authority. John, however, prefers an alternative allegiance, summed up as Sherwood:

John: Well, then, I'll choose Sherwood.

Robin: John?

John: I loved you, Robin. You were the Hooded Man, Herne's Son, the people's hope. Now you're the king's fool.

John, as so often in the tradition, is the channel through which questions of power and hierarchy are raised. Here, Robin comes to realize the truth of John's warning and escapes from Nottingham to reunite the outlaws and continue the struggle against injustice – a struggle that in the second season's final episode, 'The Greatest Enemy', brings about Robin of Loxley's death.

The series treats Robin Hood as a sort of Arthur-figure, one who can return to serve England. A grieving Marian is left holding Robin's sword, appropriately called 'Albion'. The succession here merges John's established scepticism about sociopolitical matters with the series-makers' practical need to defuse audience's potential unease about a new actor playing a new version of Robin Hood: John's entrenched suspicion of all members of the privileged classes blights his initial relation with the new Hooded Man, who is Robert Earl of Huntingdon. The enemies of the Sherwood men are a class, not merely particular instances of corrupt power, such as the traditional foe, the Sheriff of Nottingham. This John says to Huntingdon, the new Robin:

> How could you understand? You? Ever starved? Ever been whipped because you forgot to lower your eyes when your masters rode by? No, not you. Because you're one of them![23]

The traditional quarter-staff encounter brings the two finally into mutual respect and their future loyalty is based on shared passion to fight injustice and oppression, not personal loyalty or master-squire loyalty.

The series' influence, together with the BBC *Legend* and *Robin and Marian*, re-orientated the characterization of little John, as we see in two 1991 films, *Robin Hood Prince of Thieves* and *Robin Hood*.

Prince of Thieves is a mess of a movie. With Kevin Costner and the outlaws playing their roles straight and Alan Rickman playing the sheriff as pantomime, the film suffers from multiple personality disorder. One of the few bright spots is Nick Brimble's performance as Little John. Tall, bearded, physically powerful, this John is already, like Conrad Asquith's John, the leader of a band of fugitives in Sherwood when he meets Robin. The quarter-staff fight, won by Robin's superior brains, impresses John, who listens to Robin's plans. John and his fellows are, in an unfortunate slip back to an earlier conception, presented, in the Arab Azeem's words, as 'simple men'.[24] This John does not simply speak dialect, such as Mantle's Derbyshire accent in *Robin of Sherwood*, but is crudely ungrammatical: John is inferior in class and intelligence to the aristocratic Locksley. But not here, in any sense, a channel for scepticism about rank. Although the film makes a lot of noise about nobility being something earned by character rather than being granted by birth, the manner in which the men and women of Sherwood are presented here, in contrast to *Robin of Sherwood*, sends a different message. In the film, which focuses on one heroic figure, who may have sidekicks and allies, but never equals (save for the impossibly perfect and politically correct Azeem), Little John is not permitted to be the equal of his new friend. Somewhat making up for the absence of closeness between Robin and John, whose place has been

'AND FOR BEST SUPPORTING HERO... LITTLE JOHN'

taken by Morgan Freeman's Azeem, is the film's depiction of John, as a married man, loved by his stalwart wife, Fanny, and respected by the rest of the outlaws. In their affection, resembling that of John and Meg in *Robin of Sherwood*, they are the most appealing and believable characters in the film. A married John also disrupts the traditional concentration of John's emotional dramas on his relationship with Robin.

Appealing is the word for David Morissey's Little John in John Irvin's *Robin Hood* starring Patrick Bergin.[25] Like Asquith and Brimble's Little Johns, this character is a fugitive from justice when he first meets Robin and Will. In the traditional fight over the stream, John has the better of the conflict, but when Robin falls in and Will says he cannot swim, John abandons hostility to aid the drowning man. In the amicable conclusion, John invites Will and Robin to his outlaw camp. They form a triumvirate, waging war against the powerful, raids against tax collectors, wealthy clerics, and the despicable Miles de Falconet who wants to marry Marian. It is John and Will who convert Robin to a war not merely for loot but against oppression. Though, as in *Prince of Thieves*, the emphasis is on the figure of Robin and his relationships with Marian, the sheriff, and the Baron de Guerre, and though there is little character-development for John and Will, the two outlaws are presented as thoughtful and politically aware men, who fight *with*, not *for*, Robin.

With the Bergin film, this paper has reached the last major Robin Hood film product to date. There are a number of parodies – such as Mel Brooks's *Robin Hood: Men in Tights*, which lampoons *Prince of Thieves*, and the BBC series *Maid Marian and her Merry Men* – and one would-be parody, the dreadful TNT series *The New Adventures of Robin Hood*, but they add nothing to the characterization of Little John, save a regression to the earlier tradition of stupidity (blended with long blond hair in *The New Adventures*).

At all periods, the relationship of the screen Robin and John has been an interesting essay in unequal power relationships, with the power in question sometimes that of comparative character and wisdom as well as actual dominance or subservience. Divisions, tensions and quarrels between the outlaws have always, from the earliest extant ballads, been shown to put into jeopardy their power to defeat their external enemies. In summary of the film traditions of Little John, one may say that, in general, the early movies lacked any interest in character development, while later TV and film versions often show either John or Robin learning and maturing through their association together. In the early films, in classic Hollywood tradition, the hero, heroine and villain monopolize screen time. These films focus on Robin's fight with the sheriff or Gisbourne, his loss and recovery of his rank, and his relationship with Marian. Other members of Robin's band, even Little John, consequently receive little attention as characters. Television series gave new scope, as the ballads had done, for concentrating on particular, quasi-discrete, episodes, often centred almost as much on a member of the band as on Robin himself. It was not until recently, notably in the 1970s, that characterization of Little John in films began to become relatively complex. Both the BBC *Legend of Robin Hood* and Lester's *Robin and Marian* stress socio-historical realism more than earlier screen versions had done but, above all, they devoted far more attention to the psychology of their characters. Perhaps the fact that the *Legend*, *Robin and Marian*, *Robin of Sherwood* and the earlier Richard Greene series were British-made partly explains the shift in them away from emphasis on the one-leader heroics of Douglas Fairbanks, Errol Flynn and Kevin Costner in American-produced and directed films and towards a theme of communal effort and consequently greater emphasis on the contributions of Little John, Scarlet and the others. With much stronger socialist tradition than that of the United States, the United Kingdom would be more receptive to retellings of the myth that stressed the values of community. Recent British productions have shown greater character depth, complexity and development, while simultaneously returning the legend to an interest in the health of the communal group which we find also in some of the early ballads.[26] In some cases John, other outlaws and even Robin have become serfs: not even the 'yeomen' of the early ballad tradition. If, as Stephen Knight wrote, Richard Carpenter's *Robin of Sherwood* truly is 'the most innovative and influential version of the myth in recent times', it is because it brings together, for the legend in particular and for Little

'AND FOR BEST SUPPORTING HERO ... LITTLE JOHN'

John in particular, both the psychologically more complex and the politically more communally grounded interpretations in contemporary films.^{27} The outlaw tradition has the potential to offer a fable of resistance, and to remind us that the Law may sometimes contain wrong and the Out-Law may contain good. The tradition has the potential also to unsettle and redraw fictionally the relationships of power and authority. The changing relationship between Robin and his lieutenant in twentieth-century films brings that drama right into the dynamics of power among the outlaws themselves.

NOTES

1. *A Gest of Robyn Hode*, ll. 9–12, in KO, p. 90.
2. DT, p. 165.
3. Jeffrey L. Singman, *Robin Hood: The Shaping of the Legend* (Westport, CT: Greenwood, 1998), pp. 36–7.
4. Extracts translated in KO, pp. 24–6.
5. Text in KO, pp. 269–80.
6. On the moral and practical dominance of John in this ballad, see Derek Pearsall, 'Little John and *Robin Hood and the Monk*', in *RHMP*, pp. 21–41.
7. 'Robin Hood and the Monk', 'Robin Hood and the Potter', the play '*Robin Hood and the Potter*', KO, pp. 31–56, 57–79, 290–2.
8. 'Robin Hood and the Monk', 'Robin Hood and Guy of Gisborne', KO, pp. 31–56, 169–83.
9. 'Robin Hood and the Monk', 'Robin Hood and Guy of Gisborne', 'A Gest of Robin Hood', the play '*Robin Hood and the Potter*'.
10. KO, pp. 227–34.
11. *Robin Hood*, videotape, 120 minutes, United Artists, 1922, directed by Alan Dwan. The ballad 'Robin Hood and Little John' (*c.*1624?) established John as a virtual giant: seven feet tall, text in KO, pp. 476–85. A lost play called '*Robin Hood and Little John*' appears in the Stationers' Register for 1594. Perhaps, like the extant ballad, it centred on the famous fight with quarter-staffs over the stream.
12. *The Adventures of Robin Hood,* videotape, 120 minutes, Warner Brothers, 1938, directed by Michael Curtiz and William Keighley.
13. Stephen Knight, *Robin Hood: A Complete Study of the English Outlaw* (Oxford: Blackwell, 1994), p. 234, says the programme ran from 1955–8. David Turner and Malcolm Baker, *Robin of the Movies* (Kingswinford: Yeoman, 1989), p. 22, says it ran from February 1956 to November 1960. Michael Eaton (e-mail to the author, 1 June 1999) reconciles the conflicting dates: the programme ran in the United

Kingdom from 17 February 1956 to 12 November 1960 and in the United States from September 1955 to September 1958.

14 Turner and Baker, *Robin of the Movies*, p. 21
15 Knight 1994, pp. 521–6.
16 *The Adventures of Robin Hood*, 'Dead or Alive', c.26 minutes, Sapphire Films, 1956, directed by Dan Birt.
17 *The Adventures of Robin Hood*, 'Good-bye, Little John', Videotape, c.26 minutes. Marathon Music and Video, Dastar Corporation, 1998, directed by Robert Day.
18 Knight 1994, p. 232. *Robin Hood*, Walt Disney Classics videotape.
19 *The Legend of Robin Hood*. Six hourly episodes, BBC, 1975, directed by Eric Davidson.
20 See George Macdonald Fraser, *The Hollywood History of the World* (London: Michael Joseph, 1996), p. 65. *Robin and Marian*, videotape, 107 minutes, Columbia Pictures, 1976, directed by Richard Lester.
21 *Robin of Sherwood*, 'Robin Hood and the Sorcerer', videotape, 115 minutes, Goldcrest, 1983, directed by Ian Sharpe.
22 *Robin of Sherwood*, 'The King's Fool', videotape, c.50 minutes, Goldcrest, 1983, directed by Ian Sharpe.
23 *Robin of Sherwood*, 'Herne's Son', videotape, 101 minutes, Goldcrest, 1985, directed by Robert Young.
24 *Robin Hood: Prince of Thieves*, videotape, 144 minutes, Morgan Creek Productions, 1991, directed by Kevin Reynolds.
25 *Robin Hood*, videotape, 104 minutes, Morgan Creek productions, directed by John Irvin.
26 See Singman, *Robin Hood*, p. 37.
27 Knight 1994, p. 239.

'Begone, knave! Robbery is out of fashion hereabouts!' Robin Hood and the Comics Code

ALLAN W. WRIGHT

Let's make one thing perfectly clear, Robin Hood was not a thief. He was a servant to the king, an honourable, good-natured cop. At least, that is the impression you would get from reading his adventures in 1950s' American comic books.

Comic books are normally overlooked in the study of the Robin Hood legend. However, they have much in common with the traditional media of Robin Hood adventures. Comics borrow a visual language from film; were printed on cheap paper much like broadside ballads; in the 1950s many stories could be collected in one comic not unlike a ballad 'garland'; and comics were generally perceived as being for children and the less-educated.[1] And like the other media, comics aroused the ire of various authority figures.

In late 1954 most American comic book publishers adopted a self-regulatory code. A recent senate investigation had linked comic books with juvenile delinquency. Church groups led boycotts against comics; legislators attempted to control comics. The industry felt the Comics Code would calm critics and prevent government interference. The Code killed horror comics, cleaned up crime comics, and superheroes were already in a slump.[2] So, comic publishers cashed in on popular TV shows. The 1955–8 *Adventures of Robin Hood* series starring Richard Greene inspired at least seven publishers to produce Robin Hood comics – four of them producing monthly Robin Hood comic series.[3] However, an outlaw was an unlikely hero for the time when the Code was most strictly enforced. Provision number one of the Code was: 'Crimes shall never be presented in such a way as to create sympathy for the criminal, to promote distrust of the forces of law and justice, or to inspire others with a desire to imitate criminals.'[4] The Robin Hood of the Comics Code was very different from his medieval counterpart. According to Stephen Knight, even the most courtly of early Robin Hood stories, the *Gest of Robin Hood* 'advocates massive theft from the church, civic insurrection against and murder of a properly appointed sheriff, breach of legitimate agreement with a king; and it imagines that all those things can lead to a lengthy and happy life'.[5] Every point in Knight's description violates a provision of the Comics Code. However, the greenwood legend had changed in the five to six hundred years since the earliest ballads. And the Code-approved comics are the best example of how in the twentieth century the stories which gave names and inspiration to rebels and robbers had become safe and harmless.

First, the Code whitewashed the violence of comic book adventure stories. Maurice Keen describes the early Robin Hood as a 'full-blooded medieval brigand' – a man who killed and sometimes beheaded his enemies.[6] J. C. Holt calls the early ballads a 'glorification of violence to young and old alike'.[7] That violence had already been cleaned up before the comics got a hold of Robin in the 1950s. In 'children's books, such as Howard Pyle's 1883 classic (continuously in print to the present day), Robin Hood orders his men to avoid killing if at all possible.[8] Yet Robin does still kill enemies on occasion in children's books – most notably in Roger Lancelyn Green's children's novel from 1956.[9] Also Robin kills opponents in the 1952 film *The Story of Robin Hood and His Merrie Men* and some episodes of the 1950s Richard Greene TV series.[10] Dell's comic adaptation of the 1952 Disney film shows Robin shooting an arrow into the chest of his father's killer.[11] Dell comics, the leading publisher at the time, never subscribed to the Code, claiming their standards were higher than the Comics Code's.[12] However, a scene like this would have never been published in a Code-approved comic, where arrows were not allowed to enter the body.[13] So instead of shooting at people, the Code-approved Robin Hood demonstrates more fantastic feats of archery. Robin Hood shoots rope-arrows to scale castle walls.[14] His arrows shatter the bows of his enemies.[15] He shoots at tavern signs,[16] chandeliers,[17] and beehives[18] to stop his foes. Even when Robin Hood jabbed an arrow into the talon of a giant hawk, the picture does not show the arrow entering the hawk.[19] However, some of the same improbable but appealingly visual tricks are used in the British comic book series of the 1950s, published by Amalgamated Press, where Robin also kills.[20] Fancy archery aside, the Code-approved Robin Hood was not completely emasculated. He still beats his opponents into submission. But his enemies never have cuts nor bruises. There is swordplay, but the foes never truly hurt each other. In the Middle Ages of Code-approved comics, there was no bloodshed. And, although in the non-Code Robin Hood comics arrows sometimes find human targets, they never draw blood. The violence seems more like good clean fun than that of a hardened, anti-establishment criminal. This is true of other historical or legendary outlaws in Code-approved comics, Billy the Kid was said to be following the path of peace in his long-running series by Charlton comics.

The Code-approved Robin Hood comics could not show the outright violence of the original tales, but there was probably some leniency in certain areas of the Code. Although it has long been a saying that the Robin Hood ballads were 'good for fools', the legend did have a literary, however dubious, pedigree.[21] Laws passed against comic books in Los Angeles county and Wisconsin state granted exemptions to historical or literary stories, which presumably would have included Robin Hood stories.[22] Medieval English outlaws causing trouble for medieval English barons were not as great a concern as comics of gangsters gunning down G-Men.

In fact, with the Middle Ages in the safe and distant past, the comics address certain political issues which the ballads avoid. Holt observes:

> 'There is nothing in the ballads of the great economic and social issues which lead to the peasants-rising of 1381; nothing of manorial service, nothing of villeinage, nothing of rent or labour-services'.[23]

And, true, the comics give very little indication that the peasants owe service to their lords. Complex medieval laws might be mentioned in one- or two-page educational features in the comics, but they were not woven into the plots of the stories in the way the Greene TV series used real medieval issues.[24] Still, a great peasant uprising does appear in the comics, even if it is not exactly historical in tone. In Magazine Enterprise's *Adventures of Robin Hood* no. 6 (with a Richard Greene photo cover) Robin incites a 'Revolt of the Peasants'. While the historical Peasants Revolt involved violence, murder, and massive destruction of property, the comic book version is a bloodless affair. The peasants merely stop working. The knights and barons have to till their own land and cook their own meals. It is not the threat of violence or some instinct of social justice that prompts Sir Gui to repent his cruel ways; rather Robin tempts Sir Gui to reduce his taxes by offering an anachronistic turkey dinner.[25]

The only tax mentioned in the early Robin Hood ballads is the one Robin Hood himself exacts on a potter.[26] But a recurring theme in Robin Hood movies, television shows, and comic books is the unfair taxation imposed by Prince John and his robber barons. In one comic plot, a tax collector is so cruel he steals the rags off peasants. In another Robin Hood 'reclaims' the money from the tax collectors and returns it to the poor. The tax collector exclaims that: 'Unless we get rid of Robin Hood, we'll never keep what we steal!'[27] The taxes are called 'unfair',[28] 'unjust' and 'illegal'.[29] The Robin Hood of the Middle Ages did not seek explicitly to overturn social structures and conventions, but in 1950s' America, royally imposed taxes were a thing of the past. In a country which was founded by people protesting tea and stamp taxes, fighting corrupt tax collectors was not insurrection but patriotism. Robin sounds like a medieval American revolutionary when he shouts slogans such as 'neither hawk nor prince can tether freedom'![30]

Robin Hood's patriotism is best seen when he defends England against invaders. In comic books Robin Hood fights the Vikings,[31] the French on more than one occasion,[32] and even the Picts, straight from the Arthurian back-up story in the same issue.[33] After foiling the French and saving Prince John, Robin says: 'You are the king's brother, sire. And my liege lord – at least where invaders are concerned!'[34]

The rest of the time, of course, Prince John is Robin Hood's enemy. He makes an excellent villain, because the Comics

Code cautioned against creating 'disrespect for established authority'.[35] As most of Prince John's comic book appearances carefully point out, he is a 'usurper'.[36] In the first ten-page story of Magazine Enterprise's *Robin Hood* comic series Prince John is called a usurper seven times, and twice more variations of the verb 'usurp' are used to describe his practices.[37] The usurper is also a villain in the Richard Greene TV series and the 1952 Disney movie. He has little role in Howard Pyle's children's book, but Roger Lancelyn Green makes him a major adversary of Robin's. In the Green book, the prince is described as 'cruel lawless John'.[38] Therefore, John's authority is neither established nor to be respected. The barons who hold their power from John are doing so illegally. They are the crooks, not Robin Hood. Both the 1950s series by Quality Comics and the 1963 non-Code one-shot by Dell make Prince John King Richard's evil half-brother.[39] John's rule is made illegitimate by – well, making John himself illegitimate.

By contrast, Robin Hood is very loyal to King Richard. Robin's battle cry is: 'For England and King Richard!'[40] In National, better known as DC, Comics any money Robin Hood reclaims usually goes to pay Richard's ransom.[41] Once Robin Hood flies in a twentieth-century style box-kite to rescue his king.[42]

In ballads, Robin is in the words of Maurice Keen 'the arbiter of an unofficial justice'. When the king pardons Robin Hood, he recognizes the outlaw's moral right.[43] But that pardoning comes towards the end of the story. In an ongoing series (either on TV or in the comics), that end will only come with cancellation Therefore, in most Code-approved comics, the king recognizes Robin Hood's moral and legal rights at the beginning of the story. Three of the four companies to publish regular Robin Hood stories made the hero the Earl of Huntingdon, a trusted friend of King Richard, who sends the earl from the Holy Land to England on a mission to check Prince John's power.[44] Once there, Robin is outlawed for his support of the proper legal authority. Thus, as an emissary of King Richard, Robin Hood has greater legal authority than his enemies.[45] This is almost the same construction of Robin's origin used in the Greene TV series, except that there Robin Hood is only a knight, Sir Robin of Locksley.[46] However, this was not the only origin story in the Robin Hood legend. Of the Code-approved books, only Charlton uses the story from the ballad 'Robin Hood's Progress to Nottingham', where Robin is outlawed for killing fifteen foresters. This story was also used by the non-Code publishers, Dell and Classics Illustrated. In all cases though, Robin Hood does not kill his enemies.[47] In Pyle's novel, Robin still kills, but only one of the foresters.

The Code said the criminal lifestyle should not be glorified or glamourized. So, it was stressed repeatedly that Robin Hood is not a thief. Almost every time he takes money from a tax collector or robber baron, Robin Hood calls his enemy a thief.[48] This concept was already present, in one sense, in the modern Robin Hood tradition. Eric Hobsbawm in his book on social banditry, *Bandits,* sees Robin Hood as the archetype of a noble robber who cannot be 'a *real* criminal by the moral standards of his community', otherwise he could not have 'unqualified support'.[49] When in the Charlton series Robin Hood becomes the leader of the Merry Men he makes it quite plain: 'Outlaws we will be ... but not thieves!'[50] Similar sentiments are expressed in children's books.[51] For example, since Little John plundered the sheriff's silverware on a day when the sheriff had not harmed or 'despoiled' anyone, Robin gives the silverware back to the sheriff.[52] Robin is acting as a juster form of the law here.

Perhaps Robin Hood's most frequent enemy in the Code-approved comics are so-called 'robber barons': greedy noblemen with names like Sir Gunder, Dhru the Dark, or Baron Grote, plunder townsmen, farmers, and travellers.[53] They are not portrayed as authority figures, but more as private individuals, medieval Mafiosi operating outside the law, with only support from a usurper prince. Maid Marian on one occasion describes a cruel knight/baron as 'an evil man who does not obey any laws but his own'.[54] In such a situation Robin Hood is clearly more law-abiding than his foes. But robber barons and knights, who also appeared in British Robin Hood comics, were not simply comic book villains.[55] They were a staple of nineteenth-century novels and pantomimes, and bedevilled the television Robin Hood in many episodes of the Richard Greene series.[56] On television, however, it seems the barons are shown more often abusing their feudal authority. In the comics the barons had about the same authority as any common brigand.

In the comics Robin often stops gangs of real outlaws. Sometimes the thieves are impersonating Robin to blacken his good name – a plot used from the medieval romance of Fouke Fitz Waryn to the 1952 Disney film.[57] Of course, Robin Hood had not always had a good name to besmirch. In 1521, the most flattering of the early Scottish chroniclers, John Major, praised Robin's manners and morals, but added 'the robberies of this man I condemn'.[58] The medieval Robin Hood was unequivocally a robber. But in a 1956 Robin Hood comic, Robin fights robbers who are attacking a returning crusader. Robin charges out of the forest shouting: 'Begone, knave! Robbery is out of fashion hereabouts! The Merry Men keep the law here since Prince John and his barons prey on one and all!'[59] Robin Hood is not merely a force for justice as he is in the ballads, but a force for law.

In a DC comic, Prince John actually makes Robin Hood the new Sheriff of Nottingham as part of a nefarious scheme to ambush the hero. Although Prince John revokes his appointment at the story's end, Robin Hood declares: 'As long as good people heed me I shall continue to be their sheriff.'[60] It strongly suggests that in a democracy, Robin would legally be the sheriff.

In the ballads, the sheriff is corrupt. Maurice Keen observes that the ballads detail his moral offences: the sheriff breaks his word and 'if he takes an outlaw in the wood, there will not even be the mockery of a trial'.[61] In the Richard Greene series, the sheriffs, played by Alan Wheatley and later John Arnatt, are scheming and underhanded. But while the sheriff might bend the law for a bribe or plot in secret, openly the sheriff was still seen as a force for law – no matter how corrupt or unjust that law is. In one episode, the sheriff lets Robin Hood go because to pursue the outlaw would reveal the sheriff had given a safe conduct in exchange for a bribe.[62] Although trying to retain outward respectability, the TV viewer had no doubt that the sheriff was crooked and corrupt. But the Comics Code did not want authority figures to be corrupt. So not only is the moral authority of the sheriff weakened, but his legal authority as well. In history and the ballads, the sheriff was a crown official. He appeals to the king in *Robin Hood and the Monk*, the *Gest* and *Robin Hood and the Golden Arrow*, as well as in Howard Pyle's book. The King (not Prince John in those cases, but Edward, Richard I, and Henry II) confirms the sheriff is the legal authority in Nottinghamshire and should arrest Robin Hood.[63] But in one DC story, the sheriff is dismissed as 'Prince John's infamous hireling!'[64] The sheriff derives his power from the 'usurper': he is not a legitimate authority figure. The sheriff is called 'Prince John's man' in the television series as well, but he also refers to himself as 'a man of the law'.[65] In the comics that is rarely the case. Just as there is no sense that greedy landlords, the 'robber barons', have proper feudal rights, there is little sense that the sheriff has a legal right to govern the shire. The sheriff may gather taxes and try to capture Robin, but he is little different from any other robber baron in the comics. There are rare exceptions where the sheriff clearly has some legal power. Sometimes Robin Hood actually turns real outlaws and robbers over to the sheriff; but in those cases, the sheriff's authority is not defied.[66]

In the *Gest* Robin Hood tells his men: 'These bisshoppes and these archebishopppes,/Ye shall them bete and bynde' (57–8).[67] In some tales, it is a prior who makes Robin an outlaw. In others, he is killed by a treacherous prioress, as in the *Gest* and the ballad of 'The Death of Robin Hood'. He robs bishops, opposes the Abbot of St Mary's Abbey, and Little John decapitates a monk. And when Robin Hood himself was being cleaned up in the post-Reformation sixteenth and seventeenth centuries, the anti-clerical element of the legend was increased. The medieval catholic clergy are among Robin's most important adversaries in the ballads and in the children's versions by Pyle, Creswick and Green. But they are completely missing from the comic books. One of the Code's provisions was: 'Ridicule or attack on any racial or religious group is never permissible.' The driving force behind comic-book censorship were church groups like the Catholic National Office of Decent Literature.[68] Villainous bishops were a thorny issue for the makers of the 1938 Errol Flynn film too, when crafting their Bishop of the Black Canons,[69] and in the 1952 Richard Todd movie, the church and the archbishop of Canterbury are among the heroes. The Richard Greene TV series does adapt the story of the impoverished knight and greedy abbot from the *Gest*. But when asked about the abbot's character, Tuck says: 'Abbot? He's nothing but a Norman captain who's grown too old for active banditry! He probably wasn't even ordained.'[70] This episode makes the abbot's spiritual authority as illegitimate as the sheriff and prince's temporal authority is elsewhere. The normal solution of the comics was to avoid the subject of religion completely. Robin Hood had been a devout Catholic in the early, pre-Reformation, ballads, but in the comic books, there are no bishops good or bad, no abbots, no monks, no nuns. There is only Friar Tuck, who was different from the other Merry Men in dress only, and the occasional reference to the Crusade. The comic book Middle Ages were strangely secular. When the Quality series Robin Hood Tales adapts the knight's story from the *Gest*, the villain is not an abbot at all, but merely a secular robber baron.[71]

The Quality series adapted many Robin Hood ballads, but when the series was taken over by DC Comics with the seventh issue, Robin Hood Tales takes a turn for the fantastic. Robin fights tigers,[72] panthers,[73] man-sized hawks and eagles,[74] and even falcons trained to catch his arrows.[75] This menagerie rivals any kept in the Tower of London. The plots of the DC stories were both imaginative and absurd. For example, in one, one of Prince John's men glue a long beard on a sleeping Robin, tries to convince him that he has slept for a year, and then lead him into an ambush.[76] In another, Robin vows not to set foot on English soil until he recovers Richard's ransom. After making that rash vow Robin discovers the thief stayed in England rather than fleeing across the Channel as Robin originally thought. In order to storm the robber baron's castle, Robin has to swing through the trees, roll down the river in a barrel, ride on a stag, and finally run up a long carpet given to him by a conveniently passing draper.[77] When Robin is visited by a time-travelling Green Arrow from 1959 and Lois Lane from 1961, the archer has a secret identity – a mild-mannered chimney sweep.[78] But when J. C. Holt remarks that, 'Robin foreshadows the world of superman and the comic strip',[79] could he have possibly known about 'The Masked Marvel of Sherwood Forest'? In Robin Hood Tales No. 12, Robin goes to the Nottingham archery contest in purple tights and a green mask and cape, a costume so gaudy that even most superheroes would give it a miss.[80]

DC was the only company publishing superhero comics at the time. One of the writers on DC's Robin Hood Tales was Bill Finger, co-creator of Batman. So it is not surprising that the DC Robin Hood seems so much like a superhero. But there is another reason. The Comics Code of 1954 was inspired by an early attempt at an industry-wide Code in 1948, and both codes were inspired by various in-house codes. National (or DC) had one of the earliest in-house codes, created in the early 1940s.[81] Amy Kiste Nyberg in her book *Seal of Approval: The History of the Comics Code* notes that DC comics were so clean that, 'it was business as usual after the implementation of the code'.[82] By making Robin Hood into a superhero, DC made him even less controversial a figure than the other Code-approved books.

And yet, DC published perhaps the most socially realistic portrayal of Robin Hood too. In 1964, Robin was a guest-star in the adventures of 'Rip Hunter – Time Master'. This Robin is old, dresses in rags, and is a poor shot – but he has one great scheme. He wants to rob the King's ransom. Of course, Rip Hunter stops Robin. Although this story returns Robin Hood to his thieving roots, it also subverts the tradition. That the whole encounter is being played for laughs can be seen in how the Merry Men respond to Robin's scheme. 'Gold! Hear that? No more stealing chickens! From now on, we can buy them!' 'Yipeee!'[83]

For the most part, the comic book Robin is thoroughly respectable. He is a force for law and order. His enemies are not only corrupt thieves but usurpers with no legitimate right to their power. If the comic book Robin met his medieval counterpart, he'd have to arrest that thieving rogue.

NOTES

[1] For the art theory behind comic books, I recommend Scott McCloud, *Understanding Comics* (New York, 1994). Comics, particularly those of the 1950s, are hard to cite using conventional methods. Often the writers and artists were uncredited, and often unknown. Comic books changed titles, numbering systems and publishers. I have adopted styles

found in Allen Ellis, *Comic Art in Scholarly Writing: A Citation Guide*, available at *http://www.comicsresearch.org/CAC/cite.html*. Information which appears in square brackets was not mentioned in the published comic book, and is added for general interest. Such information includes the name of writers and artists, if known, and the more familiar name of the publisher. When locating comic books, publishers are important. And while few will have heard of the official name of 'Comic Magazines', most collectors will be familiar with 'Quality Comics'. In terms of credits (w) stands for writer, (a) for artist, (p) for penciller: the person who does the art in pencil, and (i) for inker, the person who draws over the pencils with ink, often affecting the style. Most comics of the time contained many stories. Page numbers (usually are in square brackets) are counted from the first comic page, including letter pages, text features and public service comics, but not ads. The page numbers in round brackets are those of the story itself, which is usually how they are numbered in the comic.

2   The history behind the Comics Code is detailed in Amy Kiste Nyberg, *Seal of Approval: The History of the Comics Code* (Jackson, 1998).
3   Michelle Nolan, 'Seven Robins!', *Comic Book Marketplace* (May 1998), 15–17.
4   Quoted in Nyberg, *Seal*, p. 166.
5   Knight 1994, p. 81.
6   Maurice Keen, *The Outlaws of Medieval England*, rev. edn (London: Routledge, 2001), p. 3.
7   J. C. Holt, *Robin Hood*, rev. edn (London, 1989), p. 10.
8   Howard Pyle, *The Merry Adventures of Robin Hood of Great Renown, in Nottinghamshire* (New York, 1985), pp. 47, 54; Paul Creswick, *Robin Hood* (New York, 1957), p. 181.
9   9 Roger Lancelyn Green, *The Adventures of Robin Hood* (Middlesex, 1956), pp. 205–6; Pyle, *Merry Adventures*, pp. 330, 370, and Creswick, *Robin Hood*, p. 314.
10 Episodes where Robin kills includes 'The Moneylender' and 'Isabella'.
11 [Uncredited (w), Uncredited (p), Uncredited (i).] *Walt Disney's Robin Hood [Four Colour]*, no. 669 (December 1955), Dell Publishing Co., Inc., 11 (reprinted from *Walt Disney's Robin Hood/Four Colour*, no. 413, August 1952).
12 Nyberg, *Seal*, pp. 116–77.
13 Ibid., p. 115.
14 Bob Haney (w), Russ Heath (a). 'Three Arrows Against Doom'. DC Special, vol. 6, no. 23 [*The 3 Musketeers and Robin Hood*], National Periodical Publications, Inc. [DC Comics], 25 (7). (Reprinted from *The Brave and the Bold*, no. 9, December–January 1956–7.)
15 [Bob Haney (w), Ross Andru (p), Mike Esposito (i).] 'The Secret of Robin Hood's Name!' *Robin Hood Tales*, no. 14 (March–April 1958), National Comics Publications, Inc. [DC Comics] 8.
16 [Bill Finger (w), Ross Andru (p), Mike Esposito (i).] 'The Town Crier of

Peril', *Robin Hood Tales*, no. 12 (November–December 1957), National Comics Publications, Inc. [DC Comics] [21] (2).

17 [Bill Finger (w), Ross Andru (p), Mike Esposito (i).] 'Robin Hood: Court Jester', *Robin Hood Tales*, no. 14 (March–April 1958), National Comics Publications, Inc. [DC Comics], 17 (7).

18 [Bill Finger (w), Russ Heath (a).] Robin Hood: 'The Secret of Sherwood Forest', *The Brave and the Bold*, no. 14 (October–November 1957), National Comics Publications, Inc. [DC Comics] 28 (8).

19 [France Herron (w), Ross Andru (p), Mike Esposito (i).] 'The Falcon Master', *Robin Hood Tales*, no. 12 (March–April 1958), National Comics Publications, Inc. [DC Comics] 7.

20 *Robin Hood Annual 1959* (London, 1958). He uses a rope-arrow in 'Robin Hood's Jest', 8, and 'Robin Hood's Winter Adventure', 46, his arrows cause a chandelier to drop on his foes. But in 'Robin Hood and the Prince's Assassin', 77, Robin stabs two of Prince John's men.

21 Knight 1994, p. 59.

22 Nyberg, *Seal*, pp. 132–4.

23 Holt, *Robin Hood*, p. 37.

24 Jeffrey Richards, *Swordsmen of the Screen: From Douglas Fairbanks to Michael York* (London, 1977), p. 202.

25 [Uncredited] (w), Frank Bolle (a), 'Robin Hood: The Revolt of the Peasants', *The Adventures of Robin Hood*, no. 6 (June 1957), Sussex Publishing Company, Inc. [Magazine Enterprises],14–20, pp. 1–7.

26 DT, p. 31; Richard Kaeuper, *War, Justice, and Public Order: England and France in the Later Middle Ages* (Oxford, 1988), p. 329; Holt, *Robin Hood*, p. 37.

27 [Uncredited] (w), [Matt Baker] (p), [Chuck Cuidera] (i), 'Ambush of the Merry Men', *Robin Hood Tales*, no. 4 (August 1956), Comic Magazines [Quality Comics]: p. 6.

28 [Uncredited] (w), [Matt Baker] (p), [Chuck Cuidera] (i), 'The Scourge of the Bailiff!' *Robin Hood Tales*, no. 2 (April 1956), Comic Magazines [Quality Comics]: p. 12 (2).

29 [Uncredited (w) and Uncredited (a).] *Robin Hood* (May–July 1963), Dell Publishing Co.: p. 5; Ibid. 25.

30 'The Falcon Master'.

31 [Bob Haney (w), Ross Andru (p), Mike Esposito (i).] 'Attack of the Sea Raiders!' *Robin Hood Tales*, no. 7 (January–February 1957), National Comics Publications, Inc. [DC Comics], pp. 1–10.

32 [Uncredited (w) and Uncredited (a)] 'Robin Hood and the French Campaign', *Robin Hood and His Merry Men*, no. 32 (May 1957), Charlton Comics Group, pp. 1–6 and [Uncredited] (w) and [Frank Bolle] (a), 'The Human Arrow', *The Adventures of Robin Hood*, no. 8 (November 1957), Sussex Publishing Company, Inc. [Magazine Enterprises], pp. 1–7.

33 [Uncredited] (w), Frank Bolle (a), 'The Warrior Maid', *Robin Hood*, no. 4 (May 1956), Sussex Publishing Company, Inc. [Magazine Enterprises], pp. 1–6, and in the same issue Sir Gallant of the Round Table: 'The Dungeons of Sir Blamas' [pp. 13–19] (1–7).

ROBIN HOOD AND THE COMICS CODE

34 Robin Hood: 'The Human Arrow', *The Adventures of Robin Hood*, no. 8, p. 7.
35 Comics Code 1954 A.3
36 [Uncredited] (w), Frank Bolle (a), Robin Hood: 'Sir Robin Hood', *Robin Hood*, no. 4 (May 1956), Sussex Publishing Company, Inc. [Magazine Enterprises], [pp. 8–9] (1–2) and [Uncredited] (w), [Matt Baker] (p), [Chuck Cuidera] (i), 'The Scroll of Doom', *Robin Hood Tales*, no. 3 (June 1956), Comic Magazines [Quality Comics], p. 2 for two of many examples.
37 [Uncredited] (w), [Frank Bolle] (a), Robin Hood: 'The Prince and the Poacher', *Robin Hood*, no. 52 [1] (November 1955), Sussex Publishing Company, Inc. [Magazine Enterprises]: 'Usurper', 1, 2, 3, 4, 7, 8, 10; 'usurps', 4; 'usurping', 5. (Despite being officially numbered no. 52, this is, in fact, the first issue of the series. A common practice, the numbering of the first two issues was carried over from an unrelated series.)
38 Green, *Adventures of Robin Hood*, p. 42.
39 [Uncredited] (w), [Matt Baker] (p), [Chuck Cuidera] (i), 'Rescue of Maid Marian', *Robin Hood Tales*, no. 2 (April 1956), Comic Magazines [Quality Comics], p. 2 (2) and *Robin Hood* [Dell], p. 1.
40 [Bill Finger (w), Ross Andru (p), Mike Esposito (i).] 'The Bantam Bowman!', *Robin Hood Tales*, no. 13 (January–February 1958), National Comics Publications, Inc. [DC Comics], [p. 13] (3); Bill Finger (w), Russ Heath (a), 'Robin Hood vs. The Merrie Men', *DC Special*, vol. 6 [*The 3 Musketeers and Robin Hood*], no. 24 (October–November 1976) National Periodical Publications, Inc. [DC Comics]: [p. 26] (8), reprinted from *Brave and the Bold*, no. 11 (April–May 1957), p. 8; Robin Hood: 'The Warrior Maid', *Robin Hood*, no. 4 (May 1956), Sussex Publishing Company, Inc. [Magazine Enterprises], p. 5.
41 For example, Robert Kanigher (w) [Bob Haney listed as writer in different reprint of the same story], Russ Heath (a), 'The Apple of Peril', *The Best of The Brave and the Bold*, no. 4 (Winter 1988), DC Comics Inc.: [p.48] (8), reprinted from *The Brave and the Bold*, no. 12 (June–July 1957), 8; [France Herron (w), Ross Andru (p), Mike Esposito (i).] 'The Masked Marvel of Sherwood Forest', *Robin Hood Tales*, no. 12 (March–April 1958), National Comics Publications, Inc. [DC Comics] [p. 16] (8).
42 Robert Kanigher (w), Joe Kubert (a), 'The Battle of the Kites!', *The Best of the Brave and The Bold*, no. 3 (December 1988), DC Comics Inc.: [p. 46] (6), Reprinted from *The Brave and the Bold*, no. 6 (June–July 1956).
43 Keen, *Outlaws*, p. 157.
44 'Rescue of Maid Marian', *Robin Hood Tales*, no. 2 (April 1956), Comic Magazines [Quality Comics], pp. 2–3, 'The Secret of Robin Hood's Name!'; 'The Prince and the Poacher'; [Uncredited] (w) and Frank Bolle (a), 'Sword from the Sky!', *Robin Hood*, no. 4 (May 1956), Sussex Publishing Company, Inc. [Magazine Enterprises]: [pp. 26] (6).

BANDIT TERRITORIES

45 Robin Hood: 'Sir Robin Hood' [9] (2).
46 'The Coming of Robin Hood'.
47 [Uncredited] (w) and [Uncredited] (a), 'The Outlaw of Sherwood Forest', *Robin Hood and His Merry Men*, no. 28 (April 1956) Charlton Comics Group, p. 1; [Uncredited] (w) and [Uncredited] (a) 'Robin Hood', *Classics Illustrated*, no. 7 [Ed. 16, HRN 153] (1959) [Revised version of no. 7, with updated story and art appeared with Ed. 14, 1957] Gilberton Company, Inc.: pp. 2–3; *Robin Hood*, (1963) Dell, pp. 2–4.
48 *Robin Hood* (1963) Dell, p. 26; [Uncredited] (w) and [Uncredited] (a), 'Robin Hood and the Tax Collector', *Robin Hood and his Merry Men*, no. 29 (July 1956) Charlton Comics Group, [p. 7] (2); 'Rescue of Maid Marian', *Robin Hood Tales*, no. 2 (April 1956), Comic Magazines [Quality Comics], p. 10; [Uncredited] (w), [Baker, Matt] (p) and [Cuidera, Chuck] (i), 'The Miserly Miller of Mimms', *Robin Hood Tales*, no. 3 (June 1956), Comic Magazines [Quality Comics]: [p. 12] (2) are just a few examples.
49 Eric Hobsbawm, *Bandits*, 2nd edn (Harmondsworth: Penguin, 1985), p. 42.
50 'The Outlaw of Sherwood Forest', *Robin Hood and His Merry Men*, no. 28 (April 1956), Charlton Comics Group, 4.
51 Green, *Adventures of Robin Hood*, p. 45; Creswick, p. 183, and Pyle, *Merry Adventures*, p. 208, among other examples.
52 Pyle, *Merry Adventures*, pp. 94–7.
53 'Rescue of Maid Marian'; 'The Scroll of Doom'; 'The Bantam Bowman!'.
54 [Uncredited] (w) and Frank Bolle (a), 'Trial by Combat', *Robin Hood*, no. 52 [1] (November 1955), Sussex Publishing Company, Inc. [Magazine Enterprises], [24], p. 4.
55 *Robin Hood Annual 1959*; Sir Randolph Fitzstephen of Barnsdale in 'Robin Hood's Jest', pp. 3–16.
56 'The Coming of Robin Hood', 'Friar Tuck', 'Checkmate', 'The May Queen', to name but a few examples.
57 [Uncredited] (w) and [Uncredited] (a), 'How Robin Aided a Weary Traveler', *Robin Hood and His Merry Men*, no. 31 (February 1957), Charlton Comics Group, 16–21 (2–6); [Uncredited] (w), Russ Heath (a), 'The Forest of Traps', *The Best of the Brave and the Bold*, no. 2 (November 1988), DC Comics Inc.: [pp. 35–40] (1–6). Reprinted from *The Brave and the Bold*, no. 7 (August–September 1958); [Uncredited] (w), [Matt Baker] (p), [Cuidera, Chuck] (i), 'Arsenal of Hate', *Robin Hood Tales*, no. 4 (August 1956), Comic Magazines [Quality Comics]: [pp 17–24] (1–8). For the Fouke story see *Two Medieval Outlaws: Eustace the Monk and Fouke Fitz Waryn*, Glyn Burgess (ed. and trans.) (Cambridge, 1997), p. 157.
58 Quoted in Knight 1994, p. 37.
59 'Sir Robin Hood'.
60 [Bill Finger] (w), [Ive Novick] (a), 'Robin Hood: New Sheriff of

ROBIN HOOD AND THE COMICS CODE

Nottingham!' *Robin Hood Tales*, no. 8 (March–April 1957), National Comics Publications, Inc. [DC Comics], 8.
61 Keen, *Outlaws*, p. 149.
62 'Too Many Earls'.
63 Pyle, *Merry Adventures*, pp. 33–5.
64 'The Battle of the Kites!', *The Best of the Brave and The Bold*, no. 3 (December 1988), DC Comics Inc., [p. 43] (3), Reprinted from *The Brave and the Bold*, no. 6 (June–July 1956).
65 'Goodbye, Little John'.
66 [Uncredited] (w), [Uncredited] (a), 'The Robber Baron', *Robin Hood and His Merry Men*, no. 31 (February 1957), Charlton Comics Group, p. 6; [Uncredited (w), Uncredited (a)] 'The Traitor of Sherwood Forest', *Robin Hood and His Merry Men*, no. 32 (May 1957), Charlton Comics Group: [p. 21] (5).
67 Text in KO, pp. 80–168.
68 Nyberg, *Seal*, p. 113.
69 Rudy Behlmer, 'Introduction', in *The Adventures of Robin Hood*, Warner Bros. Screenplay Series (University of Wisconsin Press, 1979), p. 27.
70 'The Knight Who Came to Dinner'.
71 [Uncredited] (w), [Matt Baker] (p), [Chuck Cuidera] (i), 'The Capture of Robin Hood', *Robin Hood Tales*, no. 5 (October 1956), Comic Magazines [Quality Comics], [pp. 17–24] (1–8).
72 [France Herron (w), Ross Andru (p), Mike Esposito (i).], 'Robin Hood and the Tiger!', *Robin Hood Tales*, no. 13 (January–February 1958), National Comics Publications, Inc. [DC Comics], pp. 7–8.
73 [Bob Haney] (w), [Ross Andru] (p), [Mike Esposito] (i), 'The Sleeper of Sherwood Forest', *Robin Hood Tales*, no. 10 (July–August 1957), National Comics Publications, Inc. [DC Comics], pp. 7–8.
74 'The Falcon Master', 'The Apple of Peril'.
75 'The Falcon Master'.
76 'The Sleeper of Sherwood Forest'.
77 [Bill Finger (w), Ross Andru (p), Mike Esposito (i).], 'The Strange Vow of Robin Hood', *Robin Hood Tales*, no. 9 (May–June 1957), National Comics Publications, Inc. [DC Comics], pp. 1–8.
78 [Uncredited] (w), [Lee Elias] (a), Green Arrow: 'The Green Arrow Robin Hood!', *Adventure Comics*, no. 264 (September 1959), National Comics Publications, Inc. [DC Comics]: [pp. 22–8] (1–7) and [Uncredited] (w), [Kurt Schaffenberger] (a), 'Sweetheart of Robin Hood', *Superman's Girlfriend, Lois Lane*, no. 22 (January 1963), National Comics Publications, Inc. [DC Comics], [pp. 21–9] (1–9).
79 Holt, *Robin Hood*, p. 10.
80 'The Masked Marvel of Sherwood Forest'.
81 Nyberg, *Seal*, pp. 106–7.
82 Ibid., p. 127.

83 Jack Miller (w), Bill Ely (a), 'The Rip Hunter – Robin Hood Band' [Chapter 2 of 'The Stowaway from A.D.'] *Rip Hunter ... Time Master*, no. 22 (September–October 1964), National Periodical Publications [DC Comics], 12–17, p. 15.

Robin Hood is Alive and Well in Cityton Prison

JOHN BEYNON

Introduction

What follows is not about the historical Robin Hood (whoever he was) or his literary and filmic personas (although we start with them), but his appropriation as a 'mitigation strategy' by inmates in the Young Prisoner Unit in Cityton Prison in south Wales. However, before moving to Cityton, let us start with Robin.

Robin Hood (like, for example, the global pop star Madonna) is polysemic:[1] he is differently received by different constituencies in different circumstances and, indeed, in different media.[2] As a child, I well remember an early 1950s 'comic and colouring' book in which invading Second World War German paratroopers were ambushed in Sherwood Forest by Robin and his merry men: machine guns were no match for their arrows, shot from behind camouflaging foliage with deadly effect. With the War over and won, this was the opportunity not only to explore the victory (won at great cost and against the odds), but to celebrate a nation gloriously saved and a re-invigorated sense of national pride, history, destiny and nationhood. The 1950s 'retro-Second World War' was an event with which Robin – ever available in time of national need to rise again and fight the good fight on the side of justice and the underdog – could be readily associated.

Robin's cultural evolution

There is uncertainty and debate about the original Robin Hood: aristocrat or yeoman, roaming Nottinghamshire or

Yorkshire, in the twelfth century, or the late thirteenth or fourteenth. It has been suggested that by the latter half of the thirteenth century the name had become widely associated with any fugitive from 'unjust justice'.[3] At some point, he became a figure of a bandit who gave out money to the poor as well as flouting authority.

This version of Robin as the heroic rebel has been sedimented into the public consciousness for over six hundred years in the form of ballads, broadsheets, novels, dramas, comics and, more latterly, cinema, television, video and computer games. He is mentioned by writers from Chaucer to Shakespeare, through Keats and Tennyson on into the twentieth and twenty-first centuries. Already in fifteen and sixteenth century there is evidence of real-life troublemakers identifying with the flamboyant and popular outlaw.[4] His skill and cunning are celebrated in the early ballads, with the forest symbolic of fertility and freedom. In the late sixteenth and early seventeenth century, he is gentrified and given a nationalistic character in the late nineteenth century. As a wronged aristocrat (since the late sixteenth century), he was falsely outlawed and therefore has natural justice on his side. Forced into exile, he becomes (like Jesse James and Ned Kelly) a symbol of resistance to corrupt authority.[5] Above all, he is a fearless leader, resolute and brave. Washington Irving captures something of this:

> 'Poets in old times had the right notions on this subject,' continued I, 'witness the fine old ballads about Robin Hood, Alan a'Dale and other staunch blades of yore.'
>
> 'Right sir, right,' interrupted he, 'Robin Hood! He was the lad to cry Stand! To a man and never flinch.'[6]

His high-minded morality and sense of the injustice of poverty becomes an essential part of his up-standing masculinity. Here, for example, is Alfred Noyes (1911) on the matter:

> you shall never do the poor man wrong
> Nor spare the priest or usurer. You shall take
> The waste wealth of the rich to help the poor,
> The baron's gold to stock the widow's cupboard,
> The naked ye hall clothe, the hungry feed,

> And lastly shall defend with all your power
> All that are trampled under by the world,
> The old, the sick and all men in distress.[7]

His is a masculinity, too, associated with a rural innocence, a long-lost and much lamented, pre-industrial, verdant and unpolluted Merry England. Washington Irving, lamenting the latter's demise, places Sherwood Forest at its heart:

> What's to become of Merry Old England when all its manor houses are all turned into manufactories and its sturdy peasantry into pin-makers and stocking weavers? I have looked in vain for merry Sherwood and all the greenwood haunts of Robin Hood: the whole country is covered with manufacturing towns.[8]

Robin crossed over into other cultures and languages. In Wales there emerged the Robin-like figure of Twm Siôn Cati, still geographically associated with a mountainous recess known as Twm Siôn Cati's Cave near Ystraffin in Carmarthenshire. Celebrated orally for centuries he was finally enshrined in literature in 1828 in what is commonly regarded as among the first novels in Welsh.

Although writers continue to embroider the Robin Hood story (and he still re-appears each Christmas in pantomime), cinema and television have opened up new avenues of representation in the last hundred years. In the 1990s alone, there were a number of films on the myth, notably *Robin Hood, Prince of Thieves* (1991), starring Kevin Costner and Alan Rickman, and featuring Bryan Adams's global hit 'Everything I do I do it for you'; *Robin Hood* (1991); and Mel Brooks's parodic *Robin Hood, Men in Tights* (1993). Robin regularly appears in one form or another on television.

Robin Hood as an identity resource

For Stephen Knight, Robin is a 'resource':

> right round the world the myth of Robin Hood, the good outlaw, is a matrix of ideas and conflicts that is still a resource for reference and representation . . .[9]

Just as there have been many versions of Robin Hood, similarly the authority against which he rebels has taken different forms

– as in the case of the invading Germans in the 1950s comic. He is a powerful image of resistance to corrupt authority and, in his rebellion, comes to represent a higher, purer, law. Indeed, he has become:

> A thief who only steals from those who should not possess so much. This concept has power in all periods and its strength seems only to increase in the present world . . . the myth repeats itself because of the simple power of its structures and their recurrent appeal . . . In all the texts the only notion that recurs is the sense that Robin hood resists bad authority . . . a spirited central figure and a force of oppression: the form the ground on which the potent myth operates: all else is local, contemporaneous, capable of alteration . . . set in the past, yet somehow able to recreate the issues of the present.[10]

It is therefore unsurprising that many working-class uprisings in the past have invoked the name of Robin. For example, in 1839 and then again in 1842, the Rebecca Riots broke out in West Wales, the immediate object of the rioters' anger being the toll gates of the gentry. In his study of the events, Williams writes:

> By day the countryside seemed quiet, but at night fantastically disguised (as woman) horsemen careered among highways and through narrow lanes on their mysterious errands. They developed uncanny skill in evading the police and the infantry and, although their mounts were unwieldy farm horses, they also succeeded in outwitting the dragoons.[11]

Both Williams and D. J. V. Jones present Rebecca as a Robin-like figure, administering natural justice and humiliating their oppressors' foot-runners. A link was made between Robin and Rebecca at the time in that Rebecca was variously described as 'Robyn mewn ffroc' ('Robin in a dress'), 'chwaer Robyn' ('Robin's sister'), even 'gwraig Robyn' ('Robin's wife').[12]

Similarly the Poll Tax protesters who skirmished with the police in Trafalgar Square in the early 1990s, were reported as perceiving themselves as latter-day Robin Hoods, standing up for ordinary people against what was seen as a corrupt and uncaring Tory government. Knight provides a witty example of how Robin's story endures in the public mind and can be clothed in the contemporary idiom when he tells of how a car crashed through the plate glass window of the exhibition shop of the 'Tales of Robin Hood' theme park in Nottingham in 1990. The damage was boarded up and the next day someone had written on the boards 'The Sheriff Strikes Back', the reference being to the then popular sequel to '*Star Wars*'.[13]

The recycling of the figure of Robin as a generous miscreant continues in the media. Here are just three examples, stumbled upon in the UK media during 2000 alone.

A shop worker who disobeyed orders to dispose of smoke-damaged football shirts after a fire and, instead, gave them to a local boys' football club, was subsequently sacked. A local paper (*The Barry Gem*, south Wales) took up her case, dubbing her 'our Robin Hood' and mounted a campaign to elicit public support to have her reinstated, which was eventually successful.

On a popular UK morning television programme (*Kilroy*, BBC1), this time on the subject of theft, a woman described herself as 'Robin Hood'. She worked in a confectioners and regularly stole boxes of chocolates which she would drop into an old people's home: 'They [her employers] had plenty of chocolates whereas for the old ladies they were a treat they couldn't afford. I saw myself as a Robin Hood, never a thief. I remain unrepentant, totally!'

The Daily Telegraph reported that children with learning difficulties (such as Dyslexia, Dyspraxia and Asperger's Syndrome) often find it extremely difficult to obtain appropriate education and this ordeal can tear families apart. Since retiring, Sheila Delaney, a psychologist, has acted as an independent advocate for dozens of such children:

> Vague about her caseload and dismissive when asked about fees, she describes her approach as 'rather like that of a Robin Hood'. One guesses that many of the less well-off families she helps will never get a bill. (Buxton, 2000)[14]

The shared theme is clear: Robin-the-Philanthropist lives on and is still busy doing good works on behalf of the poor, the under-privileged and those in need of help. The fact that this can involve breaking the law does not destroy the morality of his or her actions. It is interesting that each of the above examples featured female Robins. Although the traditional Robin figure displays stereotypical masculine characteristics (fair-mindedness, physical courage, skill at fighting, determination, loyalty, even probity), the modern (bisexual?) Robin encapsulates a 'masculine' way of behaving, boldly independent of the law and norms, that is equally available to both biological men and women.[15]

The figure of Robin Hood and myth

Why does Robin Hood continue to have such appeal? To help address this question I want to introduce four closely related terms drawn from literary and cultural studies, namely 'myth', 'allegorical form', 'allegorical interpretant' and 'writerly text'.

Myth

The key to Robin's continued popularity lies in the fact that he has long moved from being a historical figure or the hero of a fictional narrative and has, instead, become a myth. Myths, Roland Barthes shows, contain essential truths and moral lessons that help resolve dilemmas, contradictions, conflicts and problems.[16]

Allegorical form

One definition of myth is a story in which heroic actions are narrated in allegorical form. Brooker (1999) defines allegorical form as 'a way of encoding a broad world view or a complex message in a more focused, accessible and entertaining narrative form'.[17]

Allegorical interpretant

Frederic Jameson argues that society is so complex, especially in the post-modern age, that it can only be understood indirectly, through what he terms allegorical interpretants.[18] The Robin myth is an allegorical interpretant in that the meaning of its characters and events symbolizes a deeper moral message about good, evil, and the eventual victory of natural justice.

Complex moral lessons are conveyed in simplified, entertaining forms and, in the case of film, by means of visually alluring and hugely palatable entertainment.

Writerly text

The Robin Hood myth is an open, 'writerly' text, in that succeeding generations can readily identify with its eternal characters and dramatic events and even interpose into it aspects of their own biographies and experiences as part of their 'meaning construction'.[19]

For Cityton's young criminals Robin was a way of thinking about, and making sense of, their lives, of explaining to themselves and others the awful predicament in which the majority now found themselves, namely of having been found guilty of serious crimes and imprisoned for sizeable sentences. Repeatedly castigated by officers in my hearing as the 'scum of the earth', for them Robin was an invaluable identity resource, a virtual space into which they could step and within which they could change the relationship between them and their criminality. They 'cherry-picked' the bits of the Robin Hood myth that spoke directly to and served their immediate needs. I take this to be part of what Jameson means when he asserts that myths are best regarded as 'horizontal rather than vertical'.[20]

Cityton Prison and its clientele

Cityton Prison is a large Victorian building, with many more recent additions, an all-male prison divided into a number of units as follows:

1 The main galleries, where the bulk of the adult prisoners are housed, usually two to a cell, and ranging from small-time thieves to crooked accountants.
2 The High Security Unit, which houses 'lifers', murderers, IRA terrorists, and highly violent or disruptive men placed in solitary confinement.
3 The Vulnerable Prisoner Unit, in which sex offenders

(ranging from rapists to paedophiles) are segregated from the rest of the prison population for their own protection.

4 The Young Prisoner Unit, which contains young male criminals in the age range eighteen to twenty-three some being held on remand until their case comes to court, while others are already engaged on what could be sizeable sentences of between two to five or more years. There is a high degree of recidivism among these young offenders and many are well embarked upon criminal careers. Robberies, car theft, drug dealing and acts of violence (including manslaughter) are the most common offences and the majority of the inmates are local: that is, from the coastal belt from Barry to Newport, including Cardiff and the Valleys.

In October 2000, Lord Justice Woolf (in his review of the future of the killers of the toddler Jamie Bulger) described Young Prisoner Units as 'hotbeds of violence, bullying, sexual intimidation and drugs' (*Daily Telegraph*, 27 October, p. 10). Although there are obviously some exceptions, prisons are generally hostile male environments, where a high degree of violence is normal.[21] Bullying is ever-present and there exists 'a culture of masculinity which . . . equates personal power with physical dominance'.[22] Masculinity is continuously placed under threat and so has to be constantly displayed, with respect earned on the basis of physical dominance through 'showing hard', threat or actual acts of violence.[23]

Nevertheless, prisons are also places where there is a lot of banter and good humour between prisoners and with officers. Having said that, order in Cityton was strict and the establishment was run according to a well-established, unvarying daily routine (classes and activities in the morning, visits or 'free association' time in the afternoons). The occasional outbreaks of violence were suppressed with ruthless efficiency by well-trained and equipped officers. Most were male, although there were a number of female officers, and the overall atmosphere was heavily macho: for example, many of the officers had military backgrounds and the majority had clearly been recruited for their physical bulk and intimidating demeanours.

The data that follows was gathered in the Young Prisoner Unit over a three-year period, 1994–7, by means of ethnographic fieldwork, including life history interviews with some sixty young males prisoners, the average age of whom was approximately twenty. It was part of two inter-related projects on masculinity, criminality and violence.[24]

Mitigation strategies

In spite of the austere, Bastille-like appearance and macho environment of Cityton Prison, the regime within was surprisingly progressive. The policy was not just to lock these young men up for the duration of their sentences but, rather, to attempt to intervene in their criminal careers by confronting them with the consequences of their crimes in the hope that they would, thereby, eventually come to a full understanding of the damage they were inflicting upon themselves, their neighbourhoods, and society in general. This was a delicate and difficult process and, unsurprisingly, many resisted it, finding it too intrusive and painful a process.

On entry into Cityton (as in the case of all prisons) many insisted they had been falsely convicted of a crime:

> Guilty? Me? You must be joking! I was nowhere near the scene of the crime. I was with me girlfriend over at her place. Tell me how I can be guilty then? Oh I'll be appealing, definite!

> I was asked to work on the ground plans, advise them on how to knock out the alarms, how to do the job, the clever bit, but I wasn't involved in the actual ram raid. I wasn't even here. I was clubbin' in Manchester. I realised later, too late, that I'd been set up. The boys who shopped me are now sunning themselves in Spain! The bastard judge clobbered me good and proper. He was just as bad as they were, worse in fact! You're looking at an innocent man rottin' in prison for eight years for a crime he never done! Put that down in yer notebook!

As they embarked on their sentences, and as they slowly began to come to terms with the awful reality of their predicament, some began to accept some responsibility for their actions en route to the actual outcome (that is, acceptance of their actions and, maybe, even an end to their criminality). But between these poles of alleged wrongful imprisonment and full acceptance of their guilt was a mid-way stage, when a man would accept responsibility and seek to 'explain' it. These 'explanations' often came in the form of 'mitigation strategies', depending on factors such as the nature of the crime; to what extent culpability could ever be mitigated; and what stage a man was in the rehabilitation process. Two examples of mitigation strategies, drawing on data gathered outside the Young Offender Unit, are as follows.

Example 1

A prisoner in the Vulnerable Prisoner Unit had been convicted for raping a ten-year-old girl. So appalling was this crime and so firm the evidence against him it would be difficult to imagine what 'explanation' or mitigation could possibly be forthcoming. He argued, however, that he was very drunk and it wasn't the 'real him' who had committed this terrible crime ('The real me would never have done such a thing, never'). Also, he implied the child herself had 'led him on', and looked far older than she was, etc.

Example 2

A prisoner in the High Security Unit had been involved in a daylight raid on a high street Post Office. As the gang made their getaway, the owner deliberately stood in the way of their car. In the pandemonium that ensued, the man had drawn a gun, had leant out of the window and fired a warning shot, purposely aiming to miss the owner. Unfortunately the bullet had ricocheted off a nearby wall and embedded itself in the head of a young woman who happened to be passing. She died later in hospital. Stricken by genuine grief, this prisoner talked of accident and chance, emphasizing time and time again that he had no intention of hurting anyone, let alone killing anyone, and that the gun had been 'just to wave about and frighten, nothing more. I'd have killed myself rather than that lady'.

Both mitigation strategies above had the effect of distancing the perpetrators from the horror of their respective crimes and, in the process, allowed each to admit that they were guilty but, at the same time, sought to absolve them of (some, at least) responsibility: they were means of mitigating the offence, finding a way of 'explaining' it and rendering it something with which one could live.

Returning to the Young Prisoner Unit, the Robin myth was appropriated as such a mitigation strategy and was repeatedly referred to throughout the time I data-gathered there. This can partly be attributed to the fact that most had seen both *Prince of Thieves* and the 1991 *Robin Hood*, with Bergin and Thurman. Indeed, the former was shown on video one morning when, owing to the funeral of an officer, normal activities and education classes were suspended and the prison operated on a skeleton staff. As I shall now demonstrate, many of the young inmates selected from the Robin myth those elements that both justified and mitigated their criminality. Robin proved an ideal resource (in Knight's sense) for criminalized young men who could turn Robin into what Foucault terms a 'discursive regime' and so try to represent themselves as the heroic, hard-done-by victims of a corrupt judiciary and a callous, uncaring, society.[25] In summary, then, a 'mitigation strategy' is an attempt to 'explain' and 'excuse' the inexcusable to oneself and others and thereby, seek to build a bridge between incarcerated ostracization and the outside world of freedom and acceptability.

'Me, I'm Robin Hood'

I was granted a free run of the Young Prisoner Unit and could interview any of the 'subjects' (in the language of Social Studies) or 'numbers' (in prison lingo), as long as they were willing to talk to me (which for the majority was a welcome diversion from the crushing tedium of prison routine). I was amazed to discover how often Robin's name cropped up, both in casual chats and in more formal interviews, held both with individuals as well as with pairs and groups. In what follows I have made no attempt to identify the individual speaker. Most were very ill-educated and illiterate, albeit highly articulate, while others were clearly highly intelligent and thoughtful:

indeed, two of the convicted drug dealers (or "ed barons') were university drop-outs. These 'voices' are drawn from a considerable volume of recorded (subsequently transcribed) and notebook-recorded interviews, gathered over the fieldwork period, and are representative of the very many references made to Robin of Sherwood:

> Me, I'm Robin Hood, just like him. Pushed around, punched out, treated like shit, hunted like a dog by the boys-in-blue (police), but fighting back, man, fighting back hard, using 'up-here' (taps head).
>
> I'm Robin Hood, stealin' from the rich to feed the poor. We do break-ins, take CDs, TVs and videos from people like you. For you it's nothing – five minutes fillin' in a form for the insurance. Our people could never have goods like that, never. We have to rob them, no other way. Fully justified, no doubt about it.

I noted in my fieldnotes:

> I said to one of the officers, 'Michael over there compares himself to Robin Hood'. He smiled and replied, 'You'll discover that a lot of them do. In here you quickly learn that Robin Hood is the patron saint of crooks! That is true wherever you go in the prison, not just in the YPU (Young Prisoner Unit). Over the years, the number of times I've heard a young man say he fancies himself as Robin Hood! I always say, "And I'm Superman, mate!" That's my way of handling it, because, unbelievable though it may seem to you, they're often dead serious about it, really caught up in the idea. Many of them end up living in a fantasy world of their own making. It's sad and pathetic, but I suppose it gives them some sort of self-respect.'

The young inmates systematically selected from the Robin myth to serve two groups of needs, namely as a means of:

- Redefining justice. If they had already been sentenced, they turned to Robin to mitigate their criminality; or, if they were yet to be sentenced and were held 'on remand' prior to a court appearance, to 'disprove' their guilt (rather than 'prove' their innocence).
- Recovering masculinity. Robin empowered a man to reclaim a sense of 'normal', even valorous masculinity, given that entry into prison was held to strip a man of the capability of being 'a proper man'.

ROBIN HOOD IS ALIVE AND WELL IN CITYTON PRISON

Redefining justice

Robin was used to distinguish between 'unjust justice' (that is, the way the judicial system habitually operates) and 'natural justice' (something far more mystical, but to which Robin's name could be attached).

'UNJUST JUSTICE'

Robin was perceived to have been unfairly victimized and outlawed by those in authority, themselves corrupt, for something he had not done or, alternatively, something he had done but which was, in the circumstances, 'understandable' (and, thereby, in the inmates' eyes, 'excusable'). Moreover, he was a man of principle in that he was understood to have stolen from the rich in order to benefit the poor. He was, therefore, a man of principle whose actions were fully justified, albeit deemed criminal. He was assumed (and this was mentioned on a number of occasions) to have had 'a heart of gold', ever willing to take up the cause of the underdog.

> I was stitched up by some boys I'd fallen in with over a robbery wot I'd not done. No way! Then this big fat judge geyser sends me down for three years! He's robbed more than I've ever robbed in my life, fiddling his expenses an' taxes an' all that. You could tell by looking at 'im that he was a right crooked bastard! All those judges an' that are as crooked as ****, everyone of them.

'NATURAL JUSTICE'

Robin was held to embody the promise (even the inevitability) of justice that would eventually lead to the exoneration and redemption of the inmate. The upholders of formal, judicial justice may be corrupt, but one day 'natural' and 'genuine' justices will supersede it. In the meantime the wronged man must bide his time, suffer ignominy stoically:

> In here I see myself as Robin Hood hiding in Sherwood, with my mates around me, always in danger. It's the price I've got to pay before I get justice which I know that one day justice will be mine. I'm just waiting until that happens and I can start living again. Like Robin Hood, one day I'll be able to hold my head up high again. I'll

245

have done my bird (time inside) and paid my so-called 'debt to society'. I'll be a free man again.'

'One day the truth will out. All those corrupt bastards wot stitched me and my mates up will be swept away and justice will be mine. I know it, just know it!'

Recovering masculinity

In his study of homicide (the vast majority of these being, throughout the world, male-on-male), Polk concludes:

> Confrontational homicide involves behaviour which is essentially a contest of honour between males . . . Extreme violence in defence of honour is definitely masculine.[26]

Similarly, being in prison is, like unemployment, hugely emasculating. Throughout Cityton one witnessed numerous desperate attempts to assert and bolster a flagging sense of masculinity, often through bravado attempts at hyper-masculinity, like manic weight training (not only in the gym, but even in the cells), fighting and generally 'showing hard'. Small, weak or old men were picked upon and bullied if only to give their persecutors a sense of masculine dominance. Most prisoners were haunted by their powerlessness and the concomitant loss of the masculine:

> You parks and padlocks your manhood at the gates when you come in here. You become less than a man. You're powerless; you've got no say in anything. You're not a proper man any more, just a number, a blob of flesh. You can't do the things that make a man a man, like having a woman, going to the pub, having a job, holding your head high and providing for your family. You're reduced to a wanker, literally! You manhood is ripped from you. That is, without doubt, one of the most terrible things prison does to you. They might as well cut off your balls, make you into a eunuch, 'cos that's what you are inside, a eunuch.

How did a sense of the masculine self survive in Cityton's emasculating environment and what part did Robin play in this process?

Before tackling this question it will be helpful to turn first to I. M. Harris, on 'messages' contemporary men 'hear'. The messages ('broadcast' by parents, religion, sport, peer group, media, etc.) play a crucial role in the construction of socially acceptable and commendable ways of 'being a man'.[27] The study is, in some ways, problematical, but it is grounded in a considerable amount of data and produces a useful 'map' of how contemporary (American) men view masculinity. I have previously pointed to the open, malleable, even 'writerly' nature of the Robin myth. Indeed, the figure of Robin-as-a-man incorporates many of the messages shaping what is regarded as valorious masculinity today: for example, he is a 'warrior'; an 'adventurer'; a 'leader'; a resilient 'tough guy', even a 'superman', in control of the situation and able to overcome obstacles; a 'rebel', albeit a responsible one, justified in his actions; a lover, even a debonair playboy; a skilful 'technician' (as a bowman); a self-reliant and cunning 'strategist'; a nature-love; and a 'good Samaritan'.

Robin-as-man offered a highly attractive and wide-ranging role model for Cityton's young, emasculated men as they strove to retrieve a modicum of 'proper masculinity' and self-respect. A number of 're-masculinating strategies' were employed, many making direct reference to the Robin myth, namely: 'Mr Ordinary'; being a rebel; defending territory; the value of mates; compulsive heterosexuality; and 'me little Maid Marian'.

'MR ORDINARY'

Robin stands alongside the equally misty historical figures of Kings Arthur and Alfred as national myths connoting Englishness, but he is the 'flip-side', the non-regal 'outsider', the 'ordinary man' wronged. It is this 'ordinariness' that impressed the young inmates:

> I'm dead ordinary, a dead ordinary bloke me. Mr Ordinary! Like I imagine Robin Hood to have been. No airs and graces, like him. What you see is what you get. Dead straight and speaks me mind, no messin' about.

'DEVIL-MAY-CARE' REBEL

Robin was admired for his 'devil-may-care', 'don't give-a-damn', 'fingers-up' cheeky insurrection. He was a rebel, even a guerrilla fighter, renowned for his skill and cunning in making fools of his adversaries. He was held to embody a valorous, streetwise (forest-wise) masculinity. Indeed, the romanticization of the rebel and outsider was held to be one of his most endearing qualities.

> I've always been a rebel, me, always. Rebelled against me parents, father especially, truanted all the time. If a teacher told me to do this, then I'd go and do that! Just can't stand people tellin' me what to do. Just can't take it! It does me 'ed in! Prefer to do me own thing in me own way. Always have, always will!

DEFENDING TERRITORY

Defending your own territory against intruders (and, thereby, exerting your 'rights') was an important aspect of 'being a man' in inmates' estimation. The Robin myth celebrates a particular geographical location in which the invading forces of official law and order (the Sheriff of Nottingham and his men) were ritually ambushed and humiliated. For Sherwood Forest substitute the bleak estates in Barry, Penarth, Cardiff, Newport, Merthyr and the south Wales valleys from which these young men originated and where the police were on foreign ground. Robin and his Sherwood triumphs spoke directly to these young men as the powerful were beaten back by the powerless, who need their intimate knowledge of their home patch to humiliate 'the pigs' (police).

> There was a car chase one night up on the Gurnos and these two pigs were in an unmarked pig wagon, but everyone knew who they were. They got ambushed in this lane with high walls on either side. They were way outa order being there. They should 'av never been there, never! We just out-classed them. Then, just as the driver realised he was trapped, he got rammed from behind. When the pigs got out the boys were ready for them and they got all this paint nicked from Homebase poured down on them! Laugh! In the end they hoofed it on foot and we torched the pig wagon!

'MATEDOM': 'ME AND ME MATES'

Matedom involved close friendships with like-minded and trusted mates. It was the central platform of these young men's lives both outside and inside the prison. The rebellious, 'warrior' masculinity to which these young men aspired was highly reminiscent of the archetypal portrait of Robin and his band of men.

> I'd willingly lay down my life for my mates. Wouldn't think twice. You've got to have mates in life. They're more important than anything.

I asked him to define a mate:

> Someone you can trust with your life. Turn yer back and they'll watch out for you. Someone you know will always be there for you and will never, ever, let you down. Like in here I've got three close mates: Gareth, Garin and Lloyd. We share everything, try to make life easier for each other, help each other out. Once I leave here I may never see them again, but they'd still be mates even if we met in fifty years time. Mates are forever.

COMPULSIVE HETEROSEXUALITY

Theirs was what Judith Butler terms a 'compulsory heterosexuality', even a hyper-masculinity, but with a soft, romantic side in respect to a 'good woman', a Maid Marian (see below).[28] This homosociability involved a lot of joking and ritualized physical contact (like baseball-style hands-on-hands greetings, football match-style hugs and mock fights, etc.), but it was strictly non-sexual.[29] The young men were highly homophobic and there was a lot of disparaging talk of 'bum raiders', 'queers', 'pansies', 'nancy boys' and 'poofs': indeed, any boy suspected on the slightest pretext of having homosexual tendencies was branded a 'nonce' and would have to be removed immediately to the Vulnerable Prisoner Unit for his own safety.

> There's no sex in here! That's one of the hardest things about prison. All the boys have porn on the walls and their girls send them in nude photos, but the officers steal those! There's no bumboys here – if there were they'd be castrated, straight off!

Maid Marian was mentioned by name a number of times and took a number of forms, none of them as a figure in her own right but only as a male appendage. First, she was an honorary 'mate', very much one of the boys, who was a trusted accomplice in a young man's crimes and could even, as the occasion demanded, fight on behalf of her man:

> Me missus, me little maid, she's with me all the time. 100%! If she sees me in a fix, then she'll simply fly in, her little fists flying!

Secondly, a 'good woman', upon whom the young man could pin his future dreams and with whom he hoped to escape into a paradisiacal future, often expressed in (Sherwood Forest-like) terms of a rural idyll:

> One day I'll be out of here. Then I'm going to find a really good missus, a right Maid Marian, someone who'll stick with me. We'll take off to somewhere in the country, a little cottage or something in the woods, get away from it all . . .

Thirdly, she was someone to whom these highly patriarchal young men could off-load domestic duties such as shopping, cleaning, child-rearing, etc.:

> She's my little Maid Marian. She'll do anything for me and the kid – washin', cookin', ironin'. You name it, she does it! Bloody loves it all!

Conclusion

Robin 'lives' in Cityton Young Prisoner Unit as a 'mitigatory overcoat', which can be put on to excuse wrong-doing and exorcise guilt. He spoke directly to these young men because they felt so strongly that they had been 'set-up', 'clobbered', and wrongfully outlawed. They empathized with Robin because he held out transformatory possibilities of asserting a non-criminal, even commendable, rebel identity. He was a way of rendering their criminality as the understandable outcome of being victimized by corrupt authority. Without pushing the case for him being a secularized version of Christ-as-Saviour too far, Robin encapsulated the possibility, even the promise, of eventual redemption. In the short term he constituted an escape chute from taking personal responsibility for one's criminality, as way of not so much explaining criminality as explaining it away. The myth provided a host of exonerating narratives that transferred responsibility from the individual onto those held responsible for rendering the young man a victim. Allied to this, Robin-as-man was an alluringly masculine and courageous figure with whom to identify for young men who felt they had been stripped of their masculinity by the judicial process and an unyielding, often brutal, prison regime.

Whereas Robin provided them with hope and consolation, for me he became a means of analysis that allowed me to make sense of the young men's perceptions of their lives and actions. The Robin myth proved malleable enough to encompass the justificatory and rehabilitative needs of the two cohorts:

- first, those who, against the odds, doggedly maintained their innocence and argued that they had been unjustly accused (even 'set up'), imprisoned and criminalized and who saw in Robin the promise that one day the truth would out; and
- secondly, those who reluctantly admitted their crimes but saw in Robin justification for their criminal actions because they had been dealt a rotten hand (a 'shit deal') by an unequal and corrupt society in the first place and were, therefore, entitled to respond as they had. They argued that they had been forced into crime and outlawed and that crime had been their best, if not only, option in the circumstances.

By recourse to Robin they sought to 'legalize' crimes that could be demonstrated as instances of 'robbing the rich to help the poor'. So, for example, robberies from banks, post offices, building societies, shops, houses and ram raids against warehouses and storages units were justified ('They're all rich, they're all insured, they don't lose out'). On the other hand, any inmate who was known to have committed a robbery against the poor, old or handicapped often had to be segregated and placed in a 'secure' cell (collecting his meals on his own after all the other inmates had been locked in their cells, or 'banged up', where meals were eaten) for his own protection.

Another way of conceptualizing myth is, of course, as ideology,[30] and as a route to false consciousness, a way of lying to oneself that everything is 'explainable' and will turn out fine in the end. From this angle Robin becomes an escape for these young men into an illusory, imaginary life, bearing very little resemblance to the reality of their proven criminality and subsequent imprisonment.

Postscript

As a postscript I refer to two additional facets of Robin associated with, first, racism and nationalism; and secondly, homosexuality.

Although Robin is often described as 'British', he is essentially in modern centuries 'English': the verdancy of Sherwood forest is very much part of England's 'green and pleasant land'. It was interesting, therefore, to hear Robin invoked not only as 'British' but as an upholder of 'white Britishness'. Towards the end of my fieldwork an interesting little exchange occurred as I interviewed a group of six inmates, two black and four white.

One of the black boys said: 'Me, I'm Robin Hood, just like him, honest to God'. To which one of his white and Welsh companions responded in a threatening and uncompromising tone of voice, raising laughter in the process:

> You could never be Robin Hood. He weren't black. He was British, man, through and through! Combat 18 boy, just like me!

So Robin was invoked for yet another purpose – to link race and nationality and uphold the 'purity' of white 'Britishness'.

Secondly, in July 1999, Robin was yet again in the news for a somewhat novel reason. In spite of appropriation by women as a 'masculine space' (as I have earlier demonstrated), his heterosexuality had hitherto remained unquestioned. Perhaps because the macho image of the honourable hero is so well established, Stephen Knight's suggestion (see the essay here by Knight and Hahn), in a paper delivered to an international conference in Nottingham that Robin was a gay outlaw created a media furore. Jonathan Leake and Mark Macaskill of the *Sunday Times* led the charge: in an article entitled 'Meet Robin Hood, Queen of the Woods' (and illustrated by a lascivious Erroll Flynn 'hitching a ride on Friar Tuck'), they announced, in good old journalistic 'nudge, nudge, wink, wink' style, that 'new studies of medieval texts . . . suggest that the robber with a heart of gold was actually a gay outlaw who had been exiled from 'straight' society. Little John, not Maid Marian, was his true love'. Knight's argument in essence was that careful study of the ballads reveal clear homoerotic overtones. In the *Sunday Times* article he was quoted as saying that:

> Robin Hood and his men are all very male and live exclusively without women. The ballads could not say outright that he was gay because of the prevailing moral climate, but they do contain a great deal of erotic imagery. The greenwood itself is a symbol of virility and the references to arrows, quivers and swords make it clear too.

Early ballads, he argued, do not contain any reference to Maid Marian who was added by sixteenth-century authors, intent on making their work more respectable to heterosexual readers. This controversial reading of the ballads was supported by Barrie Dobson, Professor of Medieval History at Cambridge University, who was quoted as saying that 'in the twelfth-century homosexuality was accepted but in the thirteenth the Church became much less tolerant and such people were driven underground'. Meanwhile Boyer in the *Western Mail* came up with the clever line, 'Knight on quest for truth outs the green queen', and the comment:

> The Robin Hood Society has defended its hero from the gay twist and says the claim could do untold damage to the folk hero. But gay rights campaigners say they are pleased with the outing.

As I read this, I could not help wondering how the homophobic young criminals in Cityton, who had invested so heavily in Robin, would have responded. And neither could I but marvel at Robin's continued relevance to contemporary life.

NOTES

[1] Cathy Schwichtenberg (ed.), *The Madonna Connection: Representational Politics, Subcultural Identities and Cultural Theory*, (Boulder, Colorado: Westview, 1993); James Lull, *Media, Communication, Culture: A Global Approach* (Cambridge: Polity Press, 1995).

[2] Knight, *Robin Hood: A Complete Study of the English Outlaw* (Oxford: Blackwell, 1994); Yosjiko Ueno, 'Murayama's Robin Hood: The Most Radical Variant in Japan', in *Robin Hood in Popular Culture: Violence, Transgression and Justice*, Thomas Hahn (ed.) (Cambridge: D. S. Brewer, 2000), pp. 265–73.

3. J. C. Holt, *Robin Hood* (London: Thames and Hudson, 1983), pp. 52–4, 189–90, suggested 'Robin Hood' or 'Robehood' became a nickname for a fugitive.
4. Knight 1994, pp. 108–9.
5. Eric J. Hobsbawm, *Bandits* (London: Wiedenfeld and Nicholson, 1969).
6. 'A Literary Dinner', Tales of a Traveller, in Washington Irving, *Bracebridge Hall, Tales of A Traveler, The Alhambra*, ed. Andrew B. Mynors (New York: Library of America, 1991), p. 487.
7. Alfred Noyes, *Sherwood* (London and New York: Frederick A. Stokes, 1911), quoted in Lois Potter, 'Robin Hood and the Fairies: Alfred Noyes' Sherwood', in *RHMP*, pp. 167–80, pp. 176–7. Potter points out that the Christian Socialist colouring of this passage was removed and the passage greatly shortened in the 1926 edition, perhaps because of the context of the Great Strike.
8. Irving, 'English Country Gentleman', *Bracebridge Hall*, p. 203.
9. Knight 1994, p. 259.
10. Knight 1994, p. 261.
11. David Williams, *The Rebecca Riots: A Study in Agrarian Discontent* (Cardiff: University of Wales Press, 1955), p. vii.
12. See D. J. V. Jones, *Rebecca's Children: A Study of Rural Society, Crime, and Protest* (Oxford, 1975).
13. Knight 1994, p. 259.
14. Ibid.
15. John Macinnes, *The End of Masculinity: The Confusion of Sexual Genesis and Sexual Difference in Modern Society* (Buckingham: Open University Press, 1998).
16. Roland Barthes, *S/Z*, A. Lavers (trans.) (London: Jonathan Cape, 1972).
17. Peter Brooker, *Concise Glossary of Cultural Theory* (London: Arnold, 1999), p. 6.
18. Frederic Jameson, *Post-Modernism, or the Cultural Logic of Late Capitalism* (Durham, NC: Duke University Press, 1991).
19. Stuart Hall, *Representation: Cultural Representations and Signifying Practices* (Milton Keynes: The Open University Press, 1997); for 'writerly', see Barthes, *Mythologies*, A. Lavers (trans.) (London: Jonathan Cape, 1972).
20. Jameson, *Post-Modernism*, p. 168.
21. T. Parker, *Life After Life* (London: Secker and Warburg, 1990).
22. *Prisons Under Protest*, Phil Scraton, Joe Sim and Paula Skidmore (eds) (Buckingham: The Open University Press, 1991), p. 67.
23. *Just Boys Doing Business? Men, Masculinities and Crime*, Tim Newburn and Elizabeth A. Stanko (eds) (London: Routledge, 1994).
24. See, for example, John Beynon, *The Joy Generation: Young Men, Masculinity and Crime* (Swindon: The Economic and Social Research Council, 1996); R. Thurstan and J. Beynon, 'Men's own Stories, Lives and Violence: Research as Practice', in *Gender and Crime*, R. E.

Dobash, R. P. Dobash and I. Noaks (eds) (Cardiff: University of Wales Press, 1995), pp. 181–201.

25 On discursive regimes, see Michel Foucault, *The Archaeology of Knowledge*, A. M. Sheridan (trans.) (New York: Harper and Row, 1972); *Discipline and Punish: The Birth of the Prison* (Harmondsworth: Penguin, 1991).

26 Kenneth Polk, 'Masculinity, Honour, and Confrontational Homicide', in Newburn and Stanko, pp. 187–8

27 I. M. Harris, *Messages Men Hear: Constructing Masculinities* (London: Taylor and Francis, 1994).

28 See Judith Butler, *Gender Trouble: Feminism and the Subversion of Identity* (London: Routledge, 1990); R. W. Connell, *Masculinities* (Cambridge: Polity Press, 1995).

29 On homosociality, see Eve Kosofsky Sedgwick, *Between Men: English Literature and Male Homosocial Desire* (New York: Columbia University Press, 1985).

30 Terence Hawkes, *Structuralism and Semiotics* (London: Routledge, 1977), pp. 39–49, 106–16; Terry Eagleton, *Ideology: An Introduction* (London: Verso, 1991), 185–91.

Bibliography

Primary Texts

Aled, Tudur, *Gwaith Tudur Aled*, ed. T. Gwynn Jones, 2 vols (Cardiff: University of Wales Press, 1926)

Andrew of Wyntoun, *The Orygynale Chronicle*, ed. D. Laing, 5 vols (Edinburgh: Edmondson and Douglas, 1903–14)

Anglo-Norman Dictionary, ed. William Rothwell, Louis W. Stone, T. B. W. Reid, with Dafydd Evans, et al. (London: MHRA, 1992)

Anon., *Annales monastici*, ed. H. R. Luard, 5 vols, Rolls Series 36 (London: Longman, 1864–69)

Anon., *Fouke Fitz Warin*, ed. Louis Brandin, Les classiques français du moyen âge (Paris: Champion, 1930)

—— *Histoire des ducs de Normadie et de rois d'Angleterre*, ed. Francisque Michel (Paris: J. Renouard, 1840; repr. London and New York: Johnson Reprint, 1965)

—— *Fouke Le Fitz Waryn*, ed. E. J.Hathaway, P. T. Ricketts, C. A. Robson, A. D. Wilshere, Anglo-Norman Text Society (Oxford: Blackwell, 1975)

Anonimalle Chronicle 1333–1380, ed. V. Galbraith (Manchester and New York: Manchester University Press, 1970)

Barczewski, Stephanie, *Myth and National Identity in Nineteenth-Century Britain: The Legends of King Arthur and Robin Hood* (Oxford: Clarendon Press, 2000)

Bolton, Philip, 'Playing Rob Roy as Robin Hood', in *Scott in Carnival: Selected Papers from the Fourth International Scott Conference, Edinburgh 1991* (Aberdeen: Association for Scottish Literary Studies, 1993)

Bower, Walter, *Continuation of John of Fordun's Scotichronicon*, ed. T. Hearne (Oxford: Sheldonian Theatre, 1722)

Burgess, Glyn (ed. and trans.), *Two Medieval Outlaws: Eustace the Monk and Fouke Fitz Waryn* (Cambridge: D. S. Brewer, 1997)

Child, F. J. (ed.), *English and Scottish Popular Ballads*, 5 vols, reprint edn (New York: Dover, 1964)

Creswick, Paul, *Robin Hood* (London: Nister, 1902)

Cywyddau Iolo Goch ac Eraill, ed. H. Lewis, T. Roberts, and I. Williams (Cardiff: University of Wales Press, 1925)

BIBLIOGRAPHY

Dafydd ap Gwilym, *Gwaith Dafydd ap Gwilym*, ed. Thomas Parry (Cardiff: University of Wales Press, 1959)

Dictionary of Welsh Biography Down to 1940 (Cardiff: University of Wales Press, 1959)

Drayton, Michael, *Works*, ed. J. W. Hebel, 5 vols (Oxford: Clarendon Press, 1961)

Dunbar, William, *Selected Poems*, ed. Priscilla Bawcutt (Glasgow: Association for Scottish Literary Studies, 1999)

Fraser, Antonia: see Pakenham

Furlong, Monica, *Robin's Country* (London: Hamish Hamilton, 1994)

Gaunt, William, *Bandits in a Landscape: A Study of Romantic Painting from Caravaggio to Delacroix* (London: The Studio, 1937)

Green, Roger Lancelyn, *The Adventures of Robin Hood* (Harmondsworth: Penguin, 1956)

Hary's Wallace, ed. Matthew P. McDiarmid, Scottish Text Society, 2 vols (Edinburgh: Edinburgh University Press, 1968, 1969)

Hayes, Sarah, *Robin Hood* (New York: Walker Books, 1989)

Iolo Goch: Poems, ed. and trans. Dafydd Johnston (Llandysul: Gomer, 1993)

Irving, Washington, *Miscellaneous Writings 1803–1859*, ed. Wayne R. Kime (Boston: Twayne, 1981)

—— *The Complete Works of Washington Irving, Journals and Note Books*, vol. 1 (1803–1806), ed. Nathalia Wright (Madison: University of Wisconsin Press, 1969); vol. 2 (1807–1822) ed. Walter A. Reichart and Lillian Schlissel (Boston: Twayne, 1981); vol. 3 (1819–1827) ed. Walter A. Reichart (Madison: University of Wisconsin Press, 1970); vol. 4 (1826–1829), ed. Wayne R. Kime and Andrew B. Myers (Boston: Twayne, 1984); vol. 5 (1832–1959), ed. Sue F. Ross (Boston: Twayne, 1986)

—— *Letters, 1823–1838*, ed. Ralph M. Aderman, Herbert L. Kleinfield, and Jenifer S. Banks (Boston: Twayne, 1979)

—— *Irving's Works, Geoffrey Crayon Edition, Complete in 27 Volumes* (New York: G. P. Putnam's Sons, 1865)

—— *History, Tales and Sketches: Letters of Jonathan Oldstyle, Gent; Salmagundi; History of New York; The Sketch Book of Geoffrey Crayon, Gent* (New York: Twayne, 1983)

—— *Bracebridge Hall, Tales of A Traveler, The Alhambra* (New York: Literary Classics, 1991)

Isidore of Seville, *Etymologies*, ed. and trans. Stephen A. Barney, W. J. Lewis, J. A. Beach, Oliver Berghof (Cambridge: Cambridge University Press, 2007)

Jonson, Ben, *The Works of Ben Jonson*, ed. C. H. Herford, F. Simpson and E. Simpson, 11 vols (Oxford: Clarendon Press, 1941)
Kingsley, Charles, *Hereward the Wake, the Last of the English* (London: P. R. Gawthorn, 1949)
Knight, Stephen, *Robin Hood: A Complete History of the English Outlaw* (Oxford: Blackwell, 1994)
—— and Thomas H. Ohlgren (eds), *Robin Hood and Other Outlaw Tales*, TEAMS (Kalamazoo: Medieval Institute Publications, 1997)
——*Robin Hood: A Mythic Biography* (Ithaca and London: Cornell University Press, 2003)
Langland, William, *Piers Plowman: A Parallel Edition of the A, B, C, and Z Versions*, ed. A. V. C. Schmidt (London: Longman, 1995)
Leeson, Robert, *The Story of Robin Hood* (Boston and London: Kingfisher, 1994)
Lleisiau'r Werin (Arfon: Cymdeithas Alawon Gwerin Cymru, 1980)
Major, John, *Historia Majoris Britanniae* (Paris, Josse Badius, 1521)
Map, Walter, *De nugis curialium, Courtiers' Trifles*, ed. M. R. James, rev. edn, C. N. L. Brooke and R. A. B. Mynors, Oxford Medieval Texts (Oxford: Clarendon Press, 1983)
Marshall, H. E., *Stories of Robin Hood* (London, New York: Dutton, 1905)
McKinley, Robin, *The Outlaws of Sherwood* (New York: Greenwillow, 1988)
McMaster, Graham, *Scott and Society* (Cambridge: Cambridge University Press, 1981)
Mammucari, Renato, *I Briganti* (Città di Castello: Edimond, 2001)
Miles, Bernard, *Robin Hood: His Life and Legend* (London: Hamlyn, 1979)
Mitchell, Adrian, *The Adventures of Robin Hood and Marian* (London: Orchard, 1998)
Morpurgo, Michael, *Robin of Sherwood* (London: Hodder, 1996)
Noyes, Alfred, *Sherwood* (New York: Frederick A. Stokes, 1911)
Ohlgren, Thomas H. (ed.), *Medieval Outlaws: Ten Tales in Modern English* (Stroud: Sutton, 1998)
Owain, Gutun, *L'Oeuvre poétique de Guton Owain*, ed. E. Bachellery, 2 vols (Paris: Champion, 1950–1)
Oxford Book of Welsh Verse in English, ed. Gwyn Jones (Oxford: Clarendon Press, 1977)
Paine, Thomas, *The Writings of Thomas Paine*, ed. Moncure Daniel Conway (New York: AMS Press, 1967)

BIBLIOGRAPHY

Pakenham, Antonia, *Robin Hood* (London: Heirloom, 1955); Fraser, Antonia, *Robin Hood* (London: Orion, 1971)

Paris, Matthew, *Chronica Majora*, ed. H. R. Luard, 7 vols, Rolls Series 57 (London: Longmans, 1872–84)

Peacock, Thomas Love, *Maid Marian*, ed. George Saintsbury (London: Macmillan, 1895)

Peele, George, *The Dramatic Works: Edward I*, ed. E. S. Hook, vol. 2 of *The Life and Works of George Peele*, ed. Charles T. Prouty, 2 vols (New Haven: Yale University Press, 1961)

Penllyn, Tudur, *Gwaith Tudur Penllyn*, ed. Thomas Roberts (Cardiff: University of Wales Press, 1958)

Percy, Thomas, *Reliques of English Poetry*, 3 vols (London: J. Dodsley, 1765)

—— *The Percy Folio Manuscript*, ed. F. J. Furnivall (London: N. Trübner, 1867)

Pyle, Howard, *The Merry Adventures of Robin Hood of Great Renown in Nottinghamshire* (New York: Scribner, 1883)

Rees, E. A., *Welsh Outlaws and Bandits: Political Rebellion and Lawlessness in Wales, 1400–1603* (King's Norton: Caterwen, 2001)

Ritson, Joseph, *Robin Hood: A Collection of all the Ancient Poems, Songs, and Ballads, Now Extant, Relative to that Celebrated English Outlaw* (London: T. Egerton and J. Johnson, 1795)

Roger of Hoveden, *Chronica*, ed. W. Stubbs, 4 vols, Rolls Series 51 (London: Longmans, 1868–71)

Scott, Sir Walter, *Rob Roy*, ed. Arthur T. Flux (London: Black, 1903)

—— *The Betrothed and the Talisman*, ed. Andrew Lang, The Waverley Novels (London: Macmillan, 1904)

—— *Ivanhoe*, ed. A. N. Wilson (Harmondsworth: Penguin, 1982)

—— *The Visionary*, ed. Peter Garside, Regency Reprints 1 (Cardiff: University College Press, 1984)

—— *Ivanhoe*, ed. Graham Tulloch, Edinburgh Edition of the Waverley Novels (Edinburgh: Edinburgh University Press, 1998)

—— *Rob Roy*, ed. Ian Duncan, World's Classics (Oxford: Oxford University Press, 1998)

Squire, J. C., *Robin Hood: A Farcical Romantic Pastoral* (London: Heineman, 1928)

Stocqueler, Joachim H., *Maid Marian or, The Forest Queen, being a Companion to 'Robin Hood'* (London: G. Pierce, 1849)

Sutcliffe, Rosemary, *The Chronicles of Robin Hood* (London: Oxford University Press, 1950)

Tilney, F. C., *Robin Hood and his Merry Outlaws* (London and New York: Dent, 1913)

Tomlinson, Theresa, *The Forestwife* (London: Corgi, 1993)
Trease, Geoffrey, *Bows Against the Barons*, rev. edn (London: Hodder and Stoughton, 1966)
Trevisa, John, *On the Properties of Things: John Trevisa's Translations of Bartholomaeus Anglicus 'De proprietatibus rerum'*, ed. M. C. Seymour (Oxford, 1975)
Vivian, Evelyn Charles H., *Robin Hood* (London: Ward, Lock, 1927)
Wailly, Natalis de (ed.), *Récits d'un menéstrel de Reims au treizième siècle*, (Paris: J. Renouard, 1876)
Williams, Marcia, *The Adventures of Robin Hood* (London: Walker Books, 1995).
Wynn, Sir John, *The History of the Gwydir Family and Memoirs*, ed. J. Gwynfor Jones (Llandysul: Gomer, 1990).

Secondary Texts

Agamben, Giorgio, *Homo Sacer: Sovereign Power and Bare Life*, trans. Daniel Heller-Roazen (Stanford: Stanford University Press, 1998)
Ailes, Adrian, *The Origins of the Royal Arms of England: Their Development to 1199* (Reading: University of Reading Graduate Centre for Medieval Studies, 1982)
Barczewski, Stephanie, *Myth and National Identity in Nineteenth Century Britain: the Legends of King Arthur and Robin Hood* (Oxford: Oxford University Press, 2000)
Benjamin, Walter, 'Ursprung des deutschen Trauerspiels', *Gesammelte Schriften*, ed. Rolf Tiedemann, 4 vols (Frankfurt-am-Main: Suhrkamp, 1980), vol. 1, pp. 203–409
Barber, Richard, *The Devil's Crown: A History of Henry II and his Sons* (London: BBC, 1978)
Barthes, Roland, *Mythologies*, trans. A. Lavers (London: Jonathan Cape, 1972)
Bartlett Robert, *England under the Norman and Angevin Kings 1075–1225* (Oxford: Oxford University Press, 2000)
Behlmer, Rudy, *Behind the Scenes* (Hollywood: French, 1990)
—— *The Adventures of Robin Hood,* Warner Bros. Screenplay Series (Madison: University of Wisconsin Press, 1979)
Bevington, David, *Tudor Drama and Politics: A Critical Approach to Topical Meaning* (Cambridge, MA: Harvard University Press, 1968)
Beynon, John, *The Joy Generation: Young Men, Masculinity and Crime* (Swindon: The Economic and Social Research Council, 1996)

BIBLIOGRAPHY

Bolton, Philip, 'Playing Rob Roy as Robin Hood', in *Scott in Carnival: Selected Papers from the Fourth International Scott Conference, Edinburgh, 1991*, ed. J. H. Alexander and David Hewitt, (Aberdeen: Association for Scottish Literary Studies, 1993), pp. 478–90

Bowen, Ivor, *The Statutes of Wales* (London: Unwin, 1908)

Brockman, Bennett A., 'Robin Hood an the Invention of Children's Literature', *Children's Literature*, 10 (1982), 1–17

Brooker, Peter, *Concise Glossary of Cultural Theory* (London: Arnold, 1999).

Brown, P. Hume (ed.), *Scotland Before 1700 from Contemporary Documents* (Edinburgh: D. Douglas, 1893)

Buchan, John, *Sir Walter Scott* (New York: Coward-McCann, 1932)

Burgess, Glyn, 'Women in the *Fouke le Fitz Waryn*', in *'Por le soie amisté': Essays in Honor of Norris J. Lacy*, ed. K. Busby and Catherine M. Jones (Amsterdam: Rodopi, 2000), pp. 75–93

Burns, Jane E., 'Portraits of Kingship in the *Pèlerinage de Charlemagne*', *Olifant*, 10 (1982–85), 161–81

Butler, Judith, *Gender Trouble: Feminism and the Subversion of Identity* (New York: Routledge, 1990)

Calhoun, Joshua and Lois Potter, *Images of Robin Hood* (Newark DE: University of Delaware Press, 2007).

Christensen, Terry, *Reel Politics: American Political Movies from 'Birth of a Nation' to 'Platoon'* (Oxford: Clarendon Press, 1987)

Classen, Albrecht, 'The Cry-baby Kings in Courtly Romances: What is Wrong with Medieval Kingship?', *Studi Medievali*, 3rd series, 39 (1998), 833–63

Commager, Henry S., *The Search for a Usable Past and Other Essays in Hagiography* (New York: Knopf, 1967)

Connell, R. W., *Masculinities* (Cambridge: Polity Press, 1995)

Crawford, Robert, *Devolving English Literature* (Oxford: Clarendon Press, 1992)

Dickinson, J., 'The Mediaeval Concept of Kingship and some of its Limitations as Developed in the *Policraticus* of John of Salisbury', *Speculum*, 1 (1926), 308–37

Dobson, R. B. and J. Taylor (eds), *Rymes of Robin Hood: An Introduction to the English Outlaw* (Gloucester: Sutton, 1989)

Duggan, Alfred L., *Devil's Brood: The Angevin Family* (London: Faber and Faber, 1957)

Duggan, Anne J. (ed.), *Kings and Kingship in Medieval Europe* (London: King's College London Centre for Late Antique and Medieval Studies, 1993)

Dwnn, L., *Heraldic Visitations of Wales and Part of the Marches* (Llandovery: W. Rees, 1848)

Eagleton, Terry, *Ideology: An Introduction* (London, New York: Verso, 1991)

Foucault, Michel, *The Archaeology of Knowledge*, trans. A. M. Sheridan (New York: Harper Rowe, 1972)

—— *Discipline and Punish: The Birth of the Prison* (Harmondsworth: Penguin, 1991)

Eales, Richard, 'The Game of Chess: An Aspect of Medieval Knightly Culture', in *The Ideals and Practice of Medieval Knighthood: Papers from the First and Second Strawberry Hill Conferences*, ed. Christopher Harper-Bill and Ruth Harvey (Woodbridge: Boydell and Brewer, 1986), pp. 12–34

Ellis, Allen, *Comic Art in Scholarly Writing: A Citation Guide*, http://www.sp.uconn.edu/~epk93002/CAC/cite.html.

Ellis, Clarence, *Hubert de Burgh: A Study in Constancy* (London: Phoenix House, 1952)

Emden, Wolfgang Van, 'Kingship in the Old French Epic of Revolt', in Duggan, *Kings and Kingship*, pp. 305–50.

Evans, Gwynfor, *Aros Mae* (Swansea and Cardiff: John Penry, 1971); translated as *Land of My Fathers* (Talybont: John Penry, 1974)

Evans, Lindsay, *The Castles of Wales: A Guide* (London: Constable, 1998)

Evans, R. Wallis, 'Prophetic Poetry', in *A Guide to Welsh Literature 1282–c.1550*, ed. A. O. H. Jarman and Gwilym Rees Hughes, rev. ed., Dafydd Johnston (Cardiff, 1997), pp. 256–74

Evans, Ruth, Helen Fulton and David Matthews (eds), *Medieval Cultural Studies: Essays in Honour of Stephen Knight* (Cardiff: University of Wales Press, 2006)

Evans, Ruth, '*Sir Orfeo* and the Bare Life', in Evans et al., *Medieval Cultural Studies*, pp. 198–212

Everitt, Nigel, *The Tory View of Landscape*, Paul Mellon Center for Studies in British Art (New Haven and London: Yale University Press, 1994)

Foucault, Michel, *The Archaeology of Knowledge*, trans. A. M. Sheridan (New York: Harper and Row, 1972)

—— *Discipline and Punish: The Birth of the Prison* (Harmondsworth: Penguin, 1991)

Foulkes, Isaac, *Cymru Fu: yn Cynnwys Hanesion, Traddodiadau yn nghyda Chwedlau a Dammegion Cymreig* (Wrexham: Hughes, 1862)

Fraser, George Macdonald, *The Hollywood History of the World* (London: Michael Joseph, 1996)

BIBLIOGRAPHY

Fraser, John, *America and the Patterns of Chivalry* (Cambridge: Cambridge University Press, 1982)

Gaunt, William, *Bandits in a Landscape* (London: The Studio, 1937)

Gilbert, James, *A Cycle of Outrage: America's Reaction to the Juvenile Delinquent in the 1950s* (Oxford: Clarendon Press, 1986)

Gillingham, John, 'The Art of Kingship: Richard I, 1189–99', *History Today*, April 1985, 17–23; repr. in Gillingham, *Richard Coeur de Lion: Kingship, Chivalry and War in the Twelfth Century* (London, 1994), pp. 95–103

Given-Wilson, C. and A. Curteis, *The Royal Bastards of Medieval England* (London: Routledge and Kegan Paul, 1984)

Gray, Douglas, 'Everybody's Robin Hood', in Phillips, *RHMP*, pp. 21–41

Gwyndaf, Robin, *Welsh Folk Tales* (Cardiff: National Museum of Wales, 1995)

Hall, Stuart, *Representation: Cultural Representations and Signifying Practices* (Milton Keynes: The Open University Press, 1997)

Hahn, Thomas, 'Robin Hood and the Birth of Cultural Studies', in Evans et al., *MCS*, pp. 39–54

—— (ed.), *Robin Hood in Popular Culture: Violence, Transgression and Justice* (Cambridge: D. S. Brewer, 2000)

Hark, Ina Rae, 'The Visual Politics of *The Adventures of Robin Hood*', *Journal of Popular Film*, 5 (1976), 3–17

Harris, I. M., *Messages Men Hear: Constructing Masculinities* (London: Taylor and Francis, 1994)

Harty, Kevin J. (ed.), *Cinema Arthuriana* (New York: Garland, 1991)

—— (ed.), *King Arthur on Film* (Jefferson, N.C.: McFarland, 1999)

—— 'Robin Hood on Film: Moving beyond a Swashbuckling Stereotype', in Hahn, 87–100

Hellman, George S., *Washington Irving Esquire: Ambassador at Large from the New World to the Old* (New York: Knopf, 1925)

Hepworth, David, 'A Grave Tale', in Phillips, *RHMP*, pp. 91–112

Hawkes, Terence, *Structuralism and Semiotics* (London: Routledge, 1996)

Head, Victor, *Hereward* (Stroud: Sutton, 1995)

Hellman, George S., *Washington Irving Esquire: Ambassador at Large from the New World to the Old* (New York: Knopf, 1925)

Hobsbawm, Eric J., *Bandits* (London: Wiedenfeld and Nicholson, 1969)

Holt, J. C., *King John* (London: Historical Association, 1963)

—— *Robin Hood* (London: Thames and Hudson, 1983)

Jameson, Fredric, *Post-Modernism, or the Cultural Logic of Late Capitalism* (Durham, NC: Duke University Press, 1991)
Jarman, A. O. H. and G. Rees Hughes (eds) *A Guide to Welsh Literature, 1282–c.1500* (rev. edn, Cardiff: University of Wales Press, 1977)
Jenkins, Henry, *Textual Poachers* (New York and London: Routledge, 1992)
Jones, D. J. V., *Rebecca's Children: A Study of Rural Society, Crime, and Protest* (Oxford: Clarendon Press, 1975)
Jones, T. Gwynn, 'Cultural Bases: A Study of the Tudor Period in Wales', *Y Cymmrodor*, 31 (1921), 161–92
Jones, Timothy S., 'Geoffrey of Monmouth, *Fouke le Fitz Waryn*, and National Mythology', *Studies in Philology*, 91 (1994), 233–49
Jonin, Pierre, 'La Partie d'échecs dans l'épopée médiévale', in *Mélanges de langue et de littérature du Moyen Age et de la Renaissance offerts à Jean Frappier*, 2 vols (Geneva: Droz, 1970), vol. 2, pp. 483–97
—— 'Le Roi dans les *Lais* de Marie de France: l'homme sous le personnage', in *Essays in Early French Literature Presented to Barbara M. Craig* (York SC: French Literature Publications, 1982)
Kaeuper, Richard, *War, Justice, and Public Order: England and France in the Later Middle Ages* (Oxford: Clarendon Press, 1988)
Keen, Maurice, *The Outlaws of Medieval England*, rev. ed. (London: Routledge, 2001)
Knight, Stephen, *Robin Hood: A Complete Study of the English Outlaw* (Oxford: Blackwell, 1994)
—— *Robin Hood: A Mythic Biography* (Ithaca and London: Cornell University Press, 2003)
—— '"Meere English Flocks": Ben Jonson's *The Sad Shepherd* and the Robin Hood Tradition', in Phillips, *RHMP*, pp. 129–44
—— 'Robin Hood: The Earlier Contexts', in Calhoun and Potter, *Images of Robin Hood*, forthcoming
Lafeber, Walter, *America, Russia and the Cold War 1945–1980* (New York: McGraw Hill, 1980)
Le Goff, Jacques, 'Le Roi dans l'Occident médiéval', in *Kings and Kingship in Medieval Europe*, ed. Anne J. Duggan (London: King's College London Centre for Late Antique and Medieval Studies, 1993)
Lloyd, Alan, *King John* (Newton Abbot: David and Charles, 1973)

Lloyd, J. Y. W., *The History of the Princes, the Lords Marcher, and the Ancient Nobility of Powys Fadog, and the Ancient Lords of Arwystli, Cedewen, and Meirionydd* (London: Richards, 1882)

Lockhart, John Gibson, *Memoirs of he Life of Sir Walter Scott* (New York: Houghton Mifflin, 1902)

Lull, James, *Media, Communication, Culture: A Global Approach* (Cambridge: Polity Press, 1995)

Lyon, Bryce, *A Constitutional and Legal History of Medieval England* (New York: Harper, 1960)

McCloud, Scott, *Understanding Comics* (New York: Harper Perennial, 1994)

Macinnes, John, *The End of Masculinity: The Confusion of Sexual Genesis and Sexual Difference in Modern Society* (Buckingham:Open University Press, 1998)

McMaster, Graham, *Scott and Society* (Cambridge: Cambridge University Press, 1981)

Mammucari, Renato, *I Briganti* (Città di Castello: Edimond, 2000)

Meisel, Janet, *Barons of the Welsh Frontier: The Corbet, Pantulf, and Fitz Warin Families, 1066–1272* (Lincoln, Nebraska and London: University of Nebraska Presss, 1980)

Morton, Graeme, *William Wallace, Man and Myth* (Stroud: Sutton, 2001)

Nagy, Joseph F., 'The Paradoxes of Robin Hood', *Folklore*, 91 (1980), 198–210

Nelson, Malcolm A., *The Robin Hood Tradition in the English Renaissance*, Elizabethan and Renaissance Studies, ed. James Hogg, Salzburg Studies in English Literature (Salzburg: Institut für Anglistik und Amerikanistik, 1973)

Newburn, Tom and Elizabeth A Stanko, (eds), *Just Boys Doing Business? Men, Masculinities and Crime* (London: Routledge, 1994)

Nollen, Scott Allen, *Robin Hood: a Cinematic History of the English Outlaw and his Scottish Counterparts* (Jefferson, N.C.: McFarland, 1999)

Nyberg, Amy Kiste, *Seal of Approval: The History of the Comics Code* (Jackson, MI: Unversity Press of Mississippi, 1998)

Ohlgren, Thomas H., and Lister M. Matheson, *Robin Hood: The Early Poems, 1465–1560, Texts, Contexts, and Ideology* (Newark DE: University of Delaware Press, 2007)

Ormrod, W. M., 'Robin Hood and the Public Record: The Authority of Writing in the Medieval Outlaw Tradition', in Evans, *MCS*, pp. 57–74

Painter, Sydney, *The Reign of King John* (Baltimore MD: Johns Hopkins Press, 1949)
Parker, T, *Life After Life* (London: Secker and Warburg, 1990)
Parry, Thomas, *Hanes Llenyddiaeth Gymraeg Hyd 1900* (Cardiff: University of Wales Press, 1979)
Pearsall, Derek, *The Life of Geoffrey Chaucer: A Critical Biography* (Oxford: Blackwell, 1992)
—— 'Little John and Robin Hood and the Monk', in Phillips, *RHMP*, pp. 42–50
Pensom, Roger, 'Inside and Outside: Fact and Fiction, in *Fouke le Fitz Waryn*', *Medium Aevum*, 63 (1994), 53–60
Peters, Edward, *The Shadow King: rex inutilis in Medieval Law and Literature 751–1327* (New Haven and London: Yale University Press, 1970)
Phillips, Helen, 'Remembering Edward I', in *Studies in Late Medieval and Early Renaissance Texts in Honour of John Scattergood: 'The Key of all Good Remembrance'*, ed. Anne Marie Darcy and Alan J. Fletcher (Dublin: Four Courts Press, 2005), pp. 270–86
—— (ed.), *Robin Hood: Medieval and Post-Medieval* (Dublin: Four Courts Press, 2005)
—— '"Merry", "Merry Men", and "Greenwood": The History of Some Meanings', in Calhoun and Potter, *Images of Robin Hood*, forthcoming
Polk, Kenneth, 'Masculinity, Honour, and Confrontational Homicide', in Newburn and Stanko, *Just Boys?*, pp. 187–88
Pollard, A. J., *Imagining Robin Hood: The Late-Medieval Stories in Historical Context* (London: Routledge, 2004)
Potter, Lois, 'Robin Hood and the Fairies: Alfred Noyes' *Sherwood*', in Phillips, *RHMP*, pp. 167–80
Pugh, Sheenagh, *Democratic Fictions* (Swansea: Seren, 2006)
Rebbert, Maria A., 'The Celtic Origins of the Chess Symbolism in *Milun* and *Eliduc*', in *In Quest of Marie de France: A Twelfth-Century Poet*, ed. Chantal A. Maréchal (Lewison, Queenston and Lampeter: Edwin Mellon, 1992), pp. 148–60
Rees, E. A., *Welsh Outlaws and Bandits: Political Rebellion and Lawlessness in Wales, 1400–1603* (King's Norton: Caterwen, 2001)
Revard, Carter, 'Scribe and Provenance', in *Studies in the Harley Manuscript: The Scribes, Contents and Social Contexts of British Library MS Harley 2253*, ed. Susanna Fein (Kalamazoo, MI: Medieval Institute Publications, 2000)

Reynolds, Susan, 'Edric Silvaticus and the English Resistance', *Bulletin of the Institute of Historical Research*, 54, no. 129 (1981), 102–5

Richards, Jeffrey, *Swordsmen of the Screen: From Douglas Fairbanks to Michael York* (London: Routledge and Kegan Paul, 1977)

—— 'From Christianity to Paganism: the New Middle Ages and the Values of 'Medieval' Masculinity', *Cultural Values*, 3, (1999), 213–34

—— 'Robin Hood on Film and Television since 1945', *Visual Culture in Britain*, 2 (2001), 65–80

Rowland, Beryl, *Animals with Human Faces: A Guide to Animal Symbolism* (London: George Allen and Unwin, 1974)

Salri, Marinella, 'Ivanhoe's Middle Ages', in *Medieval and Pseudo-Medieval Literature,* ed. Piero Boitani and Anna Torti, The J. A. W. Bennett Memorial Lecture, Perugia, 1982–83 (Tübingen and Cambridge: D. S. Brewer, 1984), pp. 149–60

Schramm, Percy E., *A History of the English Coronation*, trans. L. G. Wickham Legg (Oxford: Clarendon Press, 1937)

Schwichtenberg, Cathy (ed.), *The Madonna Connection: Representational Politics, Subcultural Identities and Cultural Theory* (Boulder, CO: Westview, 1993)

Scraton, Phil, Sim Sim and Paula Skidmore, (eds), *Prisons Under Protest*, (Milton Keynes: Open University Press, 1991)

Sedgwick, Eve Kosovsky, *Between Men: English Literature and Male Homosocial Desire* (New York: Columbia University Press, 1985)

Singman, Jeffrey L., *Robin Hood: The Shaping of the Legend* (Westport CT: Greenwood, 1998)

Spence, Lewis, 'Robin Hood in Scotland', *Chambers Journal*, 18 (1928), 94–6

Stephens, Meic, *A Most Peculiar People: Quotations about Wales and the Welsh* (Cardiff: University of Wales Press, 1992)

—— (ed.), *Cydymaith i Lenyddiaeth Cymru/Companion to the Literature of Wales*, rev. ed. (Cardiff: University of Wales Press, 1997)

Stewart, Ralph, 'The Enchanted World of The Lady of the Lake', *Scottish Literary Journal*, 22:2 (1995), 5–13

Stringer, K. J., *Earl David of Huntingdon* (Edinburgh: Edinburgh University Press, 1985)

Strohm, Paul, 'York's Paper Crown: "Bare Life" and Shakespeare's First Tragedy', *Journal of Medieval and Early Modern Studies*, 36:1 (2006), 75–103

Sutherland, Kathryn, 'Fictional Economies: Adam Smith, Walter Scott and the Nineteenth-Century Novel', *ELH*, 54 (1987), 97–127

Thurstan, R. and John Beynon, 'Men's own Stories, Lives and Violence: Research as Practice', in *Gender and Crime*, ed. R. E. Dobash, R. P. Dobash and I. Noaks, (Cardiff: University of Wales Press, 1995), pp. 181–201

Tiddy, R. J. E., *The Mummers' Play* (Oxford: Clarendon Press, 1923)

Turner, Ralph David and Malcolm Baker, *Robin of the Movies* (Kingswinford: Yeoman, 1989)

Turner, Ralph V., *The King and his Courts: The Role of John and Henry III in the Administration of Justice 1199–1240* (Ithaca and New York: Cornell University Press, 1969)

—— *King John* (London and New York: Longman, 1994)

Ueno, Yosjiko, 'Murayama's *Robin Hood*: The Most Radical Variant in Japan', in Hahn, pp. 265–73.

Umland, Rebecca and Samuel Umland, *The Use of Arthurian Legend in Hollywood Film*, (Westport CT: Greenwood, 1996)

Walker, Eric G., *Scott's Fiction and the Picturesque*, Salzburg Studies in English Literature, Romantic Reassessment, ed. James Hogg (Salzburg: Institut für Anglistik und Amerikanistik, 1982)

Warren, W. L., *King John* (London: Eyre and Spottiswoode, 1961)

Welsh, Alexander, *The Hero of the Waverley Novels* (New York: Athenaeum, 1963)

Westwood, Jennifer, *Albion: A Guide to Legendary Britain* (London: Granada, 1985), pp. 300–4

Williams, David, *The Rebecca Riots: A Study in Agrarian Discontent* (Cardiff: University of Wales Press, 1955)

—— *A History of Modern Wales* (London: John Murray, 1977)

Williams, J. E. Caerwyn, 'Guto'r Glyn', in Jarman and Hughes, *Guide*, pp. 197–221

Wilson, Richard, '"Like the Old Robin Hood": *As You Like It* and the Enclosure Riots', *Shakespeare Quarterly*, 43 (1992), 1–19

Films, TV, Videos

Fellow Traveller, BBC/HBO. Connoisseur, 1989, directed by Philip Saville

Robin and Marian, Columbia Pictures, 1976, directed by Richard Lester

Robin Hood, United Artists, 1922, directed by Alan Dwan

Robin Hood, Walt Disney, 1973, classics videotape

BIBLIOGRAPHY

Robin Hood, videotape, 104 minutes, Morgan Creek Productions, directed by John Irvin

Robin Hood, Men in Tights, Columbia, 1993, directed by Mel Brooks

Robin Hood: Prince of Thieves, Morgan Creek Productions, 1991, directed by Kevin Reynolds

Robin of Sherwood, 'Herne's Son', Goldcrest, 1985, directed by Robert Young

Robin of Sherwood, 'Robin Hood and the Sorcerer', Goldcrest, 1983, directed by Ian Sharpe

Robin of Sherwood, 'The King's Fool', Goldcrest, 1983, *directed by Ian Sharpe*

The Adventures of Robin Hood, 'Dead or Alive', Sapphire Films, 1956–60, directed by Dan Birt

The Adventures of Robin Hood, 'Good-bye, Little John', Marathon Music and Video, Dastar Corporation, 1998, directed by Robert Day

The Adventures of Robin Hood, Warner Brothers, 1938, directed by Michael Curtiz and William Keighley

The Legend of Robin Hood. Six hourly episodes. BBC 1975, directed by Eric Davidson

Index

1381 Rising, Peasants' Revolt 16, 133, 219
  see also Tyler, Wat

Abbot of Unreason, Misrule see Scotland
ABC TV, Melbourne 40
Aberdeen 101, 103–5, 113
Adam Bell, Clym of the Clough and William of Cloudesley 11
Adam de Gurdun 5
Adam de la Halle see Robin et Marion
Aeneas 105
Agamben Giorgio 14–15
Al(l)an a Dale 33, 38, 132, 133, 134, 161, 190, 200
Alfred, King 247
America 1, 7, 8, 9, 10, 39, 58, 143–66, 168–94, 217–32
  American forest 10, 151; West 10
Andrew of Wyntoun 21, 101, 105–6, 109–10, 111, 196
Arthur, King 11, 19, 64, 73, 89, 91, 99, 102, 126, 167–94, 247; *Camelot* 194
  Arthurian films 191
  The Adventures of Quentin Durward 168
  The Adventures of Sir Galahad 186, 193
  The Black Knight 168, 184, 185–7, 188, 192, 194
  The Black Shield of Falworth 168

Excalibur 194
First Knight 194
Ivanhoe 168, 169, 178, 186
Knights of the Round Table 168, 181, 183, 193–4
Lancelot and Guenevere/Sword of Lancelot 182, 194
Prince Valiant 168, 183, 186, 193
Siege of the Saxons 188, 192, 194
The Warriors/The Dark Avenger 168, 186
Arthur a Bland 34–5
Audulf/Audulph de Bracy 84, 127
Aunflor, King of Orkney 92n
Australia 40; Australian Rules football 104

Bandits/banditti 1, 4, 5, 9, 17, 21, 119, 128, 129, 134, 140n, 147, 163
  local 20
  'social bandit' figure 7, 21, 153
  see Hobsbawm, Eric, outlaws, poaching, Wales: Welsh outlaws.
Barclay, Alexander 44
Barczewski, Stephanie L. 126, 167, 192
Barnsdale (name of places in Notts, Yorks and Rutland) 20, 21, 105, 109–11, 164, 196
  and Scotland 109–11
Bart, Lionel, *Twang!* 38

INDEX

Barthes, Roland 238
'Battle of Waun Gaseg' 63
Beatte, Pierre *see* Irving,
    Washington
Becket, Thomas, St 13
Beelzebub 104
Bell Adam 11, 104, 163
    as 'Allan Belle' 113
    see Inglewood
Beery, Wallace 24, 171
Benjamin, Walter 14
Bennett, Enid
    see Maid Marion
Beowulf 105, 115
Bergin Patrick 26, 29, 213
Bevington, David 110
Bevis of Hamton 100
Beynon, John 11
Big Breakfast Show 40
Billy the Kid 220
Black Death 58
Blaise de Beautement 52
Blake, Bill 116
Blamires, David 7, 17
Blanche Lande, Blancheville
    see Whittington
Blind Hary *see* Wallace, William
Blunk, Laura 9, 17, 18, 106
Boece, Hector 108
Bolton, Philip 129
Bonacord
    see Scotland
Bonnie Prince Charlie 122
Bourdieu, Pierre 10
Bower, Walter 106, 107, 114, 196
Boy Bishop 106
    see Scotland: Bonacord
Brando, Marlon 170
Brecon 58
Brian de Bois Gilbert 127
British Forces Network 40
British Library 150–2
Brooker, Peter 238

Brooks, Mel 29, 36–7
    Blazing Saddles 30
    see Robin Hood
Bruce, Robert, King of Scotland 8,
    12, 121
Bruce, The 121
Buchanan, David 108
Buchanan, John 158
Burgess, Glyn 1, 11
Burke, Edmund
    see Irving, Washington
Burnham Beeches 116
Burns, Robert 19
Butch Cassidy 28
Butler, Judith 249
Byron, Lord 144, 145

Cahuz, son of Yvain 90
Cambridge 110
Cardiff 62
Carlisle, Sheriff of 11
Chaplin, Charlie 25
Charlemagne 73
Charles II 6
Chaucer, Geoffrey 5, 13, 12, 133,
    158, 160
    Works: *Canterbury Tales* 13
        Knight's Tale 158
        Miller's Tale 160
    Characters: Canterbury Pilgrims
        160
        Miller 133, 158
        Pardoner 37
        Prioress 158
        Yeoman 122, 140
        and Tabard Inn 160
Chepman and Myllar 113
Chester, Earl of 87
Chicago Lesbi-Gay Line 39
Christmas Carol, A (Dickens) 110
Christopher, St 122
Cinderella 102
Cityton Prison 233–55
Clanchy, Michael 31

INDEX

Clim of the Clough 21, 104, 160
   see Inglewood
Clorinda 50
Cockaigne, land of 15
Cold War 7, 167–94
Colonialism 129, 147–9, 154–64, 166n, 167
   see imperialism, postcolonialism
Comics 2, 8, 10, 217–32
Cooper, Gary 169
Costner, Kevin 18, 26, 212–14, 235, 243
   see Robin Hood
Coward, Noel 47
Cromwell, Thomas 66
Crawford, Robert 115
Creswick, Paul, *Robin Hood* 224
Crusades 7, 25–6, 74, 175, 176, 178, 180, 186, 187, 195n, 220, 225
   and the Cold War 185–8

Dafydd ap Gwilym 62
Dafydd ap Siancyn/Siencyn ap Dafydd ap y Crach 1, 63, 64, 71n
David, Prince of Scotland, Earl of Huntingdon 187
   see Robin Hood
Dean, Forest of 61
Dean, James 170
Deleuze, Gilles 10
Devil 88, 91
Dobson, Barrie 40, 109
Doctor Kildare 169
Doncaster *see* Scott, Sir Walter
Douglas, Gavin, *Pallice of Honur* 113
Drayton, Michael, *Matilda the Faire* 44
   Poly-Olbion 45
Druz de Montbener, Sir 85
Dunbar, William, 'Of Sir Thomas Norrey' 113,

'Ane Litill Interlude of the Droichis Part of the Play 113
Duncan, Ian 130
Dunfermline 121
Dyffryn, Clwyd 62

Eales, Richard 78
Eaton, Michael, *Fellow Traveller* 116
Eddy, Nelson 26
Edinburgh 114
Edith, Queen of England 4
Edmund, St 13
Ednam 111
Edric the Wild 6, 7
Edward, St 13
Edward I 8, 13, 19, 106, 107, 121
Edward II, as prince 186
Edward III 111, 186
Edward IV 63
Edward the Confessor 4, 12
Edwinstowe 51
Egan, Pierce, *Robin Hood and Little John, or the Merry Men of Sherwood Forest* 26, 33, 42
Eliot, George, *Middlemarch* 133
Elizabeth I 67, 68
Elwes, Cary 26
Englishries 58
Eustace the Monk 2, 60
Evans, Ruth 14
Evans, Thomas, *Old Ballads, Historical and Narrative* 146
Everett, Nigel 138

Fairbanks, Douglas, Jr. 7, 24, 26, 28, 43, 169, 171, 173, 198, 199, 214
Fan fiction 19
   see also Robin Hood: Robin of Sherwood
Feast of Fools 104

INDEX

see also Scotland: Bonacord
Feminism 17, 51, 55
  see also gender
Feyrer, Gayle, *The Thief's Mistress* 17
Fielding, Henry *The History of Tom Jones* 68
Fitz Waryn family 60, 76
Fitz Water, Lord 7
  see also Maid Marion
Flynn, Errol 26, 28, 39, 171, 173, 174, 177, 186, 189, 198, 214, 224, 253
Folvilles (outlaw gang) 5
Forster, E. M. 38
Foucault, Michel 14
Foulke Fitz Waryn III 1, 6, 11, 19, 20, 59–62, 65, 69n, 73–98, 107, 127
  as 'Amys del Bois' 85
  as Foulke Morgannwg 20, *Syr Ffwg* 61–2
  in Welsh tradition 20, 61–2
  Roman de Foulke le Fitz Waryn 6, 59, 73–98, 127, 223
  see also wolf 88
Foulke le Brun 75, 76
Foulkes, Isaac, *Cymru Fu* 62
Fraser, John 168–9
Friar Tuck 7, 48, 49, 51, 156, 161, 177, 189, 197, 200, 204, 210, 225, 252
  May game 'Friar' 44
Friedhofer, Hugo 173
Furlong, Monica, *Robin's Country* 46, 55

Gamelyn/Gamlin 131, 199
  Gamelyn 11, 131
Gamwell 50
  see Will a Gamwell
Gandelyn 127, 197–8
Gaudio, Tony 173
Geats 117

Gender 18–19, 21, 25–43, 45–6, 176, 209, 209, 213
  see also homosexuality; homosociality; masculinity
Geomagog 88, 91
George, St 135
Gerard, William 66
Giffard, Sir John, of Brimpsfield 61
Gilbert, Henry, *Robin Hood and the Men of the Greenwood* 17
Gilbert of the White Hand 33, 114
Gillingham, John 91
Glamorgan/Morgannwg 20, 58, 62
Glyndŵr, Owain 6, 8, 17, 58–60, 62–3, 66, 71n
Gwerin Owain (Owain's Children) 62–3
Godwin, Earl 4, 12
Gower, John 158
Grafton, John 108
Graham Norton Show 40
Green, Roger Lancelyn 46, 49, 50, 218, 221, 224
Green clothing 125–6
  fairy 64, 126
  Kendal 145
  Lincoln 32, 64, 125–6, 132
Greene, Richard 115–6, 189, 193, 201, 214, 217–18, 220, 221, 222, 224–5
Greenwood 18, 20, 27, 30, 31, 32, 33, 35, 36, 44, 46, 49, 50, 125, 131–2, 133, 134, 137, 138, 139, 145, 153, 155, 160, 190
Greer, Germaine 51
Grey, Lord Reginald 62
Gruffudd ap Dafydd ap Gruffudd 62

INDEX

Guy of Gisburne 24, 25, 28, 48, 49, 50, 51, 54, 113, 177, 198, 200, 206, 214
  see also Robin Hood
Guy of Warwick 61, 100
Gwenwynwyn, Prince of Powys 60

Hahn, Thomas 13, 18, 252
Harington, Sir John 110
Hark, Ina Rae 173
Harold, King of England 74, 92n
Harris, I. M. 246–7
Harry the Minstrel
  see also Wallace, William
Havilland, Olivia de
  see also Maid Marion
Hayes, Sarah, *Robin Hood* 47
Hellman, George S. 144
Henry I 75, 76
Henry II 7, 13, 61, 75, 76, 78, 92n, 224
Henry III 5, 106–7, 173–4, 176, 193
Henry VIII 15
Henry the Younger, Henry II's son 92n
Hereward 1, 3, 6, 8, 12, 13, 129
  Gesta Herewardi 8
  Hereward's castle 20
  see also Kingsley, Charles
Hicks, Russell 173
Hilton, R. H. 16
Hobsbawm, Eric 2, 7, 15, 222
Holcroft, Thomas, *The Noble Peasant* 121
Hollywood 11, 18, 31, 36, 167, 173
  see also Arthur, Robin Hood
Hollywood films 27, 214
  Adventures of Sir Galahad 193
  Against All Flags 177
  At Sword's Point/Sons of the Musketeers 174

Beau Geste 168
Ben Hur 169
Conan the Barbarian 192
Conan the Destroyer 192
Confessions of a Nazi Spy 172
Crossfire 180
East of Eden 170
Exodus 191
Fury of the Vikings 192
Gentleman's Agreement 180
The Heat of the Night 18
I Married a Communist 186
I was a Communist for the FB1 186
Last of the Vikings 192
Lethal Weapon 18
The Long Ships 192
Mad Max 192
My Son John, Conspirator 186
The Norseman 192
Prince Valiant 193
Quo Vadis 169
Rebel without a Cause 170
The Robe 169
Salome 170
The Spanish Main 177
Spartacus 191
The Ten Commandments 169
The Vikings 192
The Virginian 168
The Wild One 170
  see also Arthur; Robin Hood; Wallace, William
Holt, J. C. 16, 218, 219, 225
Homosexuality 21, 24–43, 252
  'gay' in Pyle 36; gay Robin Hood
  see also Robin Hood 37–42
Homophobia 29–30, 35, 36, 37, 253
Homosociality 33, 36, 249
Howell Cilan 65

275

INDEX

Howel the Good/Hywel Dda 58
Hubert de Burgh 79
Hughes, Lynn *see* Twm Sion Cati
Huntington 110
   Huntingdon 187
   see also Robin Hood
Huntingdon, Earls of 39, 109, 187, 195n
Hwde of Edname 111

Ian McLellan 116
Ieuan ap Gruffudd Leiaf 64
Ifor Hael 62
Iolo Goch 61
Iorwerth Drwyndwn, Prince 60
Iorwerth Goch, Prince 60
Imperialism 8, 9, 10, 13, 16–7, 21, 167
   see also postcolonialism
Inglewood, Cumbria 11, 21, 105, 109, 110, 111
   see also Adam Bell; Clim of the Clough, William of Cloudesley
Irving, Peter 145
Irving, Washington 10, 143–66, 234, 235
   and Beatte 159
   and boyhood reading 144
   and Burke 163
   at Newstead, Notts 155–7; with Mr Rodes 155
   and Pourtales 159
   and Ritson 145, 164
   and Scott 145–6
   and Shakespeare 152–3, 158
   works: *Bracebridge Hall* 145, 146, 147–8, 152, 154, 160, 163
   Buckthorne, or the Young Man of Great Expectations 159
   Journals 159
   Letters of Jonathan Oldstyle, Gentleman 154
   Sketch Book 147–50, 152, 158, 160, 163
   Tales of a Traveler 147, 159, 160
   Traits of Indian Character 159
   characters: Simon Bracebridge 159
   Buckthorne 159
   Geoffrey Crayon 143, 145, 148, 150, 152, 153, 155, 160, 162–3
   Julia 144
   Ready Money Jack 153
   Rip Van Winkle 154
   Slingsby; Starlight Tom 153, 155, 157
   May games and May Day 153, 154, 155
Isambart of Belame 48
Isidore of Seville 73
Ivanhoe
   see Scott, Sir Walter

Jaffé, Sam 28
James, Jesse 234
James I of Scotland, *The Kingis Quair* 158
James III of Scotland 13
James of Normandy 86
Jameson, Frederic 238
Jean II, King of France 15
Jews 174, 183–5
   Yiddish 29
Joan, daughter of Henry II 60, 82–3, 95n
Joce de Dynan 75
John, King 1, 6, 11, 12, 60, 73–98, 127, 173, 175, 179–80, 190
   as prince 25–6, 28, 44, 49, 60, 61, 171–2, 178–9, 180, 186, 189, 198, 220, 223–5
Sherwood hunting lodge 39

276

see also Leopard; Magna Carta
John de Rampaigne 84, 87, 127
John of Fordun, *Scotichronicon* 106
John the Graham, Sir 17
Jones, D. J. V. 236, 254n
Jones, Timothy 4, 22n
Jonson, Ben, *Sad Shepherd* 7, 15, 45, 56n

Katherine of Aragon 15
Keats, John, 234; 'To a Friend' 121
Keen, Maurice 218, 221, 223
Kelly, Ned 234
'King Edward' 31–3, 225
Kings and kingship 1, 8, 13, 31–3, 73–98, 99, 107, 124, 131, 176, 180–2, 197
  king and outlaw 10–14, 15, 21
  English kings 14
Kingsley, Charles, *Hereward the Wake* 8, 13, 128
Kirklees, 20–1, 48
  prioress 33, 207
Knight, Stephen 7, 9, 13, 16, 18–19, 20–1, 38–41, 45, 119, 122, 137, 218, 235, 236
Korngold, Eric 171, 173
Koven, Reginald de, *Maid Marian* 26

Lake District 128
Lancelot 182–3, 194
Langland, William, *Piers Plowman* 5, 114
Lardner, Ring, Jr. 116
Law of the Father 24–43
Law of the March 58
Le Robin Hude, ship 103
Leake, Jonathan 38–9, 40, 252
Lee, Rowland 66

Leeson, Robert, *The Story of Robin Hood* 47
Leicestershire 5
Leigh, Rowland 27
Leopard, emblem of King John 60, 88
L'Evènement
Lewys Glyn Cothi
  see also Llywelyn y Glyn
Lincoln Green, 125–6, 132; and fairy green 126
Lincolnshire 111
Little John 6, 9, 16, 18, 20, 21, 26, 30, 33, 34, 35, 37, 40–2, 105–6, 114, 127, 135, 196–216
  Grave, Hathersage, Derbyshire 20
  Little John a Begging 201
  in Scotland 103, 108, 135, 140n
  as Scottish giant 108
Llywelyn ap Moel y Pantri 62–3
Llywelyn the Great, Welsh prince 59–60, 61
Llywelyn y Glyn 64
Lockhart, Sir James 129, 146
London 16, 74, 225
Louise, Anita 173
Lucy, Sir Thomas 152

Macaskill, Mark 252
McCarthy, Senator Joseph 116, 191, 203
  McCarthyism 170, 180, 184, 189, 201, 203
  see also Robin Hood,
McDonald, Jeanette 26
McKinley, Robyn, *The Outlaws of Sherwood Forest* 17, 51–3
McMaster, Graham 140n
Madonna 233
Magna Carta 173, 175

INDEX

Maid Marion/Maid Marian 7, 9, 18, 24–7, 29–30, 33, 38, 40, 42, 44–57, 102, 144–5, 156, 171–4, 178, 190, 200, 207–10, 211–13, 222, 249, 253
  and 1922 *Robin Hood* 24–6; 171
  and 1938 *Adventure of Robin Hood* 27
  and sexual/romantic relationships 17–18, 44–5, 46, 48–51, 52–5, 171, 208–9, 213
  in children's literature 17, 44–57
  and Marina 33
  as Matilda Fitzwater/Fitzwalter 7, 44–5, 48, 55, 171–2
  and Maudlin/Witch of Papplewick 45, 53, 57n
  in *Robin Hood and Maid Marian* 18
  in *Maid Marian and her Merry Men* (TV) 213
  played by Enid Bennett 171
  Olivia de Havilland 172–3
  see also Feyrer, Gayle; Koven, Reginald de; McKinley, Robyn; Peacock, Thomas Love 17; Robin Hood: Stocqueler, Joachim; Tennyson, Alfred 17; Tomlinson, Theresa 17
Major, John, *Historia Majoris Britanniae* 107–8, 223
Malory, Sir Thomas 42, 181, 182
Map, Walter 7
Marion, heroine of *pastourelle see also* Robin et Marion
Marshall, H.E., *Stories of Robin Hood* 46, 47, 48
Mary, St 13

Mary Magdalene, St 13
Masculinity 17–18, 24–43, 45, 167, 171, 235, 237–8, 240–1, 246–50
Matilda de Caus 69n, 75, 80–1, 83, 84, 95n
Marwnad yr Hedydd 63
Melusine 7
Merlin/Myrddin 60, 64, 88, 102, 181, 182, 188, 193, 194, 210
Merry England 36, 37, 137, 235
Merry men 18, 29–32, 36, 45, 55, 124, 125, 131, 134, 154, 171, 200, 205, 222, 223, 225, 226, 233
Miles, Bernard, *Robin Hood: His Life and Legend* 51
Mitchell, Adrian *The Adventures of Robin Hood and Marian* 49, 55
Monk of Misrule 134
  see also Scotland
Morgannwg *see* Glamorgan
Morpurgo, Michael, *Robin of Sherwood* 47, 54
Morris dances 123, 144, 153–5
Morton, Graeme 19
Morys Fitz Roger, Morys de Powys 60, 81–2
Much, the miller's son 50, 210
Mummers 104, 155
Munday, Anthony, *Death* and *Downfall of Robert, Earle of Huntington* 7, 27, 44, 55, 108, 110
  and the Admiral's Men 110

National identity, nationalism 1, 5–9, 167, 252
  see also Bruce, Robert; Edric the Wild; Hereward; Glyndŵr, Owain; Wallace, William; Wales: Welsh bandits
Nelson, Eddy 26

INDEX

Nelson, Lord 104
Nicholas, St 103
Ninja Turtles 99
Normans 58, 59–60, 126–7, 137, 172–3, 177, 178–80, 186, 189–90, 204, 225
Nottingham 6, 38, 40, 50, 60, 107, 109, 177, 190, 199, 210, 212, 225, 237
   Nottingham Evening Post 41
   Sheriff of 2, 53, 60, 96n, 107, 178, 190, 204–5, 207–8, 212, 213, 215, 222, 223–4, 248
   University of 38
Nottinghamshire 20, 144–5, 233
Noyes, Alfred, *Sherwood* 37, 55, 234–5, 254n
Nyberg, Amy Kiste 226

Ohlgren, Thomas H. 118n
Oman, Carola, *Robin Hood* 47, 49
Orfeo, Sir 14
Ormrod, Mark 12
Outlaws *passim*; 'good outlaw' figure 1, 2–3
   king of 15, 130
   performance 15
   and law 2, 3, 4, 10, 12–14, 15, 58, 120, 129–30, 219–23
   and justice 5, 12–13, 172, 188, 192–3, 220–6
   and royal pardons 12
   image of writers 10
   see also bandits, poaching, Welsh outlaws, wolf 88
Oswald, St 13
Owain ap Gruffudd ap Nicolas 64
Owain Cyfeiliog 60
Owain Gwynedd, Welsh prince 60
Owen, Lewis, Baron 67

Paine, Tom 163

Pakenham (Fraser), Antonia, *Robin Hood* 50
Paris, Catherine 144
Past and Present 16
Paston family 2
Payn Peverel 88
Peacock, Thomas Love, *Maid Marian* 17, 26, 45, 49, 50, 55
Pembroke, William, Earl of 173
Percy folio manuscript 113, 207
Pennant, Thomas, *Tours of Wales* 67
Peterloo Massacre 124, 136
Phillips, Helen 9,
Planché, J. R., *Maid Marian* 26, 27
Poaching 10, 11, 51, 151–3
   image of writer 10, 152
Poitiers, battle of 16
Polk, Kenneth 246
Porteous Riots 116
Postcolonialism 10, 101, 147, 151, 154
Potter, Lois 254n
Price, Adrian 5, 9, 17, 20
Prince Valiant (film) 168, 183, 193
Pugh, Sheenagh 19
Pyle, Howard 9, 18, 33–7, 218, 221, 222

Radical politics 3, 5, 13, 16, 116, 119–20, 133, 137, 139, 145, 167 189–90, 194, 214–5, 253n
   see also McCarthy
Rains, Claude 28
Ramsay, Sir Alexander 111
Ravi 105
Rebecca Riots 236
Red Bandits of Mawddwy 66
Reginald de Bracy 126–7
Renart 3
Roman de Renart 3

INDEX

Revolution, French 146
Rheinallt ap Gruffudd ap Bleddyn 65
Rhys Gethin 63
Richard I 7, 24, 52, 126, 164, 171, 172–3, 176, 178–80, 186, 189–90, 193, 200, 207, 210–11, 221, 224
Richards, Jeffrey 7, 10, 11,
Ritson, Joseph 45, 106, 121, 145, 146, 160, 164
Rob Roy 1, 129–30, 145
  see also Scott, Sir Walter
Robert, son of Robin Hood 174
'Robin and Gandelyn' 127, 197
Robin et Marion (Adam de la Halle) 7, 102
Robin des Bois 102, 105, 115
Robin Goodfellow 154, 155, 157
Robin Hood 1, 2, 6, 8, 13, 17, 18, 19, 20, 24–55, 129, 131, 135–42, 143–66, 167–195, 196–216, 217–32, 233–39, 243–53
  ballads: *Death of Robin Hood* 207, 224
  Gest of Robyn Hode 2, 11, 13, 15, 31, 45, 48, 54, 96n, 109, 112, 113, 114, 123, 139, 196, 218, 224, 225
  Pedigree, Education and Marriage of Robin Hood, The 146
  Robin Hood and Maid Marian 27, 44
  Robin Hood and Guy of Gisburne 2, 113, 131, 197
  Robin Hood and Little John 199
  Robin Hood and the Bishop 112
  Robin Hood and the Golden Arrow 224

Robin Hood and the Monk 2, 17, 112, 114, 131, 196, 204, 224
Robin Hood and the Potter 2, 3, 36–7, 112, 114, 131, 196
Robin Hood's Birth, Breeding, Valour and Marriage 50
Robin Hood's Golden Prize 112
Robin Hood's Progress to Nottingham 112
Films 7–10; *The Adventures of Robin Hood* 1938 24, 27, 28, 167, 171–3, 175, 177, 189, 198–9, 224
Bandit of Sherwood Forest 168, 173, 176, 188, 193
A Challenge for Robin Hood 168, 189, 190
Ivanhoe 168, 169, 178, 180–1, 186
King Richard and the Crusaders 168, 186
Men of Sherwood Forest 168, 188, 190, 201
Prince of Thieves 168, 177
Robin and Marian 17, 194, 2079, 212, 214
Robin Hood (1922) 7, 167, 171, 175, 198
Robin Hood (1973) 205
Robin Hood (1991) 29, 235, 243
Robin Hood: Men in Tights 37, 42, 213, 235
Robin Hood, Prince of Thieves 18, 228–9, 194, 212–13, 235, 243
The Story of Robin Hood 221, 223, 225
Rogues of Sherwood Forest 168, 175, 188, 200
Son of Robin Hood 168, 176, 201

INDEX

The Story of Robin Hood 168, 177, 186, 201, 218
The Sword of Sherwood Forest 168, 189
The Siege of the Saxons 188, 192, 194
Tales of Robin Hood 168, 177
Opera: *Robin Hood* 33
see also Koven, Reginald de
and 1381 Rising 16
and children's literature 9, 41, 189, 222
and Crusades 7
and plays 2, 6–7
and Rebecca Riots 72n, 236
and Saxons 35, 119, 137–9, 171–3, 177, 178–80, 183, 189
Forresters Manuscript 141n
gay 18, 21, 34–43, 252–3
see also homosexuality
TV: *Adventures of Robin Hood* 115, 201–5, 217, 218, 221, 222, 223
Legend of Robin Hood 206–7, 209, 212, 214
New Adventures of Robin Hood 214
Robin of Sherwood 4, 19, 194, 199, 201, 209–13, 214–5
Whitsun May games 8, 16, 44, 101, 103, 123, 144
Winter festivities 103–4
as Earl of Huntington or Huntingdon 24, 25, 27, 157, 160, 171, 173–4, 175, 198–9, 211
as Locksley/Loxley 13, 50, 119, 121, 122–3, 129, 131, 139, 157, 171, 189, 199, 211, 260
as philanthropist 237–8
as Robert Fitzooth 160

as yeoman 15, 122
in Scotland 8, 99–118
in the landscape 109
in USA 7–9
see also *Robin et Marion*, radical politics, Brookes, Mel; Costner, Kevin; comics, Eaton, Michael; Fairbanks, Douglas; Gilbert, Henry
Robinson Crusoe 133
Rockingham Forest 110–11
Roderick Ddu 125
Roger de Bellême 75
Romanticism 128
Roosevelt, President Franklin 173
Rosa, Salvator 128
Ross, Sue Fields 159
Roxburgh 111
Ronaldo, Cristiano 105, 115
Rutland, Barnsdale 109–10, 111

Sabatini, Rafael 168
St Andrews 106
St Augustine's Chapel 89
Salri, Marinella 140n
Sanders, George 169
'Sang of the Outlaw Murray' 122
Scarlet, Will 33, 34–6, 42, 48, 203–4, 213
see also Stutely, Will
Scotland 12, 19–20, 21, 99–118, 128
Bonacord/Unreason, Abbot and Prior, 'Misrule' 20, 103, 104, 134, 197
the highlands 9, 21, 120, 127–9, 141n
plays and pageants 15, 197
Scottish outlaws 9
Scott, Sir Walter 2–3, 9–10, 99–100, 108, 116, 119–42, 145–6, 158, 179

281

INDEX

works: *The Abbot* 116, 131, 134–6
The Antiquary 125, 129
The Betrothed 128
The Heart of Midlothian 116
Ivanhoe 13, 116, 120–1, 122–3, 126, 127, 130–1, 146, 164, 178
A Lady of the Lake 123–4, 125, 134, 135
A Legend of the Wars of Montrose, 120, 127–8
Minstrelsy of the Scottish Border 122, 146
Rob Roy 120, 129–30
Rokeby 126, 129, 130, 135
The Talisman 186
The Visionary 136
Ivanhoe (film) 168, 169, 178–80
and Crabbe 158
and Doncaster area 137
characters: Alice Brand 133
Allan McAuley 128
Athelstane 137
Bertram 130
Brian de Bois Guilbert 127, 180
Cedric 127, 137, 139
Dalgetty 128; Denzil 129, 134
Douglas, Lord 123–6, 134
Edmund, 133
Ellen 126
Fitz James 125
Front-de-Boeuf 127
Glendinning, Sir Halbert 135
Gurth 137–8
Ivanhoe 122, 131, 137, 138
Locksley
  see also Robin Hood
Lovel 125
Macintyre 129
Rebecca 129, 140, 180
Reginald de Bracy 126–7
Rob Radical 136
Roderick Ddu 125
Wamba 127, 137–8
see also Allan a Dale, Foulke Fitz Waryn; Robin Hood, Rob Roy; Scotland
Sedgwick, Eve Kosofsky 24, 255n
Shakespeare, William 14, 152–3, 158, 234
  As You Like It 15
  Titus Andronicus 110
  Prince Hal 159
  and the Chamberlain's Men 110
  see Irving, Washington
Sherlock Holmes 102
Sherwood 19–20, 21, 48, 52, 109, 144, 153, 164, 174, 198, 200, 210, 211, 212, 235, 244, 245, 248, 250
Shropshire 1, 6, 20
Simon de Montfort 5, 106, 196
Singman, Jeffrey L. 196
Smith, Marcus, 10
Soviet Union 169 see Cold War
Spence, Lewis 100, 109, 113
Spiegel, Der 40
Squire, J. C., *Robin Hood* 38
Stead, Christina 116
Stocqueler, Joachim, *Maid Marian, the Forest Queen* 38, 42
Stow, John 108, 110
Straw, Jack 161, 163
Stutely, Will 33, 34
Sullivan, Sir Arthur 26
Superman 169
Sutcliff, Rosemary 46, 47–9
Sutherland, Robert, Earl of 174

Tarzan 169
Tatchell, Peter 39
Taylor, John 109
Tennyson, Alfred, Lord, 55, 234
  The Forresters 17, 26

INDEX

Theobald le Botiler 80
Thierry de la Fronde 105
Thurman, Uma 29
Tilney, E.C., *Robin Hood and his Merry Outlaws* 47, 48
Tomlinson, Theresa, *The Forestwife* 17, 53
Trease, Geoffrey, *Bows Against the Barons* 13
Tristan 3, 14
Tudur Aled 61
Tudur Penllyn 64
Twain, Mark, *A Connecticut Yankee at King Arthur's Court* 167
Twm Siôn Cati 1, 67–69, 235
    John Ross, 'Tomshone Catty's Tricks' 68
    William F. Deacon, *Twm John Catty, the Welsh Robin Hood* 68;
    T. J. Llywelyn Pritchard, *The Adventures and Vagaries of Twm Shon Catti* 68
    Lynn Hughes, *Hawkmoor* 68
Tyler, Wat 136, 163

Unreason, Abbot and Prior *see* Scotland

Vietnam War 191
Vivian, E. Charles H. 46, 48

Wales 5, 17, 21, 58–72, 236
    the Welsh in Scott 9, 128–9
    Welsh Marches 5, 58, 59, 61, 66, 128
    Welsh outlaws 5, 9, 58–72

Wallace, William 1, 3, 8, 9, 12–13, 17, 19, 105, 106, 107, 109, 111–15, 121–2, 130
    Blind Hary, Harry the Minstrel, *Wallace* 12; 111–14
    Braveheart 13, 19
    and Andrew of Wyntoun 101
    in Hyndford manuscript 114
    proposed sanctification 13
Walter, Hubert, Archbishop of Canterbury 80, 190
    see also Hubert le Botiler 80
Walter de Lacy 75
Wasserman, Julian 10
Wayne John 105
Weinstein, Hannah 116
Wertham, Frederic 170, 183
Whittington 60, 77
    see also Blanche Lande, Blancheville
Will a Gamwell 42
William I 6
William of Cloudesley 11, 104, 105, 161
    see also Inglewood
William Fitz Waryn 87
Williams, David 236
Williams, Marcia, *The Adventures of Robin Hood* 47, 49, 55
Wodehouse, P. G. 47
Wolf, 'wolfshead' 87
Woolf, Lord Justice 240
World War I 7; II 6, 168, 173, 174, 176–77, 233
Wright, Allen W. 2, 8, 10
Wynn, Sir John 64, 65

Yorkshire 20, 51, 109, 234